Freedom
FROM
HEART ATTACKS

BY *Benjamin F. Miller, M.D.*

AND *Lawrence Galton*

AND IN SPECIAL CONSULTATION WITH

Daniel Brunner, M.D.

SIMON AND SCHUSTER · NEW YORK

Second printing

SBN 671-21319-9
Library of Congress Catalog Card Number: 72-82863
Designed by Edith Fowler
Manufactured in the United States of America
by American Book-Stratford Press, Inc.

To Judith W. Miller,
  Susan, Betsy, Ruth and Joel

To Barbara Galton,
  Kit, Jill and Jeremy

who, in so many ways,
gave us the desire and encouragement
to write this book

Contents

1

An Epidemic Like No Other

Call it a fantasy: In Noland, a little country in the Western world, there is nothing of special beauty, no gambling casino, no glamorous queen. Yet this country excites the rest of the world because it harbors a disease, "cardiosis," which each year spreads to other countries.

Upon reaching the United States, it kills more than half a million people annually, and is particularly fearsome because of its predilection for active men of the middle years, forty-five to fifty-five. Thus it strikes at heads of families and is a chief cause of turning wives into widows, of depriving children of fathers. Although it does not so commonly affect very young people fatally, it is believed to sensitize even those in their teens so that later they succumb more easily to its attacks.

In addition to the vast human cost, there is a fearful economic toll; industry, government, and the professions are deprived of men at the heights of their careers, at the times in their lives when their experience has fitted them for major tasks and achievements.

Finally, the specter of the disease evokes anxiety in the whole population. Men, in particular, fret. But women do get the disease at a later age, and children are concerned that it will strike their parents.

Fortunately, now, there is being developed a protective vaccine against this killing plague. It is no absolute preventive, 100 percent effective. It requires an unusual measure of cooperation from the population. Great discipline is needed to undergo the series of preventive inoculations, which are almost as numerous and disturbing as those required to prevent rabies after the bite of a mad animal. But the danger of this epidemic disease is so great that doctors are advising everyone over the age of ten to undergo the inoculations.

As you have recognized, of course, we have fantasied—but only up to a point—about heart attack, which each year kills at least 600,000 Americans and disables many more. It is our deadliest predator, epidemic in proportions—but epidemic like no other disease.

All other diseases that strike in epidemic fashion die out in a period of months, in some cases even weeks. Even plague, cholera, and yellow fever have their limits in time. In this country, when we still had polio epidemics, they would last only a few months at a time. Moreover, epidemics typically vary in severity. Some years flu outbreaks, for example, are mild; other years, they kill large numbers of people. But the heart attack epidemic goes on constantly in this country, is present every day of the year, in every year of every decade.

It has been mounting in ferocity; the death rate from it, some studies indicate, has quadrupled since 1931.

Cancer is not to be dismissed as a threat, nor stroke, nor kidney disease. But for Americans today, heart disease ranks almost beyond compare as the prime threat to life, health, and happiness.

Despite all the advances in public health and medical science since 1900—including huge reductions in deaths from tuberculosis and pneumonia, then the chief causes of mortality—life expectancy for American middle-aged men now is only a few years greater than at the turn of the century. And it is obvious that there can be no major further advance in life expectancy extension without control of the heart attack epidemic.

At age forty, the annual rate of new heart attacks is about 3 per 1,000 among American men. At age fifty, 1 of every 100 men will develop coronary heart disease, the major cause of heart attacks, in the course of a year. Before age sixty, 1 of every 5 American men will have the disease—and in most cases a heart attack will be the first overt sign.

One victim in 4 will die within three hours of his first heart attack. Of those who survive beyond three hours, 1 in 10 will die within a few weeks. People who have had one heart attack are approximately five times as likely to die within five years after the event as people without known heart ailments.

TWO-SEX EPIDEMIC

While the magnitude of the problem among men has tended to obscure its importance among women, in one recent year coronary heart disease accounted for 212,000 deaths among American women, a toll 60 percent greater than that from cancer.

Women after the menopause begin to experience heart attacks. Up to age forty-five, men have 13 times more attacks than do women. From that age to about age sixty-two, men still have twice as many. Thereafter, women are fully as susceptible. However, since men start suffering from coronary heart disease about 20 years earlier than women, there is a disproportionate number of widows.

A Vaccine?

In our fantasy we imagined a preventive vaccine. Is there really one on the way for coronary heart disease? CHD is no bacterial or viral infection. It is not a disease even faintly resembling the types against which conventional vaccines can work. Not that chemical agents with potential usefulness for controlling some aspects of coronary heart disease are not being developed. A vaccine in the usual sense, however, is unlikely.

But knowledge about coronary heart disease and heart attacks—also known as coronary occlusions and myocardial infarcts—has now advanced to the point where there could be almost the equivalent, in a very real sense, of a vaccine.

Any vaccine carries materials to alert body defenses—to muster them to help abort the development of a specified disease.

This is possible today for heart disease.

One Reason for Optimism

Much of the realistically mounting hope for counterattacking, for bringing the epidemic under control, comes from studies of coronary heart disease around the world and the finding that there are millions of people in various areas who have minimal chances of having heart attacks, who are virtually immune.

"So what!" one might be tempted to say. "Suppose the Japanese don't get many heart attacks and the Yemenite Jews in Israel are free of coronary heart disease! We don't have the same heredity."

But the differences between various populations in coronary heart disease rates cannot be dismissed as inherited or genetic differences. Japanese living in Japan have a low frequency of heart attacks but Japanese living in Hawaii and the United States mainland have much higher rates. When the Yemenite Jews first came to Israel they were, indeed, virtually free of heart attacks; but now their children and grandchildren are not so free. This suggests that heredity cannot be the all-important factor and that resistance against, or proclivity for, coronary heart disease lies in environmental influences, in the way of life.

Only recently has it begun to become really clear how important way of life is. Differences in heart attack rates traceable to differences in way of life are far from slight. In a recent international cooperative study covering men forty to fifty-nine years of age in seven countries, the highest CHD prevalence rate—56.6 per 1,000 for East Finland—was 40 times greater than the lowest—1.4 for Dalmatia. This is a huge difference in risk for a disease that can kill instantly or damage such a vital organ as the heart.

Generally, populations of the poorer countries of the world have been thought to have lower heart attack rates. But in many countries—India is one example—the death rate from other diseases is so high that it is hard to get reliable figures on the incidence of heart disease.

And there have, indeed, been some questionable studies in the past. For example, it was once thought that Eskimos in Alaska had very little coronary heart disease. But when the studies leading to that belief were subjected to intensive scrutiny, they turned out to be full of faults. For one thing, they covered Eskimo populations with very few people over age thirty; thus few heart attacks could be expected simply on the basis of age. In addition, the medical examinations carried out for the studies were so skimpy that critics say they could hardly have identified any diseased condition of the coronary arteries. And here and there, in other instances, the same criticism could be made.

But the most recent studies are firmly grounded. They have

covered populations in many countries. And those carried out in Israel are especially impressive.

THE REMARKABLE LABORATORY: A NATION

Israel is a magnificent, virtually unique laboratory for coronary heart disease. More than a million people from diverse corners of the world have migrated to it since 1948.

Heart disease researchers everywhere would love to have plunked down in their midst a large number of people not previously exposed to the ways of life of most developed nations to the rich and fatty diets and other aspects of modern western life. Investigators in Israel got just such an unusual bonanza 20 years ago when 48,000 Jews immigrated from Yemen, where they had been isolated for 2,500 years.

Yemenites, as they arrived in Israel, were astonishingly free of coronary heart disease. For them, heart attacks were virtually unheard of. Not so for the Ashkenazi Jews from central Europe.

And yet Israeli investigators have been able to demonstrate that, in the space of just five months, they could turn Yemenites into Ashkenazis—at least so far as blood cholesterol levels are concerned—and then return them to Yemenite status again.

The Bedouins in Israel's Negev desert, seminomadic, with a way of life still much as it was hundreds of years ago—except for their sheikhs and a few of their wealthy who have adopted Western ways—are part of the unique laboratory that Israel is. The differences in the heart health and way of life of the bulk of Bedouins and the heart health and way of life of the Bedouin sheikhs and wealthy, as well as of much of the rest of Israel, are enlightening.

In Israel, too, are the kibbutzim, the more than 200 unusual communal settlements. In Western society, differences in socioeconomic status are mainly determined by occupation and salary level—not in the settlements. Kibbutz members are equal partners. They engage in different types of work, ranging from agriculture, fishing, building, and light industry to clerking, accounting, and management. And it is not at all unusual to find among the manual workers people of superior intelligence and high educational level who, because of idealistic motivation, continue to be manual laborers.

It is notable that kibbutz members have a far lower rate of heart attacks than the Jews who live in Tel Aviv and other Israeli cities yet both groups originally came from the same countries.

In the United States, efforts to study the influence of sedentary and nonsedentary living on coronary heart disease rates encounter some difficulties. Go into an American industry and it is possible to separate the sedentary from the nonsedentary workers but it is difficult to be certain of dietary influences, to make sure that they are not so varied as to prevent getting a true picture of the influence of sedentary versus nonsedentary living. In a kibbutz, all meals are from a central kitchen for adults; the diet is the same for all, sedentary and nonsedentary.

Studies of the influence of other factors are facilitated by kibbutz living. Smoking? There are nonsmokers and heavy smokers in the settlements. Any kibbutz member can draw as many packages of cigarettes once a week as he wishes. A medical scientist investigating the influence of smoking can go to the disbursement records; he need not depend upon the memory of a smoker about how long and how much he has smoked.

Almost anywhere but in a kibbutz, family eating patterns—with parents and children eating from the same pot—may help to confound the influences of environment and heredity. In a kibbutz, children do not live at home in the usual sense; they spend long evenings with their parents but live in a children's dwelling with separate dining facilities. There are no family eating patterns in a kibbutz. This has allowed investigators to compare cholesterol levels in children and parents and demonstrate how much greater is the influence of environment than heredity on those levels.

These and still other Israeli studies are all the more significant and helpful because most physicians in Israel are trained in the same tradition as American physicians. The quality of medical research is so high that there has been substantial support for it from the U.S. National Institutes of Health and other U.S. Government agencies.

Much has been learned about coronary heart disease through the work of United States investigators and those in England, Canada, and many other countries. To no small extent, the very concept of "risk factors"—the dietary and other influences that increase the hazard of developing the disease—has stemmed from the remarkable, long-term, government-supported study of more than 5,000 residents of the Massachusetts community of Framingham. Important contributions have come from many other studies, such as those of Dr. Frederick Stare and his Harvard Medical School associates on the heart attack propensities of Irishmen in Ireland and their brothers in Boston, those of industrial populations by Dr. Jeremiah Stamler, and the investigations of Professor Ancel Keys at the University of Minnesota and around the world.

It is now clear that coronary heart disease with its heart attacks is not purely a matter of heredity; not purely a matter of diet; not purely a matter of exercise or the lack of it; not purely a matter of stress; not purely a matter of any one factor. Instead, it's the result of an equation full of factors. And the factors interact; they affect each other. They may not only add to each other but in some cases multiply each other.

The Israeli experience, now added to the latest work of other scientists in this country and elsewhere, underscores the hopefulness of this. For the factors can be altered. Since there is interaction, an alteration of one often helps to change another favorably. In fact, a change in one can have profound effects on several.

The idea of preventing coronary heart disease is no longer a will-o'-the-wisp.

Undoubtedly there is much more to be learned. But we need not wait decades for more research to dot every "i" and cross every "t." These are our lives now; they are threatened right now. And prevention, as the evidence in the following pages will indicate, is possible right now.

It means making some changes in our way of life—but not necessarily a complete about-face in living.

The measures—practical and often simple, although a few in some cases may call for a determined gritting of teeth—can help, preferably at younger ages but also even at advanced ages, to minimize the likelihood of a heart attack; to maximize the likelihood of recovery and return to normal life should a heart attack occur; and, even for the person who has already experienced a heart attack, to greatly reduce the likelihood of a recurrence.

Does this sound overblown? Too much to hope for? We urge you to read the evidence, to weigh it, to consider the caliber of the latest research work, to sit in on a conversation with the distinguished Israeli physician and investigator, Dr. Daniel Brunner, to examine the suggestions for a program of prevention you can adopt. Then decide—as of course you will want to and should—for yourself.

2

What Is a Heart Attack?
What Is Atherosclerosis?
The Life Picture of the Disease

"Heart attack!"

The words have the rattling sound of machine gun fire. At least once every minute in this country somebody experiences the reality. The victim may stagger, clutch fist to breast, sweat with pain—a pain greater than that of childbirth, possibly the most intense and certainly the most terrifying of any in the catalog. Along with the pain, there may be belching of gas, retching, vomiting. Almost invariably, there is intense anxiety, a sense of doom, of death at hand.

Some victims die almost instantly; some, in hours or days; some recover.

There is a great seeming-paradox in a heart attack. Although it strikes suddenly and may kill in a moment, it has been developing for 20, 30, 50 years.

But there is nothing really paradoxical at all about a heart attack. It is not itself a disease, but an end product of disease. Unless we understand how the disease builds up over a period of years, the natural history of it (what physicians call its "clinical course"), we are helpless to prevent the end result. The preventable stages, as we shall see, occur early in the course, not an hour or two before the fatal moment.

A LATE DISCOVERY

It is now clear—from evidence to be found in Egyptian mummies, for example—that coronary heart disease is no newcomer but affected people thousands of years before Christ. Until very recently, however, it had no name; until even more recently, it had no explanation.

For millennia, the belief was that sudden death was caused by devils or demons. Even in the early eighteenth century, when several prominent citizens of Rome died suddenly, the public generally considered the deaths to be due to God's wrath with the city and, upon the order of Pope Clement XI, postmortem examinations were carried out by the papal physician, Lancisi, to demonstrate that the deaths were from natural causes. Not long afterward, a French physician published an account of a poet, very obese, who had experienced severe chest pain and then died suddenly. On autopsy, the coronary arteries were found to be so narrowed that they would not accommodate the point of a sewing needle.

In the nineteenth century, German physicians became aware of and described in some detail atherosclerosis of the coronary arteries—the deposition of fat and narrowing of the vessels feeding the heart.

But it was not until 1912 that a Chicago physician, Dr. J. B. Herrick, put all the pieces of evidence together and arrived at the concept of acute coronary thrombosis—the sudden deadly event, the blockage at a single moment in time of a coronary vessel already narrowed and ripe for blockage, thus cutting off vital blood flow and starving the heart so it died.

After that, doctors were able to diagnose a heart attack

well enough, but knew little about the mechanism of the disease behind it. Without that knowledge there was a fatalistic attitude. Once a person experienced a heart attack, death was inevitable sooner or later, usually not much later. At most, a victim might hope for three years more of life.

The fatalism extended to the little-understood disease process itself. It was supposed to be an accompaniment of aging and therefore unassailable. But the age-association notion was exploded during World War II. During the War, physicians began to note heart attacks in relatively young men in the armed forces. They gathered data on 866 cases of heart attack in men aged eighteen through thirty-nine. Most of the men had been in seemingly good health until the very moment of sudden death. Sixty-four of them were less than twenty-four years old; more than 200, all told, were under twenty-nine. Autopsy studies showed typical changes in the coronary arteries. They helped to provide convincing evidence that heart attacks were not matters of advancing age but of advancing disease.

During the Korean War, physicians went a step further. They performed postmortem studies on many soldiers killed in battle. They found clear evidence, when the coronary arteries were opened, that disease was present in these men with an average age of only twenty-two. Despite seemingly good health, artery disease had begun; in 10 percent of these very young men, the atherosclerotic process had already narrowed by 70 percent or more the channel in one or both coronary arteries.

Another fact emerging from more recent autopsy studies carried out on men of all ages is that fatty deposits in the coronary arteries are more common and more severe than 25 years ago. At age thirty, for example, men have more coronary artery disease now than forty-year-old men did a quarter of a century ago.

Still another disturbing note comes from U.S. Air Force regular annual examinations of flying personnel that have uncovered the occurrence of a considerable number of silent heart attacks in young men.

Actually, although a classic hallmark is agonizing chest pain, a heart attack can occur without such pain and without other symptoms, and apparently does so in as many as 10 percent of cases. If there is any indication at all, it may be just a sharp twinge or two in the chest followed by a continual dull ache which is passed off as not worth attention.

The occurrence may be discovered only during a routine electrocardiogram. The electrocardiograph machine picks up, amplifies, and records the pattern of electrical signals from the heart muscle. If a silent heart attack has occurred and destroyed a small part of the heart muscle, the heart continues to beat but the dead part of the muscle disturbs some of the electrical pathways, and the changes show up on the electrocardiogram. Autopsy studies, too, frequently show evidence of old heart attacks in people without previous records of them.

THE UNIQUENESS OF THE PUMP

Human disorders are many and varied, infectious and non-infectious, acute and chronic. There are people who suffer perennially from severe headaches, or joint pains, or attacks of intestinal discomfort. No disease event, however, is more dreaded than the heart attack. Why can a heart attack be overwhelming? For the answer, we need perspective on the uniqueness of the heart as a pump and of the coronary arteries that carry the blood to nourish the pump.

A tough, four-chambered, muscular organ about the size of your fist and weighing about 12 ounces, the heart circulates fabulous amounts of blood through the body—the entire 5-

quart content once through the body every 60 seconds. Daily, it pumps the equivalent of 5,500 quarts weighing 6 tons through 60,000 miles of blood vessels.

It does its work without prolonged surcease, never shutting off for repairs. A vital organ like the kidney can stop full functioning for as long as 20 days and then, if functioning returns, the body can recover normally. Not so with the heart. If it stops pushing out blood for more than a few minutes, the delicate brain is irreversibly damaged for want of nourishment only blood can supply to it.

Working away at 70 to 80 beats a minute day and night, the heart depends for its own nourishing blood supply on a couple of small arteries called the coronaries.

THE FEEDERS

When blood is ejected from the main pumping chamber of the heart, the left ventricle, it immediately enters the aorta, the great trunk artery of the body which is about the size of a garden hose. From the aorta branch off the many arteries that carry blood to all parts of the body. Almost as soon as the blood enters the aorta, some of it is pushed into the mouths of two arteries, the coronaries, which branch off from the trunk line at a point very close to the heart.

The coronaries run down the front of the heart. Behaving like other arteries, they divide into branches that cover the back as well as front of the heart. The branches divide and subdivide, finally ending in capillaries, the tiniest of blood vessels. The capillaries feed nutrients from the fresh rich, red blood to the tissues. Then the blood moves into the small vessels of the vein system and, duly, into the large veins which return it to the heart chamber that will pump it to the lungs for refreshening.

Thus, the heart muscle is not nourished directly from the blood passing through its four chambers but only through the blood brought to it by the coronary arteries. And these arteries, which carry blood continuously to an organ that must not be allowed to stop functioning for lack of it, must be supple and elastic. They must bend and sway with the heart muscle as it contracts forcefully in what is called systole to eject blood and then when it relaxes in diastole to permit blood to enter and recharge the heart chambers. And with all the stretching and bending, the coronary arteries must maintain their normal smooth interior to allow blood to pass through easily, without damage, without clotting. This they manage to do so long as they remain healthy and free of atherosclerosis.

The coronaries are built on the same pattern as other arteries in the body. They have a thin, very smooth inside wall called the *intima;* a thicker middle portion, the *media,* composed of elastic fibers and smooth muscle cells; and an outer coating, the *adventitia.*

Arteries themselves being tissue must, of course, be fed. Through the outer adventitial layer, tiny feeding vessels penetrate into the media portion. But these vessels do not go all the way through the media and do not reach the inner intima wall. The inner wall and the portion of the media next to it receive oxygen and other nourishment directly from the blood passing through the artery—and not, as do other tissues, through tiny capillaries. Thus, the inner wall receives relatively sparse nourishment. If damage to the inner wall should occur, there is no large supply of blood that can be mobilized to heal the injured area—in contrast, for example, to what happens in a very richly supplied tissue such as the skin of the face where a small cut from shaving can heal almost overnight.

Nature has cunningly contrived circulation so that blood remains constantly fluid except when a clot is needed for repairs. When, for example, a blood vessel is cut so that the blood begins to leak out, a clot forms to plug the cut. The story of the dozen or so factors in the blood involved in maintaining its fluidity yet capable of making it clot at the right moment is a long and somewhat complex one which need not be recounted here. Our primary concern is knowing that the coronary arteries must be kept smooth, otherwise there is danger of clot formation—and clot formation is one way a heart attack is produced.

THE DISEASE PROCESS

Coronary artery disease used to be called arteriosclerosis, which means artery hardening. It is now called atherosclerosis. Athero means soft swelling. And atherosclerosis is a more accurate descriptive term than arteriosclerosis because the disease process starts with a soft swelling and then progresses to hardening.

The earliest change visible to the eye when atherosclerosis begins to develop is the fatty streak. It is a thin line in the inside lining of the artery: slightly raised, yellowish in color, measuring about one-eighth of an inch in width and half an inch in length.

When such a streak is studied under the microscope, using the special tissue-staining techniques of the medical pathologist, there can be seen an accumulation of cholesterol, cholesterol compounds (cholesterol esters), and some neutral fats. Close examination shows that the elastic fibers of the artery lining are frayed and torn; and smooth muscle cells have begun to balloon out, because of a glut of fatty substances, to form the typical "foam cells" of early atherosclerotic disease.

Most experts on the pathology of atherosclerosis believe that as the disease progresses, the fatty streak grows in size until it becomes the typical "plaque" of atherosclerosis. Plaque is filled with an excess of fat and broken-down cells and looks as if it might be composed of mushy gruel.

As plaques grow in size, there develop areas of hemorrhage and areas of repair where collagen fibers are laid down. And, in long-standing plaques, there may be extensive deposition of calcium so that the plaques become almost bony-hard. Older, larger plaques often break open and resemble ulcerating sores.

In their early stages, plaques develop in the innermost part of the artery, the intima; soon, however, they may involve the media, or middle portion. When plaques are young, small, and soft, they may heal over, be resorbed, and disappear. But when they have advanced to the calcified, hardened, ulcerated stage, it is unlikely that any significant amount of healing is possible.

ANGINA, THE BREAST PANG

Once you visualize what happens during the atherosclerotic process, you can probably anticipate some of the consequences. As plaques enlarge, they begin to stick out into the channel within the artery.

A healthy coronary artery, with a diameter of 2 to 3 millimeters (²⁄₂₅ to ³⁄₂₅ inch), can admit a drinking straw. As atherosclerosis progresses and plaques shrink the internal diameter of the arteries, there may be no symptoms at all for many years. Enough blood still flows through to meet the needs of the heart.

But at some point when the disease process has progressed enough, there may come the moment when the patient experiences his first attack of angina pectoris. It may happen when he is shoveling snow, climbing stairs, playing golf or tennis, or running to catch a bus.

The plaques have built up. Artery narrowing has progressed. There is impediment to blood flow. And while enough blood has been moving through the narrowed arteries to nourish the heart muscle and cause no discomfort under ordinary circumstances, the moment has come when, under some circumstance calling for increased blood flow to the heart—during exercise, for example—the extra surge can't get through.

And now, unable to obtain all the oxygenated blood it needs to sustain its increased beat during body activity, the heart responds with pain. This is angina pectoris (breast pang). Angina involves heart pain but not heart attack. It is a danger signal, however—an indication of atherosclerotic disease in the vital coronary arteries.

Anginal pain can be agonizing. Some patients report that when the pain develops, they experience a sensation of dying. The pain is felt in the front of the chest, usually under the breastbone. It may travel down the left arm or up into the face, mouth, or teeth. It may be brought on not only by exercise but by emotional stress, sexual intercourse, cold air striking the face; in some cases, it may even occur at rest.

Fortunately, the pain usually yields quickly to rest or to use of a tablet of nitroglycerin (yes, the explosive, but in a tiny amount carrying no danger at all of explosive effect). Placed under the tongue from where it can be absorbed very rapidly into the system, nitroglycerin provides prompt relief. Many people with angina, in fact, having learned by experience the circumstances likely to bring on an attack (for example, climbing steps or sexual intercourse), take a nitroglycerin tablet in advance as a preventive measure.

Angina can be present for decades without damage to the heart provided the atherosclerotic disease does not progress further. If the angina is so severe—the pain so great and episodes so frequent—as to be truly disabling, it may be overcome now by new surgical techniques for increasing the flow of blood to the heart muscle (see Chapter 14).

THE HEART ATTACK

When an atherosclerotic plaque ulcerates and roughens, it offers a surface that may stimulate formation of a blood clot. The clot, depending upon the location, then may obstruct a coronary artery or one of its branches. Sometimes, a plaque may break open and discharge so much of its gruel-like contents that they are enough to block an artery or branch, achieving the same effect as a clot of blood.

Blockage of a coronary artery or branch deprives an area of heart muscle—the particular area supplied by the blocked vessel—of vital oxygen and other nutrients. Unless other vessels have developed, extra vessels forming what is called collateral circulation and capable of taking over much or all of the job of supplying blood to the deprived area, that area of heart muscle will be damaged. This is the heart attack, also called coronary occlusion and myocardial infarction.

The outcome will depend upon the amount and location of heart muscle damaged. If a large portion of the wall of the left ventricle, the heart's main pumping chamber, is affected, the outlook is very serious; death may result because the heart simply cannot keep on moving blood out to the body. Or the damaged area may so disrupt the pattern of normal rhythmic electric signals that govern the beating of the heart that an abnormal, useless, quivering rhythm called ventricular fibrillation develops and leads to death.

What else can happen in this serious situation? The infarcted or damaged area of muscle may be so softened that it starts to balloon out. The ballooning out may progress to the point where the ventricle wall bursts and death follows in moments. Or the damaged heart wall may trigger the formation of a blood clot underneath, in the chamber of the heart, and pieces of the clot may break off and be pushed out to block vital arteries to the lungs, brain, kidneys, or legs.

These are some of the gruesome aspects of a heart attack. They help to underscore the need for immediate treatment of a heart attack. So do the more common, less gruesome aspects.

Actually, more often than not, only a small area of heart muscle is affected by a heart attack. Just as it does in other body areas, nature provides more muscle for the heart than is needed for routine activities. It is possible to go on living—

even living virtually a normal life—after two or even more heart attacks if they are not very large ones.

Fibrillation has already been mentioned in connection with massive heart attack. It must be mentioned again here because of its additional importance. Heart attacks are not always produced by clots. A study of more than 2,000 sudden deaths by the Chief Medical Examiner of New York City revealed that 30 percent were due to advanced coronary heart disease —but three-fourths of these showed no clot. The blame may lie with fibrillation: an undernourished and very sensitive heart may, as the result of some sudden extra irritation, go into the squirming, useless fibrillation beat, causing death without complete blockage of an artery.

But fibrillation can be overcome if treated promptly enough. An electric current applied to the heart through the intact chest wall by means of an electronic instrument called a defibrillator can end fibrillation and restore normal beat in many cases. Moreover, another type of abnormal rhythm preceding fibrillation can give warning that the latter may follow, allowing measures to be taken to prevent the fibrillation.

PREVENTING DEATH

Today, most good hospitals have special intensive care units for heart attack patients. In these units, special electronic equipment monitors every beat of a patient's heart and keeps constant surveillance on other vital factors. Special teams man the units around the clock and can react instantly to save life if a crisis occurs.

Currently, the vast majority of patients reaching a hospital alive after a heart attack can later walk out of the hospital. For them, the death rate has been dramatically reduced. Unfortunately, each year in this country, 400,000 people who suffer heart attacks never reach a hospital alive. A large proportion of them could be saved if there were a chance to treat them.

It is not usually a matter of it taking too long to get to a hospital. When two University of Rochester cardiologists recently interviewed 160 coronary victims to find out how much time had elapsed between onset of symptoms and hospitalization, the average interval turned out to be 3½ hours. In some cases, the delay stretched for as long as 5 days. Transportation time from home to hospital accounted for only a tiny fraction of the delay—20 minutes on average.

The trouble was that patients were slow to seek help, even when symptoms were unmistakable. Eighty percent had experienced intense chest pain yet had delayed seeking help. (Procrastination was somewhat more understandable among remaining patients with less clear symptoms, such as seeming indigestion, dizziness, shortness of breath.) Moreover, the investigators discovered, patients with high-risk medical conditions and a tendency to develop heart attacks were those who waited the longest before seeking medical assistance.

This is consistent with findings of a recent special conference of the American College of Cardiology, an organization of specialists in heart problems. The findings: that certain attitudes about heart disease keep people from seeking medical care when they suspect they have heart symptoms; that people often deny they have symptoms of heart disease because they believe it is a completely incapacitating condition from which they will never recover.

A step in the right direction has been the recent inception of public educational programs aimed at indoctrinating people with the need to get quick help when they have the slightest suspicion that they are undergoing a heart attack.

No less important is a need for clear public understanding not only that heart attack victims often can be saved with prompt treatment, but also that more often than not a heart attack does not mean extensive damage to the heart. If abnormal rhythms can be prevented or overcome promptly, there is a high probability of survival—and survival does not have to mean invalidism.

RECOVERY FROM A HEART ATTACK

With proper care, usually extending three to six weeks in the hospital and up to three to six months at home, healing of a damaged heart can often proceed smoothly.

Many people wonder how the heart can possibly heal since it is always at work. They point, for example, to the fact that when an arm or leg is injured, it may be put at complete rest to aid healing. Actually, the heart is not literally working all the time. It is at rest between beats. And while this rest interval may seem brief, it actually extends for a longer period of time than the work interval of the heart. It is still further extended when the patient relaxes and physical activity, during the healing period, doesn't go beyond the moderate. While the heart does not rest completely overall, nature does manage to put a damaged heart area in particular at sufficient rest so it heals over just as does a cut in an arm or leg.

A fatal first heart attack is more likely to occur in a relatively young person, say of forty or fifty, than in an older individual. The young person's coronary circulation system has not developed collaterals the way the circulation system in an older person has. Blockage of an artery may cut off blood supply completely whereas in an older person, the collaterals may be well developed enough to come to the rescue and reduce the severity of the attack.

There is now evidence that people who take care to get plenty of exercise as part of a preventive program gradually build up healthy collateral circulation that may help to prevent heart attacks or lessen their severity.

Once it was thought that after a heart attack, other attacks were inevitable, the disease hopelessly progressive, and death inevitable sooner or later. Patients were advised to retire—frequently to Florida or another warm-climate area. In retrospect, doctors say that many of these patients probably died in retirement from cirrhosis of the liver rather than from heart disease; they sat around, sad, bored, and drank themselves to death. Patients who survived heart attacks and could not retire were duly warned to give up physical activity, to avoid even climbing a flight of stairs.

It is now recognized that the heart can recover completely from even a severe attack and that very often victims can be restored to normal or near-normal life and job activity. The recovery from severe coronaries of two Presidents, Eisenhower and Johnson, who then managed to carry on all the activities and shoulder all the burdens of the Presidency, perhaps did more than anything else to convince many people that it is possible to recover completely from a heart attack.

Today, many physicians encourage patients after heart attacks to return to jobs and active living and, indeed, to begin an exercise program, starting slowly and working up to vigorous activity, as a means of increasing collateral circulation, training the heart, invigorating the body generally, and instilling confidence. In almost every instance, a normal sex life is encouraged. Rarely is a change of climate advised.

Anyone who has had a heart attack should give up any notion of being inevitably doomed to invalidism. He should accept, gracefully, his initiation into the coronary club and carry out preventive measures to be discussed later—measures that can help reduce risk of another attack.

It is important for a person recovered from a heart attack to have reassurance from his physician, from his family, and from knowledge about the disease and what can be done to retard or prevent its further progress.

It is often helpful if the physician talks over the situation fully with the patient's spouse and children. A heart attack can be a frightening experience, anxiety-provoking for the whole family. It strikes at the relatively young man and threatens the family's economic support. No less important, it threatens the emotional support derived from husband and father who, at least for a time now, needs emotional buoying-up by the rest of the family.

THE FALSE HEART ATTACK

You may have heard of instances in which a patient suffering what appears to be a heart attack is hospitalized but then, after a day or two, can be released from hospital. What he has really suffered is an episode of coronary insufficiency, a condition about halfway between an attack of angina pectoris and a true heart attack. It deprives the heart muscle of enough oxygen to cause pain almost comparable to that of a heart attack but the oxygen deprivation is not sufficient to actually damage the heart muscle.

Coronary insufficiency may be triggered when a clot starts to form but then does not progress, or when a coronary artery is narrowed enough by a large plaque so that a sudden, unusual demand for more blood—as the result of unusual exertion or nervous tension—cannot be met.

Today it is possible to diagnose heart attacks not only by changes in the electrocardiogram but also by sensitive enzyme tests performed on the blood. Certain enzymes appear in the blood in increased amounts only when the heart muscle is truly damaged and they are released into the blood from the damaged area. Thus, the enzyme tests are most helpful in distinguishing between a true heart attack with actually damaged heart muscle and the coronary insufficiency type of attack without muscle destruction.

You may have wondered whether heart attacks ever occur as the result of the weakening and "blowing out" of the wall of a coronary artery. This does happen with other arteries. Some strokes, for example, are the results of the blowing out of brain arteries. An atherosclerotic aorta, the main trunk artery, rarely is blocked completely by plaque or blood clot, but when severely diseased, an area of the aorta may balloon out. The outpouching is called an aneurysm and as it becomes more extensive the artery wall may be so thinned and weakened that it finally leaks blood or ruptures completely. If discovered in time, an aortic aneurysm can be repaired surgically: the diseased area can be cut out and the remaining portions reconnected directly or with a graft between.

The coronary arteries do not undergo this type of ballooning out because they are firmly embedded in strong muscle.

The Life Picture of the Disease

We have discussed the disease changes that may take place in the coronary arteries and what happens to the patient as they do. Over a lifetime, the picture looks as shown in Table 1.

TABLE 1

Age (Years)	Artery Condition	Symptoms
0–10	Normal	None
10–20	Fatty streak	None
20–30	Plaque	None
30–45	Complicated lesions: ulceration, hemorrhage, clotting, calcification	Probably none, but there may be some angina pectoris, and even occasional mild, unnoticed heart attacks.
45 and older	Increasing severity of plaque lesions and complications	Angina pectoris; coronary insufficiency; frank heart attacks.

The picture above, of course, is based on averages and there are many exceptions either way. Some people live to age 100 and have "clean" coronary arteries, though this is extremely rare in the United States. There are people, on the other hand, like the medical school classmate of one of us who died suddenly of heart attack at the age of thirty-one, with marked atherosclerosis of the coronary vessels.

Women have much the same pattern as the table indicates but with less intense changes until after menopause.

Discussing chemical reactions, one distinguished scientist likes to classify them as slow, fast, and "too damn fast"—almost too fast to measure. All chemical and biological processes around us require time. But some involved in simple chemistry take only nanoseconds (billionths of a second). Some involved in molecular biology require only milliseconds (thousandths of a second). Some more complicated chemical processes require minutes to hours. And biological processes such as growth and aging take days to years.

However much a heart attack seems to be an instantaneous disease, it is really the manifestation of a disease that has been evolving for many years.

Pathologists are physicians trained to study diseased organs. Some are medical examiners or coroners and their work requires them to examine the bodies of people who meet accidental deaths or who die under circumstances leaving the cause of death in doubt. Pathologists see the bodies of many people, young and seemingly in perfect health when alive, victims of automobile accidents. More and more, they are impressed by the fact that so many of the seemingly healthy young, just barely out of their teens, have definite signs of beginning atherosclerosis.

More and more now it is possible to help people with incapacitating angina, to save the lives of heart attack victims who only a decade ago would almost certainly have died and, once saved, to provide for them, through medication or surgery and other measures, rehabilitation to normal or near-normal living. We will be covering this in greater detail in Chapter 14.

Obviously, it is desirable to be able to combat the effects of disease but it is far more desirable to prevent the disease or, if it already exists, to keep it from advancing.

What foments atherosclerosis has been under intensive study throughout the world.

No disease is ever the result of some one factor. This is true even of infections ranging from the common cold to pneumonia. Repeatedly, investigators have been able to demonstrate that the microorganisms, or bugs, responsible for many infections are always all around us and even within us. Their mere presence in limited numbers causes no problems. But then suddenly something happens—host resistence is lowered, for example—and infection develops. The once-in-check organisms multiply and overrun. So it isn't the bugs alone that are involved in infection; it's the host, too—and a whole series of factors responsible for determining how much or how little resistance he has.

Very clearly, this is true for heart attacks and the atherosclerotic disease that produces them. It's a multifactorial disease. Research has been pinpointing the major risk factors; it has been showing how they interact, how they can be combated, how in many cases combating one automatically combats several others.

3

The Cholesterol Story:
A Hard Look at One Factor

No one is surprised today to hear people talk about their "cholesterol values." The word cholesterol has become part of the everyday language. It is used as much as, and even more often than, such terms as blood sugar, Pap test, blood pressure, and basal metabolism. Almost everyone knows vaguely that cholesterol is related to heart attacks and perhaps the whole process of artery hardening. And almost everyone would like to have a "normal" or a very low cholesterol level.

Why all the concern about a rather complex chemical substance? Because during recent decades study after study has indicated that the level of cholesterol in the blood serum correlates with susceptibility to coronary heart disease and heart attacks.

THE INDICTMENT

Throughout the world, wherever groups of people have been found with low frequency of atherosclerosis and heart attacks, their blood serum cholesterol has proved to be on the low side in comparison with American averages.

Various long-term studies in this country—in Framingham, Mass., Albany, N.Y., and Minneapolis, Minn., for example— have established that the risk of having a heart attack rises sharply with increasing levels of cholesterol. (From now on, cholesterol value or level will refer to the concentration of cholesterol in the blood serum, and any figures used for cholesterol values will indicate milligrams of cholesterol in 100 cubic milliliters, roughly 4 ounces, of blood.)

For example, in Framingham, the frequency of coronary heart disease was found to be seven times greater in persons with cholesterol above 259 than among those with levels below 200. In the Albany study, the frequency of CHD for higher cholesterol values was three times greater, and in the Minneapolis study it was six times greater.

In one Israeli study carried out by Dr. Brunner and his associates, cholesterol in patients with heart attacks averaged 264 while the level in Yemenites free of heart attacks averaged 159.

It has now become possible for physicians, using a special x-ray movie technique, to actually make pictures of the coronary arteries and the blood flow through them. The technique is a valuable aid in diagnosis, in determining whether a patient with chest pain, for example, does in fact have heart disease or instead owes the pain to some other condition such as muscle spasm in the chest wall. In a recent study using the technique in 723 patients at the Cleveland Clinic, only 20 percent of those with cholesterol levels lower than 200 had any significant narrowing of the coronary arteries. On the other hand, 81 percent of patients with cholesterol levels higher than 275 had significant narrowing.

It can be argued, of course, that an association between higher cholesterol levels and frequency of coronary heart disease and heart attacks does not signify a cause and effect relationship. And this is true.

But evidence about the importance of cholesterol comes from other types of observations as well. Atherosclerotic arteries, it is known, contain large amounts of cholesterol both in the free form and bound to other compounds. As far back as 1910, investigators were able to determine that atherosclerotic arteries contain 6 to 7 times as much free cholesterol and more than 20 times as much cholesterol compounds as normal arteries.

At the turn of the century, too, investigators were able to demonstrate that feeding cholesterol-rich food to rabbits could produce changes in the arteries resembling the changes found in human disease. They fed the rabbits diets heavy on eggs, milk, and meat and saw fatty deposits develop in the aortas of the animals. It remained for a Russian investigator, N. Anitschkow, in 1912 to feed pure cholesterol dissolved in vegetable oil to rabbits to prove that it was the cholesterol that caused the damage to the aortas.

Since then it has been established that not all species of animals react as do rabbits. For example, the dog, cat, and rat are resistant to the development of atherosclerosis when fed cholesterol. A number of other species, however, do react like the rabbit. Dr. Louis N. Katz of Michael Reese Hospital in Chicago, knowing that birds in zoos are prone to develop atherosclerosis, decided to feed cholesterol to chicks and found them to be as susceptible as rabbits. Swine and some strains of pigeons develop atherosclerosis when fed cholesterol. And very important has been the demonstration that cholesterol feeding induces atherosclerosis in some types of monkeys and in some of the nonhuman primates such as the baboon.

Recently, working with rhesus monkeys, investigators have produced advanced coronary artery disease in as little as two years with butterfat and cholesterol added to a low-fat, commercial primate ration. And Dr. Robert W. Wissler of the

University of Chicago has reported the development in as short a time as 20 months of severe coronary and aorta lesions in rhesus monkeys fed on human foods formulated to resemble the average American diet.

It should be mentioned that the usual experiments with rabbits have required getting the animals' serum cholesterol up to a very high level—as high as 1,500—compared with the average American human level of 250. But with the high level, artery disease can be produced in the rabbits in three months whereas the disease may take decades to develop in man. More recently, investigators have shown that artery disease can be produced in rabbits with much lower cholesterol feeding and, while it may require two or three years of such feeding, the end result is disease of the arteries resembling human disease much more closely than when the experiments are carried out with much higher amounts of cholesterol for the usual three-month period.

OTHER EVIDENCE

More evidence on the importance of cholesterol in athero-sclerosis comes from two groups of humans. There are people who inherit a tendency to high blood cholesterol levels; they are prone to early development of atherosclerosis and to heart attacks. Another group of persons, those fed diets rich in cream and milk for peptic ulcers, tend to be more subject to heart attacks than do others.

It would seem, indeed, that cholesterol level is related to coronary heart disease. The evidence is somewhat like that for the relationship between cigarette smoking and lung cancer. Most of us accept the weight of statistical evidence showing that cigarette smokers have far greater likelihood of developing lung cancer than have nonsmokers. Yet, thus far, there has been no demonstration of any specific cancer-causing substance in cigarette smoke. Of course, all of us prefer direct evidence. But many criminals have been convicted on circumstantial evidence when the jury felt the weight of the evidence to be strong enough.

Since atherosclerosis is such a slowly progressive disease, it will take many years to prove definitively that lowering elevated blood cholesterol actually reduces the risk of heart attack. Preliminary evidence, however, is highly suggestive that it does.

For example, it has been reported recently that members of "anticoronary clubs" who reduced their cholesterol levels and body weights have been experiencing only one-third the incidence of coronary heart disease ordinarily expected.

It can be argued that the weight reduction in these people was more important than the reduction of cholesterol levels. Also, perhaps members of the clubs smoke less, exercise more, and have less emotional stress because of their group activities. Only time and careful observation of large numbers of people will permit cholesterol to be factored out specifically and its role in coronary heart disease established beyond doubt.

At present, however, most physicians would agree with Dr. David Kritchevsky, a gifted research worker in the field of atherosclerosis, who says: "Whatever the final definition of initiation of atherosclerosis may be, there is little doubt that cholesterol is related to this disease in some manner."

CHOLESTEROL IN WOMEN

In women, a high level of serum cholesterol may be even more of a danger signal than in men. Dr. Charles W. Frank of Albert Einstein College of Medicine, New York, studied 745 men and 228 women between the ages of twenty-five and sixty-four who developed angina pectoris or had a heart attack. The study went on for three and a half years.

As compared with men, women with high cholesterol levels

were found to have a significantly greater probability of progressing from angina to a first heart attack, or from a first heart attack to a repeat attack, and of dying. Having a high cholesterol level increased their probability of heart attack death regardless of such factors as age, weight, blood pressure, and the presence or absence of diabetes.

Just why elevated cholesterol levels appears to be even more dangerous for women than for men is something of a mystery. Coronary heart disease rarely occurs in women under the age of forty. And, whereas in men cholesterol levels tend to rise in the early years and then may change little between the ages of forty and sixty, in women it is usually only after age forty that the levels start to rise sharply. If, indeed, as it seems to do, elevated cholesterol promotes artery disease, artery disease may progress even more rapidly in women over forty with high cholesterol levels than in men over forty.

THE FORM OF CHOLESTEROL

Coronary heart disease researchers now believe that the form of cholesterol in the blood is important. Two principal forms —usually called alpha and beta cholesterol—are to be found in serum. Both are there but it appears to be the ratio between them that counts. The less beta cholesterol in comparison with alpha, the less the likelihood of heart attack. It appears that beta cholesterol is much more readily deposited on artery walls than is alpha.

For example, in an Israeli study by Dr. Brunner and his associates, while 90 percent of persons with definite heart disease were found to have elevated beta cholesterol levels, none of the Yemenite Jews (who as a group are virtually free of heart disease in Yemen and upon arrival in Israel) had abnormally high beta cholesterol levels. In the same study, workers from Israeli collective settlements, who have many fewer heart attacks than Israeli city dwellers, were found to have lower beta cholesterol values than a group of city physicians of the same age and sex.

Other Israeli research workers—Dr. M. Toor, Dr. A. Katchalsky, and their collaborators—have made similar findings. They observed that in Yemenite Jews who had been in Israel less than 5 years, total cholesterol and beta cholesterol levels were lower than in Yemenites who had been in Israel for 20 years or longer and had adapted to Israeli ways of life. Also, in this study the highest beta cholesterol as well as total cholesterol values were found in Israelis of European origin who were at higher economic levels than the Yemenites.

"NORMAL" CHOLESTEROL LEVELS

At a businessman's luncheon, the conversation may well go like this:

"I had a checkup recently and my cholesterol was 309, and my doctor said it's at the upper limit of normal and not to worry about it."

A second man reports: "But my doctor found mine to be 260 and said that was upper normal."

A third says: "My doctor is raising hell about my weight, diet, and exercise because he won't be happy until my cholesterol goes below 200."

Who is right? What is a normal cholesterol value? Nobody really knows.

You can argue that since you are born with a cholesterol level of 80 that should be considered normal. On the other hand, there are those who argue that it is a matter of statistics and if you average the values for adult Americans, you come up with a figure of 250 and that can be considered normal. Dr. Laurence Kinsell, an authority on cholesterol, considers 180 to be the upper limit of normal and says that "true normal levels may be much lower."

Until Americans are free of coronary heart disease, there will probably be no agreement on what constitutes a normal value. Any "normal" derived from statistical averaging may be invalid and deceptive. Surely an average weight, for example, which is arrived at from the weights of an overfed, overweight population can hardly be considered to be normal weight. Most physicians feel that, as for weight, our national average for cholesterol is pitched too high.

If we judge from the Yemenites in Israel who are free of heart disease, a value of 150 would seem to be closer to true normal. This value of 150 is found in other parts of the world where the populations have lower incidence of heart attacks. Most American physicians would be very happy, indeed, to have patients show cholesterol values of 150; they would even be content to settle for a 200 level.

CHOLESTEROL DETERMINATION

When cholesterol in the blood is to be measured, a sample of blood is drawn in the morning before breakfast after an overnight fast of at least 12 hours. Usually about two teaspoonsful are drawn from a vein into a syringe. The blood is allowed to clot, then is centrifuged or whirled at high speed, and the serum or liquid part is separated out and subjected to chemical analysis.

All hospitals and private clinical laboratories are equipped to make cholesterol determinations, but variations in test results between laboratories often are tremendous. There have been studies in which blood samples from individual patients were divided into six parts and sent to six different laboratories for analysis. The cholesterol determinations reported back varied by as much as 100 points.

So, in case you are tempted, our advice would be not to just march into any laboratory to have a cholesterol check made. Let your physician decide on the laboratory; he will know a reliable one. Subsequent determinations should be made by the same laboratory; usually an efficient laboratory will get consistent results in terms of its own standards even though its determinations may be somewhat higher or lower than those of another laboratory. Your physician will know what the normal should be as performed by the laboratory he selects. And he will be largely concerned about changes in the cholesterol level: whether, if elevated, it comes down in response to diet or other measures he institutes.

It is also important to realize that a single cholesterol determination may not establish your true level. From day to day, the cholesterol level in the morning fasting state may vary by as much as 20 points. Thus, your physician would be justified in having more than a single determination made. Especially if your value appears to be at what he considers the upper limit of normal, he may need another determination to make certain.

LOWERING CHOLESTEROL

If elevated cholesterol can be considered so important in coronary heart disease, if the low level found in Israeli groups relatively immune to the disease can be considered significant, why can't some simple method be found to bring cholesterol level down in CHD-prone Americans?

Elevated cholesterol can be brought down—but it is not a simple matter of a panacea, of a pill, or even of eliminating cholesterol from the diet.

Cholesterol is manufactured in the body. A small, important amount is taken in with food, and we shall have more to say about that soon. The cholesterol taken in via food is called exogenous or "outside" cholesterol. Much more important is the endogenous or "inside" cholesterol.

To understand the logic of attempts to reduce cholesterol

levels in the blood, we must first understand something of how cholesterol is manufactured, stored, distributed, changed, and excreted in the body.

Cholesterol is a large, complex molecule. Ordinary drinking alcohol has 2 carbon atoms; the acetic acid in vinegar also has only 2 carbon atoms. Cholesterol, however, has 27. In addition, it has four "ring" formations of a very stable nature in what chemists call a "sterol configuration."

We are so conditioned to thinking of cholesterol as harmful to the arteries, and as being involved in gallstones, that understandably most of us regard it as a purely deleterious, even poisonous, substance. That is not the case. The human body could not function without cholesterol.

The compound is contained in almost every cell of the body. It is probably concerned with the regulation of the passage of nutrients into and out of cells through the cell membranes. Cholesterol is found in high concentration in the brain and probably acts there in some important, though not yet well understood, capacity. Furthermore, cholesterol serves as a material from which numerous important body constituents are manufactured. For example, the corticosteroids, or hormones of the adrenal gland such as cortisone, are derived from cholesterol. Without these hormones, life is impossible. Also, the sex hormones are derived from the sterol nucleus of cholesterol. Cholesterol is changed by the body to bile acids and excreted in the bile. And digestion would be a sorry mess if the bile acids were not available to bring fats into emulsion in the intestine for absorption into the body.

It's a pity that cholesterol has to act as both friend and foe.

The big, strongly knit molecule, with its skeleton of 27 carbon atoms, is manufactured, strangely enough, from one of the simplest compounds in the body—the 2-carbon acetic acid structure. Scientists have patiently unraveled all the steps from the 2 carbons to the 27. Medical scientists can get ecstatic over the story of the unfolding of the many steps in cholesterol manufacture. However, our purpose here is to tell you about cholesterol as it applies to arteries and the heart rather than to make a biochemist of you. But if you do have scientific training and want to learn more of the cholesterol story, you may enjoy consulting latest editions of biochemistry books in a medical, university, or public library.

Although the body builds cholesterol with relative ease, it has no mechanism for breaking the compound down again readily to the 2-carbon starting material. This complicates the matter of reducing elevated levels of cholesterol in the blood. If cholesterol could be decomposed readily, we might find simple ways to reduce the blood level to favorable concentrations.

It is difficult to attempt to control cholesterol levels by hindering manufacture of the compound. If synthesis of the compound were stopped or curtailed sharply, there would be interference with normal functions of the body dependent upon cholesterol. The cure might, indeed, kill. But the situation is far from hopeless as we shall see, and some success has been achieved in partial reduction of cholesterol production in the body. Moreover, even though cholesterol cannot be decomposed completely, it can be converted into bile acids which are excreted into the small intestine; and this, as we shall also see, offers some possibilities for lowering excess blood cholesterol levels.

Most of the manufacture of cholesterol in the body is carried out in the liver. In severe liver disease, the serum cholesterol level may be greatly reduced. But damaging the liver deliberately is, obviously enough, no solution since a seriously ailing liver can be more immediately dangerous to health than damaged arteries. But there may be ways to interfere with the catalysts—the enzymes—in the liver that control the rate at which cholesterol is produced.

You might ask, logically enough: "Why worry so much about total cholesterol in the body? Why not simply control the mechanism that determines its level in the blood—and thus achieve a desirable concentration?"

But no simple method is yet known for controlling the body's "cholesterol-stat" mechanism. Each individual seems to have a built-in pattern of cholesterol regulation and for most of us in this country, the stat, or control, seems to be set too high. Unfortunately for us, nature does not seem to understand where to peg the level of cholesterol in order to protect our hearts and arteries, leaving it up to us to find measures to help ourselves.

Actually, nature's failure here is a cause for considerable scientific wonderment. For many other chemicals in the blood are controlled naturally with remarkable precision to protect health. For example, blood sugar is regulated exquisitely in almost everyone except the diabetic. Important substances such as calcium are regulated precisely within a very narrow safe range, otherwise we would all have tetany seizures from too little blood calcium or severe headaches and other symptoms from too much.

Curiously enough, it does seem possible for nature on occasion to change the cholesterol-regulating mechanism. Such a genetic change for the better has been observed in the Masai tribe in Africa. Scientists have wondered why these people are free of coronary heart disease and have low serum cholesterol levels despite a strange diet composed of huge quantities of meat, milk, and animal blood. Such a diet is anathema to any heart specialists. Yet the Masai are protected from its ill effects.

The Masai, as valuable studies by Dr. Bruce Taylor of Evanston, Ill., have shown, can turn off the manufacture of cholesterol. When they eat too much cholesterol itself or too much of foods that promote the manufacture of cholesterol, their body chemistry is alerted, the right "valve" is pressed, and their serum cholesterol level still remains about 150. This phenomenon is believed to result from a genetic change in the Masai. What a pity it has not caught up with us.

How then can we, lacking a natural, built-in, effective cholesterol control, go about achieving better control? Diet, medicines, surgery, exercise, reduced stress have all been proposed. Of these, diet is one of the easiest and safest measures.

DIETARY CONTROL

Dietary control of cholesterol level rests upon two basic principles. The first is that cholesterol content of foods varies greatly and by proper selection of food we can reduce cholesterol intake. The table in Appendix II lists common foods and their cholesterol content.

A quick glance will show that the following foods are especially high in cholesterol: egg yolk (1,500), butter (250), kidney (375), sweetbreads (250), calf brains (2,000-plus), lobster (200). The figures are for 3½-ounce portions.

On the other hand, the following have essentially no cholesterol content: fruits, vegetables, egg whites, cereals, vegetable oils, peanut butter, and vegetable margarine. Skim milk and milk powder are very low in cholesterol (it should be emphasized that fat-free skim milk or milk powder retain all the valuable protein, mineral, and vitamin content of whole milk but is free of the fats that contain cholesterol and saturated fatty acids).

The other dietary principle for reducing blood cholesterol rests upon the scientific finding that the lower the ratio between saturated and unsaturated fats in the diet, the lower will be the cholesterol level. Saturated fats are found in butter, whole milk, many meats (particularly beef, lamb, and pork). Unsaturated fats are the "soft" fats such as are contained in vegetable oils, fish and fowl, and many margarines.

In case you are interested in the chemical meaning of the terms saturated and unsaturated, both types of fats contain carbon atoms. In an unsaturated fat, there are bonds between the carbon atoms capable of taking up additional hydrogen. If a fat cannot take up any additional hydrogen at all, it is said to be saturated. If it has one bond that can take up hydrogen, it is said to be slightly unsaturated. Some fats have four bonds that can take up hydrogen; they are referred to as highly unsaturated.

Actually, no food is made up of fats that are entirely saturated or unsaturated. Wherever fats are present in foods, both types are to be found but the proportions of saturated versus unsaturated vary.

Thus, for example, corn oil, cottonseed oil, and soya oil are composed of about 55 percent unsaturated and 10 to 25 percent saturated fats, with the balance being slightly unsaturated. Butter, however, contains about 50 percent saturated, less than 10 percent unsaturated, and the remainder slightly unsaturated fats.

A practical approach to dietary control uses both principles and underscores moderation. Cholesterol intake does not have to be completely curtailed; that would be dangerous since some cholesterol is essential. Nor is there any need to try to eliminate all saturated fats—a virtual impossibility, anyhow. It really comes down to a matter of restraining ourselves, of pulling back from the overemphasis we have put upon fat in the American diet.

How the American Diet Has Changed

Few of us today really understand how drastically American eating habits have changed. Until about the turn of the century, the American diet was rich in carbohydrates and, in some cases, in meat. But the meat was lightly streaked with fat; the heavy marbling of today was unknown. At that time steers were driven long distances to stockyards; there was little of the "finishing," or final fattening which is common today. Even pork and bacon, while fatty, consisted of fat that was not saturated because pigs foraged freely or were fed peanuts.

About the year 1900 the average American diet appears to have been composed of 50 percent carbohydrates, 20 percent proteins, 30 percent fats. By 1950, this had changed greatly. Luxury foods were in lavish supply. As some observers have noted, with dairies churning out vast amounts of milk, cream, butter, and cheese, and with the American youth's taste for them, our youth diet had become "one big milk shake." A little later in life the diet became "one big beefsteak." Thick, marbled steaks had become a status symbol. By 1950, fats made up 40 to 45 percent of the diet.

So it would seem wise to set that part of our diet in order, reducing to some extent—sensibly moderating seems an appropriate term—our intake of fat. It would also seem wise to moderate our intake of foods rich in cholesterol and to put more emphasis on foods with more of the unsaturated fats and less of the saturated.

In Israel, investigators have established that the diet of the Bedouins, who have a remarkably low incidence of coronary heart disease, contains only small quantities of meat and dairy products and is characterized by a low percentage of fat calories. Yemenites, too, consume less fat—less than half of the animal fat eaten by the European Jews who have a high incidence of coronary heart disease.

Few if any of us would want to adopt a Bedouin or Yemenite diet. Nor need we. But instead of moving away from, we can move toward a healthy diet. We can forego the extreme of the too-rich diet in favor of the moderation of a diet that, while helping to promote health, need not be lacking in enjoyment.

You Don't Need an Encyclopedia

To achieve a more healthy and still enjoyable diet does not require constant consultation of a food encyclopedia and rigid rules, only keeping in mind a few simple guidelines.

Since egg yolks are very rich in cholesterol, we should limit their intake. Most authorities consider two or three eggs a week reasonable, with no limitation at all on use of egg whites in cooking; the whites are virtually all protein.

When it comes to dairy products, the emphasis should be on skim milk, buttermilk, cottage cheese, and such other low-fat cheeses as farmer, hoop, and sapsago—very much favoring such items in place of other cheeses, butter, sweet and sour cream, and ice cream.

As for entrees, a practical and healthy approach here might be called multi-moderational. We don't have to come near to giving up our beloved steaks, chops, and roasts. We can have them a little less often, and a little more often we can have lean types of poultry such as the white meat of chicken and turkey (avoiding the skin where most of the fat is concentrated). A little more often, too, we can have favorite fish and seafoods, which have high protein content and in comparison with meats lower saturated and higher unsaturated fat content.

When we do have meat, we can be moderate about portions. We don't really have to sate ourselves with 12-ounce steaks. We can trim away all visible fat. When meat is roasted, we can discard the dripping fat instead of using it as gravy. In the preparation of meat, we can do more roasting, broiling, baking, and boiling and less frying.

As for breads: French bread, corn bread, and dinner rolls tend to be relatively rich in fat; white, whole-wheat, rye, and Italian bread less so. Melba toast is low in fat. And low-calorie breads without saturated fats are to be found in some markets. Soups don't have to be banned if you enjoy them. Eat those that do not contain much fat. One procedure worth trying is to cook a soup, refrigerate it, then skim off the fat from the top before reheating.

We can put more emphasis on vegetables, salads, and fruits. They take the edge off appetites—and they do more. While they have hearty bulk, they are low or moderate in calories, contain only small amounts of fat (mostly unsaturated), are loaded with vitamins and minerals, and some, such as peas and beans, are rich in protein.

We don't have to give up desserts entirely if they are important to us. We can be sparing in their use, eating smaller portions, and sometimes substituting fruits, fresh or compote.

As for beverages, we can acquire a taste (if we don't already have it) for the real taste of coffee and tea, for example, rather than for the oversweetened taste so much in vogue, using little sugar and possibly even none at all. And we can substitute nonfat milk for cream.

ONE TEST DIET

There have been trials that have produced evidence that a change in diet may help reduce the incidence of coronary heart disease.

In 1957, the New York City Health Department formed an "anticoronary club" to test the idea that a person who eats so as to lower the cholesterol level in his blood may at least trim the odds against cardiovascular disease. A diet was worked out by the Health Department's Bureau of Nutrition that rested on two principles: moderation in the quantity of fat eaten and equal amounts in the diet of the three kinds of fat, saturated, unsaturated, and slightly unsaturated. It was called the "prudent diet."

It sounded somewhat strange: no more than 16 ounces of beef, pork, or lamb per week; fish, veal, and poultry high on the menu; no butter, ice cream, or hard cheese but instead low–saturated-fat margarines, sherbet, and cottage cheese; no rich desserts and pastries but rather baked foods low in saturated fats, made with shortenings high in unsaturated fats. Fish, a rich source of unsaturated fats, was to be eaten at least five times a week. Beef could be eaten four times. The remaining meals, except breakfasts, were to involve poultry or veal. Vegetables, fruits, cereals, and vegetable oils were fine. Only four eggs a week were allowed.

Within a few weeks of the announcement of the club, 900 men had joined up. They were New Yorkers ranging from forty to fifty-nine years of age, mostly from managerial and professional occupations. There was close supervision. Members went through weekly sessions with nutritionists and through monthly panel meetings. There were blood tests.

By 1959, the charter members had proved that they could learn to like and even love the diet. Within six months on it, they found that their blood cholesterol levels really did drop— the higher the prediet cholesterol level, the greater the fall. A prediet level of 300 was likely to drop to 240; if it had been 260, it might drop to 220.

Once the club was well under way, another group of men was asked to join the study, eating as they always had and serving for comparison. They had to be similar to the men in the club in many ways, including having an interest in maintaining and improving health.

Some eight years after the original formation of the club, there was enough experience for a preliminary comparison to be made between the cholesterol levels and the heart attack rates of the club members and of the control-group volunteers.

The results: The rate of heart attacks for the control or comparison group was 980 per 100,000 against 339 per 100,000 for the men in the diet group. The prudent diet could hardly be considered a cure-all for coronary heart disease but it did provide evidence that diet change could be helpful.

To illustrate how a prudent diet works, Table 2 gives

sample meals for a week, designed for men who want to reduce cholesterol levels while maintaining normal weight. This particular diet provides 2,300 calories a day.

TABLE 2

MONDAY

Breakfast: Half a cantaloupe, half a cup of cottage cheese, 2 slices of toast, two teaspoons of margarine (made largely with vegetable oil), 2 teaspoons of jam, coffee or tea.

Lunch: 4 ounces of poached or canned salmon, 1 tablespoon of tartar sauce, tossed green salad, 1 tablespoon of French dressing, one baked apple, 2 slices of bread, beverage.

Dinner: Veal stew (four ounces of veal with carrots and celery), ½ cup of noodles cooked with 1 tablespoon of seasoned oil, Chinese cabbage or lettuce wedge, one tablespoon of French dressing, half a cup of citrus fruit, one slice bread, beverage, 2 fruits, 2 cups of skim milk if desired.

TUESDAY

Breakfast: 1 sliced orange, 1 cup of oatmeal cooked with 2 teaspoons of oil, 6 ounces of skim milk, 1 or 2 slices of toast with 1 or 2 teaspoons of margarine, 1 teaspoon honey, beverage.

Lunch: 4 ounces of turkey or sardine sandwich, 1 tablespoon of mayonnaise, 2 slices of bread, lettuce and tomato, 1 tablespoon of French dressing, half a cup of canned apricots, beverage.

Dinner: Clear broth or bouillon, 4 ounces of curried shrimp, chutney, ½ cup of steamed rice cooked with 1 tablespoon of oil, avocado, lettuce, 1 tablespoon of French dressing, ½ cup of canned figs, 1 slice of bread, beverage, 2 fruits, 2 cups of skim milk if desired.

WEDNESDAY

Breakfast: ½ grapefruit, 2 ounces of broiled kippers, 2 slices of toast, 2 teaspoons of margarine, 4 ounces of cottage cheese, 2 teaspoons of jam, beverage.

Lunch: 4 ounces of tomato juice, 4 ounces of well-done hamburger, 1 roll, ½ cup of cole slaw with 1 teaspoon of mayonnaise, 1 cup of Jell-O or fruit ice, beverage.

Dinner: 4 ounces of marinated broiled chicken, ½ cup of peas, broiled tomatoes cooked with 1 tablespoon of oil, romaine lettuce, 1 tablespoon of French dressing, applesauce, 2 slices of bread, 2 fruits, 2 cups of skim milk if desired.

THURSDAY

Breakfast: Grapefruit cut up and mixed with ½ cup of orange juice, 1 egg scrambled with the white of a second egg in ½ tablespoon of oil, 1 ounce of Canadian bacon, 2 slices of toast, 2 teaspoons of margarine, coffee.

Lunch: 4 ounces of broiled flounder, ½ cup of lima beans or corn, lettuce and tomato salad with 1 tablespoon of French dressing, 2 slices of bread, ½ cup of fruit compote, beverage.

Dinner: 4 ounces of London broil, ½ cup of potatoes cooked with 1 tablespoon of oil, ½ cup of fried or oven-broiled asparagus or summer squash, mixed green salad with 1 tablespoon of French dressing, 1 slice of bread, ½ cup of berries, beverage.

FRIDAY

Breakfast: 4 ounces of orange juice, 2 slices of French toast (1 egg), cooked with 1 tablespoon of oil, 2 teaspoons of honey or maple syrup, beverage.

Lunch: 2 ounces of seafood cocktail, ½ cup of cottage cheese, ½ cup of fruit salad, 2 slices of bread, beverage.

Dinner: 4 ounces of broiled mackerel or swordfish, 1 medium boiled potato, ½ cup of steamed broccoli, collards or Swiss chard, slice of tomato with 1 tablespoon of French dressing, ½ cup of apricot whip, 1 slice of bread, beverage, 2 fruits, 2 cups of skim milk if desired.

SATURDAY

Breakfast: Half a cup of grapefruit sections, 1 poached egg, 2 slices of toast, 2 teaspoons of margarine, 2 teaspoons of marmalade, beverage.

Lunch: ½ cup of chicken salad with 1 tablespoon of mayonnaise, lettuce, olives, celery, green pepper, 2 slices of bread, 2-inch section of spongecake, raw fruit, beverage.

Dinner: 4 ounce ham steak, ½ cup of rice cooked with 1 tablespoon of seasoned oil, ½ cup of Brussels sprouts, green salad, 1 tablespoon of French dressing, half a cup of fresh or canned pineapple, 1 slice of bread, 2 fruits, beverage.

SUNDAY

Breakfast: ½ cup of strawberries, 1 cup of Wheat Chex, 6 ounces of skim milk, beverage.

Lunch: 4 ounces of crab-meat omelet (1 egg) cooked with 1 tablespoon of oil, green beans and mushroom salad with 1 tablespoon of French dressing, 2 slices of bread, 1 wedge of melon, beverage.

Dinner: 1 cup of chicken gumbo soup, 4 ounces of roast chicken, cranberry relish, medium baked potato (white or sweet), ½ cup of spinach, kale or mustard greens, ½ cup of fruit Betty, 1 slice of bread, 2 fruits, beverage.

EXERCISE AND CHOLESTEROL

Diet can be an important aid in reducing excessive cholesterol levels. So can exercise.

The ability of physical activity to lower blood fat levels has been demonstrated by studies in this country. Israeli physicians, too, have found exercise to be valuable.

Moreover, exercise produces other dividends: weight reduction, tension release, and stress reduction, for example. Chapter 6 covers the whole story of exercise and coronary heart disease, including its beneficial effect on cholesterol level.

MEDICINE TO REDUCE CHOLESTEROL LEVELS

As you can imagine, there is a pot of gold at the end of the cholesterol rainbow for the pharmaceutical company able to develop a safe medicine capable of reducing cholesterol to desirable levels. There has been much research by companies not only in the United States but throughout the world. So far no ideal medication has been found, but some useful progress has been made.

Physicians, however, are understandably extremely cautious when it comes to prescribing any kind of medication that must be taken for months and years after the disastrous MER-29 experience. MER-29, also known as Triparanol, was introduced with high hopes as a safe way to reduce blood cholesterol. It did, indeed, achieve reduction. But it did so by stopping the production of cholesterol at a point close to the end of the chemical assembly line, leading to the production of another material, desmosterol. Desmosterol, some experts feared, might be as toxic as, perhaps even more so than, cholesterol to the blood vessels and, before long, some severe toxic effects were discovered in some patients. MER-29 was withdrawn from the market.

At the moment, there is an apparently safe compound, *Atromid*, which provides a modest reduction of blood cholesterol. Atromid is effective in lowering excessive levels of neutral fats (triglycerides) in the blood, another risk factor to be discussed in the next chapter.

Nicotinic acid, a vitamin, which is in no way connected with nicotine in action, reduces cholesterol when administered in large doses. However, it may cause severe blushing and reddening of the skin. It nauseates some people. Also there is a question of whether it may in some cases produce slight liver damage.

Thyroid compounds are being tried because it is known that patients with overactive thyroid glands have reduced cholesterol levels while those with underactive glands have elevated levels. Since the natural thyroid hormone, levothyroxine, is a potent compound that increases body metabolism and also speeds the heart rate, there have been studies with a less active form, dextrothyroxine. Some investigators have been reporting good results with this agent; others believe that to get effective action on serum cholesterol it is necessary to push the medication dosage to the point where there might be damage to the heart.

Estrogenic hormones help reduce cholesterol to some extent and have been advocated for treatment in high-risk men. But the large doses that must be given have effects on sexual life and may cause enlargement of the breasts. Most men prefer to suffer with their heart disease rather than continue with estrogen therapy.

Still another approach is being tried. Cholesterol, as already noted, is absorbed from the intestine, and bile acids, containing the cholesterol sterol nucleus, pour into the intestine to aid in digestion. There has been a search for a resin that could combine with the cholesterol in food, or the bile acids, or both. Such a *resin* might reduce the body's absorption of cholesterol from the diet. If it also combined with bile acids, preventing the reabsorption and recirculation of the sterol compounds in the bile acids, more of the body's production of cholesterol would have to be used to make the bile acids, leaving less cholesterol available for the blood. One such compound—*cholestyramine* or *Questran*—has been developed. While it has shown some promise, the dosages required often produce gastrointestinal discomfort severe enough to cause patients to discontinue the medication.

Pectin is a soft, slippery substance found in apples and in citrus peel. It's a harmless substance which, in goodly amounts, often can produce a modest (e.g., 10-point) decrease in cholesterol levels, presumably by combining with cholesterol and bile acids as resins do and causing greater excretion in the feces. Thus people who like apples and have no trouble digesting them should use them freely.

COFFEE, TEA AND COLA DRINKS

It has been suggested by some that the caffeine contained in coffee, tea, and cola beverages may cause elevation of serum cholesterol. Most physicians, however, are not worried by any small rise that may be traceable to caffeine. As with everything else, these physicians urge moderation in the use of coffee, tea, and cola. Not only may the stimulant effect of excessive caffeine intake be dangerous to the heart and blood pressure, but the sugar contained in some cola drinks and the sugar and cream added to coffee and tea are not favored for preventing coronary heart disease. Frequently, too, the drinks are taken with doughnuts or other foods which are fried or to which butter is added, and such items should be kept to a minimum.

ALCOHOLIC BEVERAGES

There seems to be no evidence that use of alcohol increases serum cholesterol. However, heavy use of alcohol is not good for the heart. Heavy drinkers frequently are neglectful of good diet; many have vitamin deficiencies that may weaken the heart muscle.

HIGH BLOOD PRESSURE

While high blood pressure, as we will see in Chapter 9, accelerates atherosclerosis and increases the risk of heart attack, there is no evidence that it acts by elevating serum cholesterol.

DIABETES

Many diabetics have increased serum cholesterol levels. This disease, discussed more completely in Chapter 9, is associated with increased atherosclerosis and heart attack risk. As part of treatment for it, there is—or should be—a determined effort to reduce elevated cholesterol levels.

SEX LIFE

Many people today, not always jokingly, remark that since their physicians frown on smoking and on some of their favorite foods, perhaps they frown on sex as well. That's hardly the case. As far as is known, there is no deleterious effect of an active sex life on serum cholesterol. Since a good sex life reduces emotional stress (or reduced emotional stress promotes a good sex life), it can be argued that sex is, if anything, good for the serum cholesterol.

4

The Newer Triglyceride Link

When we think of blood fat that may cause damage to the arteries, almost always we have cholesterol in mind. Now, in addition, there is interest in another fatty compound, triglyceride.

This fat—and the name triglyceride simply means a combination of glycerine with three fatty acids—is common in butter, cream, many meats, and, in fact, in most fatty foods. It is also the main form in which fat is found in the body, both stored in tissues and mustered for use in producing energy.

Just as cholesterol is always present in the blood steam, so is triglyceride. And there has been increasing evidence that a marked increase in triglyceride concentration in the blood—no less than a marked rise in cholesterol level—may be associated with coronary heart disease.

Among the pioneering investigators of triglyceride was Dr. Margaret J. Albrink, now at the West Virginia University School of Medicine. Since she first, in 1956, reported an association between triglyceride concentration and coronary heart disease, many other investigators have done the same.

In one of her studies, Dr. Albrink found that as cholesterol increased from 200 to 260, triglyceride also increased. More than 70 percent of men with cholesterol levels above 260 also had elevated triglyceride levels.

In 1965, Dr. D. F. Brown and his co-workers in Albany measured both cholesterol and triglyceride concentrations in a long-term study and showed that both were important. For any given concentration of cholesterol among a group of subjects, the coronary heart disease rate increased as triglyceride concentration increased. Similarly, for any given triglyceride level, coronary heart disease increased as cholesterol concentration increased.

In the government's Framingham study, too, both cholesterol and triglyceride were found to contribute to risk. The risk associated with one rose in proportion to the level of the other. Whether cholesterol was high or low, the risk rose with the level of triglyceride. The converse was equally true. People with high values for both seemed to be worse off than those with high levels of one or the other. This suggested that each had an independent effect.

As Dr. Albrink has pointed out, "Like cholesterol, serum triglycerides are low in societies having a very low incidence of coronary heart disease, such as Japan." Investigators have found that the relatively immune groups in Israel, the Yemenites and Bedouins, have low triglyceride levels, much lower than those for European settlers in the country.

What causes abnormal elevation of triglyceride in the blood? In some cases, it appears to be an inherited tendency. Much more often, however, the major culprit may be weight gain, particularly in the twenties when many people shift from active to more sedentary life. Marriage may be an important factor since, as Dr. Albrink notes, "The acquisition of a good cook and the security of married life are frequently followed by an abrupt gain in weight by young adult men."

Many investigators now are taking a hard look at—and some

are putting outright blame on—sugar in the diet. They find a tremendous increase in sugar consumption. And there are reports of gratifying response of patients with elevated triglyceride levels to sugar restriction.

THE SUGAR LINK

Sugar is, as such things go, very much of a Johnny-come-lately in the diet. It has been an important element for less than a century. Before that, it was a luxury, often available only from apothecaries—sold, as caviar is today, by the ounce. It has been reported that in Elizabethan times, for example, the whole of England used only some 88 tons of sugar annually.

It was the discovery of methods of refining sugar from beets in the last century that allowed it to become a commonplace ingredient in the diet. And commonplace it has become. Dr. John Yudkin of the University of London, who is both biochemist and physician, was among the first to emphasize that coronary heart disease deaths have risen to epidemic proportions during the years when sugar consumption has been rising to almost incredible levels. In England, average consumption increased sixfold in the nineteenth century; today, it is about 120 pounds per person per year, or 2.3 pounds a week.

Consumption in the United States has also shot up as it has in other rich Western nations. Average intake of refined sugar now runs about 127 pounds in Ireland, 120 in Holland, 115 in Australia, 110 in Denmark. According to studies by Dr. M. A. Antar and other researchers at the State University of Iowa, average American sugar intake now may be as high as 170 pounds a year, more than 3 pounds a week.

We consume much more than the visible sugar we add to coffee and tea, sprinkle on cereals and fruits, and use in cooking. The visible, in fact, may account for only about half or less of total intake. There is sugar in pies, cakes, pastries, candies, jams, jellies, ice cream, gelatin desserts, soft drinks.

Soft drinks may contain as much as 10 to 12 percent sugar. It is not uncommon now for food manufacturers to add sugar to such items as soups, vegetable juices, and salad dressings.

Some investigators believe that there is a closer correlation between the rise in heart attack rates in the past half century or so in Western countries and the increase in sugar consumption than the increase in fat consumption. Others dispute this, arguing that the correlation with fat intake is better, but that the best correlation is to intake of both saturated fats and sugars.

Clearly, the richer a country becomes, the more its average diet increases in total calories and in the amount of fats and sugars. Commonly, diets in rich countries are 50 percent higher in calories than those in the poorest countries, 400 to 500 percent higher in fat intake—and while there is no significant difference in total carbohydrate intake, there is in sugar intake. In rich countries, people tend to eat less of the complex carbohydrates found in bread, cereals, potatoes, and starch, and more of the simple carbohydrates in sugar.

In the United States, since 1900, the average total daily carbohydrate intake has actually decreased from about 18 ounces to 13. But the share from wheat products has been almost halved; from potatoes, halved; from corn products, much more than halved. In their place refined sugar consumption has shot up. Where once complex carbohydrates in the diet outweighed simple carbohydrates by two and a half to one, now the simple outweigh the complex.

Israeli investigators have found that a significant change in the diet of Yemenites after long residence in Israel is the greatly increased consumption of sugar. Some suggest that if a nutrient is a causative factor in coronary heart disease, the increased consumption of sugar could play a role, direct or indirect, in the higher prevalence of the disease—and of diabetes as well—among Yemenites who have lived for many years in Israel.

Dr. A. M. Cohen and his colleagues at the Rothschild Hadassah University Hospital, Jerusalem, questioned several hundred Yemenites about their food habits in Yemen. Then they studied in detail 20 Yemenite families who had lived in Israel less than 10 years and another 20 who had lived in Israel for more than 25 years. A careful check was made of present eating habits, to the extent of having a dietitian visit the families daily for a week, checking menus, measuring quantities served.

Comparing the diets in Israel and in Yemen, Dr. Cohen and his associates found a slight increase in calorie intake and in average body weight among the Yemenites long-resident in Israel. They found virtually no change in total protein and only a small increase in total fat. But there had been a marked change in sugar consumption. In Israel, about 20 percent of the Yemenites' carbohydrates were consumed as sugar compared with nearly zero in Yemen.

Several years ago, in England, Dr. Yudkin and an associate investigated the diets of patients who had suffered heart attacks. They made comparisons between a group of patients who had had a first heart attack in the previous three weeks and another group of normal healthy people. They questioned the heart attack patients closely and for their comparison study used only those who indicated that they had not changed their diets in the past five years. They found that the heart attack patients had double the sugar intake of the healthy people.

From his work, Dr. Yudkin believes that people consuming more than 110 grams (approximately ¼ pound) of sugar a day are five times as likely to develop a heart attack as those taking less than 60 grams (approximately ⅐ pound).

The exact mechanism, or mechanisms, by which sugar may play a causative role in atherosclerosis and coronary heart disease are still unknown. Intensive research is currently under way to try to find out.

Dr. Yudkin believes that not all people are sensitive to sugar. He fed to human volunteers diets high in cholesterol and also high in either starch or sugar. All developed high blood cholesterol levels but the group on the high cholesterol-high sugar diet had increases in serum triglyceride as well. About one-third of the volunteers seemed particularly sensitive to a high-sugar diet, responding with greatly increased triglyceride levels.

One of the most distinguished authorities on triglyceride in heart disease in the United States is Dr. Peter Kuo, a professor of medicine at the University of Pennsylvania. Dr. Kuo has found that most patients with heart disease who show elevated trigylceride levels are sensitive to excess sugar in their diet.

Dr. Kuo's own work, and the work of others, has shown that the body can convert excess carbohydrate calories into fats, which is a normal process. It appears to be exaggerated, however, in atherosclerosis-prone people. Moreover, sugar is more lipogenic or fat-forming than equivalent amounts of starches.

Dr. Kuo's findings indicate that all of us, whether or not we have a tendency to high blood fats, would show higher levels of them (especially of triglyceride) if we were to eat a lot of carbohydrates, although we wouldn't have as great a response as people with a tendency to high levels. Also, in normal people, the carbohydrate-induced triglyceride elevation tends to go down with time, as if the body adjusts to the new increased carbohydrate intake.

A very high intake of starches would raise blood fat levels in the same way that sugar does but people are unlikely to eat the amounts of starches required. When we eat a chocolate bar, for example, it is the equivalent of half a dozen slices of bread. In the average American diet, there is likely to be more sugar than complex carbohydrate and there is little doubt, Dr. Kuo says, that many of us are getting excessive amounts, exceeding what we would normally metabolize or use up.

Dr. Kuo has found that many patients with high blood fat levels who are referred to him have carbohydrate-sensitive elevations which tend to disappear when they are placed on a diet that sounds rather rigorous. It calls for the elimination of ordinary sugar, jams, honey, berries, fruits, fruit juices, candies, and pastries; elimination of butter and coconut oil (some margarines contain coconut oil), cream, whole milk, ice cream, and fried foods; elimination of all forms of alcohol; and the use of three evenly divided meals a day without snacks.

As we have obtained them directly from him, Dr. Kuo's recommendations for a daily diet are in Table 3.

TABLE 3

Breakfast: 1 or 2 slices of bread or toast with margarine
V-8 or tomato juice
Crisp bacon, Canadian bacon, ham, or smoked fish
Tea or coffee, with artificial sweetener if desired

Luncheon and dinner: Soup of all kinds except creamed varieties
Fish, fowl, meat of all kinds (with extra fat trimmed off)
Cooked vegetables—1 serving of starchy vegetables such as corn or potatoes, but no sweet potatoes or beets; leafy vegetables, as much as desired
Salads—fresh vegetables with lemon juice or olive oil
Bread—1 or 2 slices with margarine
Tea or coffee, with artificial sweetener if desired

Dr. Kuo is suspicious that some so-called skim milks contain appreciable amounts of butterfat so he eliminates all milk at first.

The diet is, indeed, rigorous. It takes great will power to give up all sweet foods, give up all alcoholic beverages, and space meals so that snacks are eliminated. Dr. Kuo permits all meats; other physicians, perhaps your own, might place more emphasis on fish and fowl. And most doctors would permit skim milk.

But there is logic to the diet for the individual who is seriously at risk for coronary heart disease because of carbohydrate-sensitive blood fat elevation. There are medications that can be used to reduce greatly elevated triglyceride levels. However, as Dr. Kuo told one of us recently: "While the diet is difficult, it works, and it can be continued safely for a lifetime—but do we feel that confident about the effectiveness and safety of a medicine that would have to be given year after year?"

One advantage of the Kuo diet—or a modification of it that some physicians may use—is that almost automatically it brings a weight loss as the intake of concentrated sugars is curtailed.

As far as most of us are concerned, whether or not we presently have blood fat elevations, a cardinal fact coming out of the many studies of dietary influences is that what we eat does influence the levels of blood fats associated with coronary heart disease. It makes sense to minimize the likelihood of such elevations, as well as control them when present, by modifications in intake of both fats and sugars.

THE FIVE PATTERNS OF BLOOD-FAT DISORDERS

So rapidly has research been moving that in the last few years it has become possible to distinguish five major patterns of blood fat disorders. They can be tested for, and once a particular pattern is determined for an individual, control of the disorder may be greatly facilitated.

The test, which is rapidly becoming a routine procedure offered by many hospital and commerical laboratories, uses a sample of a patient's blood serum. A spot of the serum is placed on a paper strip which is then exposed to an electric field. The electric field causes lipoproteins—the combinations of fats and proteins in the serum—to move along the paper strip at varying rates. After a time, the amount of each blood fat is marked by a band on the paper, and the density and size of the bands indicate normal or abnormal levels.

The test and its interpretation are the work of researchers at the government's National Heart and Lung Institute led by Dr. Donald S. Fredrickson and Dr. Robert I. Levy.

Type I. An individual with this abnormal pattern shows only slightly increased cholesterol but tremendously increased triglyceride, often above 5,000 mg percent. Such an individual is unable to clear dietary fat from the blood. Recurrent abdominal pain attacks and skin outbreaks are associated with eating fats. The disorder, which is rare and appears to stem from an inherited deficiency in an enzyme, is readily controlled by diets containing not more than 20 percent of total calories as fat. The low-fat diets produce prompt relief of pain and skin outbreaks. The reduction in elevated triglyceride level is dramatic.

Type II. A common pattern, this is characterized by a marked increase in cholesterol level, with normal or only mildly elevated triglyceride. The Type II individual may have yellow-tinted, cholesterol-filled bumps on knees, elbows, and heels; they disappear with diet treatment and medication. There is premature coronary artery disease; and often there is a striking family history of early death. The Type II pattern can result from excessive dietary cholesterol intake, thyroid disease, liver disease, or kidney disorder. These causes can be quickly evaluated. If they can be ruled out, a physician will want to check the patient's family for the mother or father and 50 percent of brothers, sisters, and children (diagnosable as early as one year of age) will have the same pattern.

When a disease such as thyroid, liver, or kidney impairment is involved, treatment can be directed at it. Thyroid replacement for underfunctioning of the thyroid, for example, can eliminate both the thyroid problem and the Type II pattern.

When no such disease in involved, treatment is directed at the Type II pattern itself. Dietary treatment emphasizes a reduction in cholesterol intake to under 200 milligrams a day (with avoidance of eggs, many dairy products, and fatty meats) and increased consumption of unsaturated fats. When necessary, a cholesterol-lowering drug—such as D-thyroxine, niacin, or cholestyramine—may be used to provide effective control.

Type III. This, like Type I, is relatively uncommon. Both cholesterol and triglyceride levels are high—in the 350 to 800 mg percent range. In the third or fourth decade of life, the individual with Type III pattern often has orange-yellow fat deposits in the creases of the palms of the hands. Premature coronary vessel disease is likely. Many individuals with Type III pattern are overweight. Dietary treatment puts emphasis on calorie control and a balance of fat, carbohydrate, and protein intake along with a reduction in cholesterol intake. The drug clofibrate, Dr. Robert Levy has reported, is effective, especially when coupled with the balanced diet, producing a complete normalization of cholesterol and triglyceride levels and disappearance of fat deposits in the skin.

Type IV. This is a very common pattern. Cholesterol levels are often normal; triglyceride levels are increased. There are no external signs in the skin. Often the individual with Type IV pattern is overweight. He may be mildly diabetic. People with this pattern form a sizable fraction of the population suffering from coronary heart disease.

Diet treatment emphasizes reduction to ideal body weight, and reduction in the carbohydrate content of the diet with an increase in the amounts of unsaturated fats. Diet treatment alone often produces normalization of the triglyceride level. Drugs like clofibrate, D-thyroxine, and nicotinic acid sometimes may be used; they are variably effective.

Type V. This pattern is often seen associated with diabetes, pancreatitis, alcoholism, and kidney disease though it may be familial. While cholesterol level may be mildly to markedly elevated, the triglyceride level is way up—in the 1,000–6,000 range. An individual with Type V pattern appears to be intolerant to dietary fat. Diet treatment calls for restriction of calories and reduction to ideal body weight, with a diet high in protein and low in carbohydrates and fat. Medications such as clofibrate, D-thyroxine, and nicotinic acid may reduce the triglyceride concentration but not to a significant degree.

The establishment of the five patterns promises to have considerable value. Physicians now can go beyond just getting a measurement of cholesterol level. Knowing which pattern an individual has, the physician knows what underlying diseases—such as thyroid, kidney, etc.—may possibly be involved. He can look for them and treat them if he finds them. If the pattern is familial, he can not only treat the patient at hand but seek out others in the family and provide early treatment for them. And, knowing the individual's pattern, he can provide more specific and thus more effective treatment to return elevated blood fat levels to normal.

While medication may sometimes be a helpful addition to treatment, dietary manipulation is the major instrument. And many physicians now are reporting that especially with Types III, IV, and V—and IV is perhaps the most common of all—patients respond very well to caloric restriction, which is usually indicated anyhow for their accompanying obesity.

Excess weight is, indeed, a factor to be reckoned with in the total picture of who gets premature coronary heart disease, why, and what can be done about reducing our soaring heart-attack rate.

5

The Matter of Weight:
Does It Matter? How?
Who Is Really Obese?

Does excess weight directly cause coronary heart disease? An honest answer to that must be: nobody knows.

What complicates clear evaluation of any *direct* role of obesity is that it is so often associated with other factors known to contribute directly—high blood pressure, high blood fats, high blood sugar, for example.

Such association is enough to make excess weight of major consequence, and its importance is underscored by the fact that such high-risk factors can be overcome. Even abnormal electrocardiographic changes can be eliminated in many cases simply by adequate weight reduction.

Moreover, cardiologists would all agree that obesity is undesirable for another reason: it puts an excess burden on the circulation, adding to the work of the heart.

Insurance statistics show, beyond doubt, not only that excess weight goes along with a higher death rate from cardiovascular disease but from many other diseases as well. The insurance data on adverse effects of obesity are grim. Excess mortality rises rapidly with increasing degree of overweight, amounting to 13 percent for men 10 percent overweight, 25 percent for those 20 percent overweight, and exceeding 40 percent for those 30 percent overweight. When mortality among the overweight is compared with the rate among the "best weight" group (who are somewhat below average weight), men 10 percent overweight have an excess death rate of one-third; for those 20 percent or more overweight, the excess is nearly one-half. For women, excess mortality relates more precisely to the degree of excess weight so that, for example, there is a 30 percent excess of mortality among women who are 30 percent overweight.

When it comes to individual diseases, insurance figures show that as compared with the population in general over-weight men and women have these excesses of mortality: 142 percent and 175 percent respectively for heart attacks; 159 percent and 162 percent for cerebral hemorrhage (stroke); 191 percent and 212 percent for chronic nephritis (kidney disease); 168 percent and 211 percent for liver and gallbladder cancer; 383 percent and 372 percent for diabetes; 249 percent and 147 percent for cirrhosis of the liver; 154 percent and 141 percent for hernia and intestinal obstruction.

Actually insurance figures may be too conservative, under-rating the excess death rate associated with obesity, since insurance companies base their statistics on experience with people they insure and they have been increasingly cautious in selecting overweight risks to insure. Recently, for example, an American Cancer Society study of 800,000 persons has shown that the obese have as many as three and a half times the number of fatal heart attacks and strokes as do the non-obese.

Many diverse health hazards are associated with excess weight. There may be breathing difficulties, for example, since the greater the weight in the chest wall, the greater the work required for breathing. With increased breathing difficulty, obese people have less tolerance for physical activity.

That obese adults have higher rates of respiratory infections has long been known. So, a very recent study indicates, do fat children. Confirming an impression of many physicians, investigators in England checked on a large group of three-month- to two-year-olds through six months of a British winter, and found among the overweight a clear preponderance of respiratory illness sufficiently severe to make the mother call a doctor and lasting for at least three days. Infant obesity appears to be associated with early introduction of solids into the diet, and as one English medical observer put it: "Just what have we achieved for the human race by altering infant diets so radically in recent decades? So our children are bigger, and we still subscribe to the myth that biggest is best, although if we took a look at the little Gurkhas and the Japanese we might realize that all bigness does for you is to give you a hard time in theaters and the economy class of airplanes."

Their bigness tends to make many of the obese diabetic. Most people who develop diabetes in adulthood are or have been obese. Difficulties during anesthesia and surgery are associated with excess weight. In women with significant obesity, menstrual abnormalities and abnormal hair growth occur with some frequency.

The ability of weight reduction to bring significant benefits for people with many health problems is well established. The problems include high blood pressure, angina pectoris, congestive heart failure, varicose veins, ruptured spinal disks, osteoarthritis, and other varieties of bone and joint disease. Not to be omitted from even a partial list, many common foot troubles and backaches may be relieved considerably, sometimes completely, by weight loss.

When a study by the Society of Actuaries in 1959 revealed that 30 pounds of overweight cuts four years off life expectancy, insurance companies began to use that statistic in their daily operations. They issue policies to people who are obese, but premium rates go up proportionately with the amount of excess weight. And the same companies cut their premium rates as overweight policyholders reduce to accepted normal levels.

Before taking a hard look at the relationship between excess weight and coronary heart disease, let's consider the extent of the obesity problem in this country and how it came about.

SIZE OF THE PROBLEM

Even now the true dimensions of the American blubber problem have yet to be accurately determined.

Estimates of how many Americans are carrying around too much weight range from 20 to 25 percent. Preliminary results of the first national nutrition survey have convinced Dr. Arnold Schaefer, the Department of Health, Education, and Welfare nutritionist who has directed the survey, that 25 percent is definitely closer to the truth.

Once, several generations ago, it was the middle-aged person who gained weight. By then, the children had grown up and life on the whole was more tranquil. Today, the picture in this country is that many people are, in terms of body weight, middle-aged by the time they are twenty-nine. They weigh as much then as their forebears weighed in their middle and late forties.

HOW IT CAME ABOUT

The change in our mode of life—toward far more sedentary living—must receive some of the blame. There has also been the change in diet.

As we've noted previously, the tremendous change in American eating habits within a relatively short period of time is not always fully appreciated. We are somewhat aware of the increase in the proportion of fats in the diet; but there has also been a marked increase in the amount of meat and concentrated carbohydrates and in the overall amount of calories.

It was not so long ago that many, if not most, American families had no regular refrigeration. Blocks of ice had some cooling effect in summer. But food storage in the home was limited. Butter became rancid and sweet milk sour before long. Meat in large quantities could not be kept without difficulty even in winter.

For many families, there was then, as there is *not* now, greater dependence on vegetables and cereals. Fresh fruits and vegetables were eaten in large amounts in the summer months. They were canned for winter use—peas, beans, corn, peaches, apples, pears, pickles, relishes. And fruits canned at home had none of the heavy syrup of today's commercial products. There was heavier reliance on poultry. Beef, veal, and pork were much leaner than now; they were not raised and fed and finished as now.

Came modern refrigeration, modern mass production, modern supermarkets, along with a rise in general affluence, and the American table has tended to groan. We eat more meats—from very fat, penfed animals. Ice cream is readily available, and we have become accustomed to many rich desserts.

For most of us, eating is no longer something done for survival; it's a social function, and all about us are invitations to eat. In addition to family meals, there are coffee breaks with doughnuts or Danish pastry; candy counters and peanut, soft-drink, and other types of vending machines in office buildings; business and club luncheons; popcorn and soft drinks in movie houses; etc., etc.

And while we have thrust upon us too many opportunities for consuming calories, we have to make opportunities for spending them. The way we live—riding to work, riding in elevators, being bused to school, even riding in golf carts—provides few opportunities for meaningful caloric expenditure. We are, we might well say, victims of the system. And not just losing weight but avoiding excess poundage in the first place requires outsmarting the system.

Perhaps the nature of man's appetite-regulating mechanism is partly responsible for the prevalence of obesity. As some researchers like Dr. Lawrence E. Hinkle, Jr., of Cornell Medical College note, the mechanism developed at a time when the big threat to man's survival was inadequate food supply and long periods of semistarvation were common for almost every individual. So it features an insistent hunger drive that spurs a man to look for food again within a few hours after a meal. And accompanying this a weaker satiation apparatus which permits a man faced with large quantities of food to eat much more than he immediately needs.

It was a good arrangement with high survival value in hunting and fishing societies and in primitive agricultural societies. But in the last 75 years, modern techniques of producing and marketing food have made the supply abundant, perennially abundant, uninterrupted by periods of inadequacy except during wars.

"Living in such a setting of abundant food," writes Dr. Hinkle, "men have to make almost a conscious effort to avoid becoming obese. As a result, not isolated men but whole populations have become relatively overweight, and have relatively high levels of fat and cholesterol in their blood. This is thought to be a primary reason for the high level of coronary heart disease in such societies."

A Hard Look at Obesity and CHD

As far back as the turn of the century, evidence for an association between overweight and heart disease was first noted. Studies in Finland, the Netherlands, and elsewhere show that during World War II, when caloric intake was drastically curtailed because of Nazi occupation, atherosclerosis and heart attack deaths dropped sharply. Not long after the war, insurance studies revealed a much higher death rate from heart and blood vessel disease among the overweight.

It was easy enough for many people to assume from such findings that obesity causes heart disease, but such an assumption had no scientific valdity. It was necessary to recognize the involvement of many contributory factors, and interactions between the factors had to be taken into consideration.

Thus high blood pressure contributes to coronary heart disease and obesity contributes to blood-pressure elevation, as shown by the fact that high blood pressure in obese patients is frequently lowered by weight reduction. High blood cholesterol levels are associated with coronary heart disease— and cholesterol level (and possibly deposition of cholesterol on artery walls) increases during periods of weight gain. There is evidence that physical inactivity favors high blood cholesterol and, of course, physical inactivity also favors weight gain.

Considering such interactions, it was easy to jump to the other extreme and assume that while obesity has indirect effects, it has no direct ones on coronary heart disease. And, for a time, the Framingham study seemed to suggest this.

That study, begun in the early 1950's, following more than 5,000 men and women under the direction of National Heart Institute scientists, has helped to highlight many of the factors involved in CHD. For example, it was the Framingham study (along with similar analyses elsewhere) that indicated that men with blood cholesterol levels of 260 or higher have double the rate of new heart disease compared with the general population, while those with readings below 200 have only half the general rate—a four to one difference. Framingham also showed among other things that people with systolic blood pressure below 120 have one-fourth the rate of CHD expected for their age and sex but those with 180 or higher have twice the expected rate.

At first, these studies seemed to indicate that obesity, if not accompanied by high blood pressure or high cholesterol levels, did not increase the risk of CHD unless the obesity was extreme. They indicated that there was greatly increased risk of a fatal coronary attack if obesity was present along with either high blood pressure or high cholesterol level, or both.

More recently, however, as the studies have gone on for longer periods, the findings have been that in men weight gain after the age of twenty-five strongly correlates with the risk of developing angina pectoris and that while the weight gain is unrelated to the risk of developing a heart attack, it is strongly related, when a heart attack does develop, to the risk of dying from the attack. In other words, obese men, whether or not they have elevated blood pressure and cholesterol levels, have an increased risk of angina pectoris and sudden death, indicating that obesity by itself contributes to these manifestations of heart disease. Essentially, what the studies show is that obesity is dangerous when it adds to the work of a heart that already has some impairment of coronary circulation.

Israeli experience, too, suggests the importance of obesity in CHD and the desirability of leanness. Israeli physicians who survived the Nazi concentration camps and compared notes found themselves unable to recall in all the years of internment a single case of heart attack or angina among their skin-and-bones fellow prisoners, even among those over fifty. They recalled that among their fellow prisoners were people who had been patients before, patients with heart disease, but with the loss of weight from near-starvation in the camps they had no manifestations of heart disease.

By any Western concept, the immune groups of Israel—the Bedouins and newly arrived Yemenites—are strikingly thin. In this country, we think that a man of average height who weighs between 140 and 150 pounds is thin; but a Yemenite or Bedouin of corresponding height might weigh no more than 120 pounds. Men in the kibbutzim are not as thin but they tend to be muscular and in tough condition. A kibbutz dweller weighing 160 pounds would have a solid band of muscle around his waist rather than the thick pad of fat to be found in an American of similar weight.

How to Tell if You Are Really Obese

Merely stepping on scales and then comparing your weight with what an old standard weight table suggests you should weigh does not necessarily provide a true indication of whether or not you are obese.

To be sure, height-weight tables have been improved. The older ones used for many years indicated weights for each year of age from fifteen on for men and women of different heights. They were based on average weights of 200,000 men and women accepted for life insurance at about the turn of the century. Their value was questionable—first, because of the imprecision of the measurements, which were made with various types of street clothes and shoes on, and, also, because the 200,000 people were not necessarily representative of the population as a whole. In addition, the tables indicated a steady increase of weight with age. If this occurred, it was not necessarily desirable.

More recent tables abandon the age criterion. And they introduce the concept of desirable rather than average weight. In effect, they acknowledge the fact that average people may tend to put on weight with the passing of years and this is not desirable. They acknowledge, too, that desirable weight is different from average weight because the latter reflects the fatties who make up the upper part of the average. The newer tables also take into account body frames although they still do not define the frames precisely.

Table 4 is a modern table of desirable weights.

The table may be used for general guidance but we would caution against complete dependence upon it. Obviously, if your weight is much above what the table calls for there is

TABLE 4

DESIRABLE WEIGHTS FOR MEN AND WOMEN

Weights in Pounds, According to Frame (as ordinarily dressed, including shoes)

MEN

Height Ft. In.		Small Frame	Medium Frame	Large Frame
5	2	116–125	124–133	131–142
5	3	119–128	127–136	133–144
5	4	122–132	130–140	137–149
5	5	126–136	134–144	141–153
5	6	129–139	137–147	145–157
5	7	133–143	141–151	149–162
5	8	136–147	145–160	153–166
5	9	140–151	149–160	157–170
5	10	144–155	153–164	161–175
5	11	148–164	157–168	165–180
6	0	152–164	161–173	169–185
6	1	157–169	166–178	174–190
6	2	163–175	171–184	179–196
6	3	168–180	176–189	184–202

WOMEN

4	11	104–111	110–118	117–127
5	0	105–113	112–120	119–129
5	1	107–115	114–122	121–131
5	2	110–118	117–125	124–135
5	3	113–121	120–128	127–138
5	4	116–125	124–132	131–142
5	5	119–128	127–135	133–145
5	6	123–132	130–140	138–150
5	7	126–136	134–144	142–154
5	8	129–139	137–147	145–158
5	9	133–143	141–151	149–162
5	10	136–147	145–155	152–166
5	11	139–150	148–158	155–169

an obesity problem. But it is possible for a person to be overweight without having any excess fat (often the case with college football players, for example). And it is also possible for people to have excess fat without being markedly overweight (often the case with very sedentary people).

Quite often, a more direct measurement of adiposity, or the actual amount of fat on the body, is needed before a decision can be made as to whether an individual is or isn't obese.

There are several simple tests by which you can assess your fatness:

The mirror test. Just look at yourself naked in the mirror. If you appear to be fat, you probably are—and it is virtually certain that you are if you also weigh considerably more than you did at twenty-five if you are a man, or more than you weighed at twenty-one if a woman.

The ruler test. This is based on the fact that if there is no excess fat, the abdominal surface between the flare of the ribs and front of the pelvis usually is flat. If you lie on your back and place a ruler on the abdomen, along the midline of the body, it should not point upward at the midsection. If it does, you are probably carrying excess fat.

The skinfold, or pinch, test. With thumb and forefinger, grasp a "pinch" of skin—at the waist, then at the stomach, upper arm, buttocks, and calf. At least half of body fat is directly under the skin. Generally, the layer beneath the skin— which is what you measure with the pinch since only fat and not muscle pinches—should be between one-fourth and one-half inch. Since you are getting a double thickness with the pinch, it normally should be one-half to one inch. A fold much greater than an inch indicates excess fatness; one much thinner than half an inch indicates abnormal thinness.

The circumference test. In men, the chest measurement at the level of the nipples should be greater than the abdominal measurement at the level of the navel. If it is the other way around, it usually means an excess of abdominal fat.

By the use of such measures of adiposity and others as well, investigators have found that even if the same weight is maintained throughout adult life, we tend to become fatter, very literally, as we grow older, with active tissue being replaced by fat. In one study, for example, 33 younger men (twenty-two to twenty-nine years) were matched with 33 older men (forty-eight to fifty-seven) so each young man was paired with an older man of the same height and weight. The older men were found to have a 50 percent greater fat content than the younger men. Women, too, have been found to show an increase in fat content with age. Active people who continue to exercise into the later years have a proportionately greater lean body mass than do sedentary people, but even in the active some fat does replace lean with age.

The lesson for all of us seems to be that if we are to slow the rate at which we progressively accumulate fat, we will do best to stop gaining weight after the age of twenty-five and in later years we will do best to actually lose some weight.

An "Age of Caloric Anxiety"

With the increased risks of ill health associated with even moderate obesity now well recognized, and with many people experiencing fear, guilt, and shame because of overweight, this has been aptly termed an "age of caloric anxiety."

Reducing seems to be the preoccupation of a large segment of the population. It has been estimated that 75 percent of over-weight Americans have made some attempt, however half-hearted, to control their weight. Polling organizations have reported that in this country at any one time some 20 million people are on some reducing diet or other.

There are relatively little hard data about how successful

most people are. Sales of commercial appetite reducers boom but indicate only intentions, not results. The number of people joining popular weight-reducing clubs does the same. One organization, TOPS (Take Off Pounds Sensibly), has been reported to have 147,000 members and at an international convention announced that its members had lost a combined 677 tons. But more useful weight-loss information for large populations is not available.

The City of New York has obesity clinics in which approximately 2,000 people voluntarily enroll each year for help in weight reduction. A survey of 2,600 of these patients showed that 26 percent were successful in reducing to within 10 percent of their normal weight range. Of those who reached normal weight, 30 percent gained back their weight by one year.

Dieting has been termed the Number 1 American pastime—and much of the time is passed in searching for some panacea, some easy and hopefully effortless way to get rid of excess pounds. Not only are diets churned out almost like cars on an assembly line, but they are often bizarre and all too often self-defeating and even health-impairing.

Fad Diets

There are supposedly magic diets that concentrate on some single food—for example, six to nine eggs a day—and others, also purportedly possessed of magic capabilities, that use food pairs varying from eggs and spinach to bananas and skim milk. There are crash diets that focus on grapefruit and coffee for days on end, or cottage cheese and little more. The intent seems to be to melt away a lot of fat in a short period of misery. But acute malnutrition states may develop and crash diets have, in fact, been known to produce fatalities.

A low-protein, low-fat diet was in vogue a few years ago. It was followed by a very low-protein diet, named the "Rockefeller" diet by its promoters. A trouble with such diets is that they usually fail to supply adequate amounts of all vital nutritional elements.

Periodically a high-fat, low-carbohydrate, or even carbohydrate-free diet achieves popularity under varied names (DuPont, Pennington, Mayo). With alcohol added, the same type of diet becomes another fleetingly popular one called the "drinking man's" diet. The idea advanced is that a high fat intake depresses fat manufacture in the body itself and that may be true; but it does not prevent fat accumulation in the body when the fat comes in from the outside.

When they are not outrightly dangerous, fad or crash diets —however in vogue they may be at any given time and however attractive their promoters may make them sound—are self-defeating. While they may lead to some initial weight loss, much of the loss may be of water rather than of body fat. Because such diets differ markedly from normal meal patterns, they are not acceptable for long periods and so weight is quickly regained once the diets are over.

And on-again-off-again dieting can be dangerous.

THE DANGERS OF UPS AND DOWNS

The frequent gains and losses of weight that many people go through as they alternate between excessive caloric intake and this or that diet may actually be more harmful than if they maintained steady excess weight.

It has been shown, for example, that blood cholesterol levels increase during periods of weight gain, thus increasing the risk that cholesterol will be deposited on artery walls. But there is no evidence that once cholesterol has been deposited it can be removed by weight reduction. Thus, a person whose weight has fluctuated up and down repeatedly may be more subject to artery-hardening stress than the person with stable though excessive weight.

Laboratory studies have established that animals of normal weight have longer life expectancies than obese animals. But they have also shown that obese animals repeatedly reduced have shorter life expectancies than obese animals never reduced.

SENSIBLE AND SOUND WEIGHT REDUCTION

The principles of effective, and healthy, weight reduction and then maintenance of proper weight are simple enough.

A man who is moderately active can count on the fact that he requires an intake of 15 calories a day for each pound of weight. If, therefore, he weighs 150 pounds and wants to maintain that weight, he will need 2,250 calories a day. If he is to take off weight, he will need to reduce his caloric intake, or increase his physical activity so he burns up more calories, or he may do both.

Some 50 years ago, when hormones were discovered, there was a common notion that obesity must be due to some hormone problem. We know now that this is the exception rather than the rule. In a few cases, improper functioning of the thyroid gland may account for obesity. The gland, which is located at the side and in front of the windpipe, just below the Adam's apple, acts somewhat like a thermostat, regulating the rate at which body organs function and the speed with which the body uses the energy from food. With an overactive thyroid, body functions speed up. There may be a perceptibly faster heart beat, nervousness, difficulty in sleeping at night, and weight loss. With underactivity of the thyroid, there is a tendency toward lethargy and weight gain.

When thyroid dysfunction is suspected, there are tests (basal metabolism and others) to determine whether there is, indeed, a thyroid problem. If there is, effective treatment to correct it is available.

But the vast majority of people with obesity have no thyroid problem. They are simply eating too many calories considering the amount of calories they expend. They pour, so to speak, more gas into the tank than the car uses up and so the tank overflows.

They must redress the balance. But if they are to do so successfully—if they are to achieve desirable weight and keep it, if they are to gain benefits for their general health and for their heart and circulatory health—they must avoid fad and crash diets. They must use a diet for reducing that is compatible with what is known about dietary influences on heart disease. And they must use one that lends itself, with some modification, to later use for maintaining proper weight and health.

To get rid of one pound of body weight requires a deficit of 3,500 calories—that many less of intake as against outgo. A sound reducing diet should help achieve that and should also have other essential characteristics:

1. It should produce the weight loss at a safe pace.

2. It should get rid of body fat, not healthy lean body tissue.

3. It should provide balance and variety, so it maintains health and provides some pleasure in eating as well as some satisfaction of hunger pangs.

4. It should teach new, and enjoyable, eating patterns so there is no prompt return to old, weight-gaining eating patterns.

In most cases, coupled with a sound reducing diet, there must be a sound program of physical activity that will increase the expenditure of calories, thus easing the dieting regimen and also contributing to general body fitness, vigor, and cardiovascular health.

We consider in some detail in the next chapter the exercise story as it relates to the health of the heart and circulatory system; we consider there, too, the values, too often overlooked, of exercise in reducing and maintaining proper weight.

If weight is to be lost, what should the pace be? Since a

pound of excess tissue in the body is the equivalent of 3,500 calories, a daily deficit of 500 calories can lead to a weight loss of a pound a week. A deficit of 1,000 calories daily can produce an average loss of two pounds a week.

There is a temptation to try to get rid of pounds quickly and be finished with the job. It's a temptation to be avoided. A loss of about two pounds a week is as much as should be attempted by anyone who is not under very close medical supervision. Except possibly in grossly obese people, this is probably as much as is desirable even under close medical supervision—and in many cases a pound a week, sometimes even less, may be suitable. Even a loss of half a pound a week totals up to a considerable loss—26 pounds—in a year.

Let us say that your objective is to lose an average of a pound a week. That requires a deficit of 500 calories a day. Let us say that you decide to add half an hour of walking a day, thus expending about 150 more calories than you have been. That leaves you with the need to cut down 350 calories on your daily food intake. That is an eminently reasonable goal.

If, for example, you are a 150-pound man and thus need 2,250 calories a day to maintain your present weight, you would need a diet providing 1,900 calories in combination with the half hour of walking a day to lose a pound a week.

Whatever your present weight, you can use the 15× factor —multiply your weight by 15 (the 15 represents the number of calories needed to maintain a pound of weight)—to arrive at the total number of calories needed to maintain you weight. Set a reasonable goal for caloric expenditure through exercise after reading the next chapter and consulting the Table of Spending Calories in Appendix I. Subtract the exercise caloric expenditure from your total maintenance caloric requirement. Then, considering how much you reasonably wish to lose a week, arrive at how many calories you can allow yourself in food.

You will want to become familiar with the caloric values of various foods and for this the table in the appendix listing such values will be useful.

But more than calories alone must be considered in arriving at your diet. It should be a balanced and varied diet, providing suitable amount of proteins, carbohydrates, and fats. If it does this, it will almost certainly provide suitable amounts of vitamins, minerals, and all essential nutrients.

In view of what we know now of the importance of types of fats and limitation of cholesterol intake in minimizing the risk of atherosclerosis and coronary heart disease, the diet should take all this into account.

Many authorities believe that a balanced diet, containing at least 14 percent protein, at most 30 percent fat (with saturated fats cut down), and the rest carbohydrates (with sugar cut to a low level) is the best diet. It contains every nutrient needed for life-long nutrition, avoids excessively high fat content which promotes cholesterol levels, avoids excessively low carbohydrate content which may cause fatigue and irritability. The protein and fat content are enough to help promote satiety.

After its own considerable studies and consultation with authorities, the American Heart Association has produced a valuable fat-controlled, low-cholesterol meal plan which you will find in the appendix. It can serve as a useful guide in your diet planning—a guide to what is probably the most helpful type of planning in terms of heart as well as general health. You can use it in conjunction with the calorie table to arrive at a healthy diet which will provide the amount of calories you need to take off excess weight and which you can later modify, adding a suitable number of calories, to maintain your optimal weight.

Your physician can be of great help in the whole process of determining what your weight should be and in deciding upon an exercise program and a diet that will most satisfactorily allow you to achieve and then maintain desirable weight. In addition to its fat-controlled, low-cholesterol meal plan, the American Heart Association has drawn up diets providing specific numbers of calories which it makes available when a physician prescribes them.

Even for the Extremely Obese

No case of overweight—not even the extreme case of obesity —today is hopeless. A considerable amount of medical research is devoted to the problem and programs are being developed which, upon careful testing, prove capable of producing dramatic results.

As just one example, there is the six-month diet program developed recently at Duke University Medical Center to meet the needs of very obese working people whose work week would not make hospitalization practical. Most of the participants are low on the socioeconomic scale (some are illiterate) and weigh between 200 and 400 pounds. The very carefully supervised program, developed by Dr. Siegfried H. Heyden, associate professor of epidemiology, combines intermittent fasting with a nutritionally sound diet containing 700 calories a day between the fasting periods. The two-and-a-half-day weekend fasting periods start Friday afternoons and run through Sunday nights. Only specified noncaloric liquids are allowed during the fasting periods.

Depending upon an individual's prior salt intake and therefore water accumulation in the body, a weight loss of as much as 15 pounds occurs during the first weekend fasting period. In each subsequent fasting period, the loss is 3½ to 4 pounds for women, 4½ to 5 pounds for men.

The 700-calorie diet between fasts has been carefully calculated to maintain the weight loss. Even an extra 100 calories beyond the 700 might produce a weight gain, reports Dr. Heyden, because in very obese people, unlike the relatively normal-weighted, the metabolic rate, the burn-up rate, is incredibly low.

Participants are advised to limit breakfast and lunch to 140 calories each, leaving approximately 400 for dinner. Meat or fish accounts for 250 to 300 of the dinner calories, vegetables for the remainder.

In ten weeks, most women lose at least 30 pounds and most men 40 to 50. Many require three to six months to get their weight down to reasonable levels.

The program is proving to be remarkably successful, perhaps in no small part because participants are required to take it seriously. Before being admitted, they must fulfill half a dozen requirements. They must buy new scales for weighing themselves at home; must agree to weigh themselves at the same time each morning after emptying the bladder and record the weight; must keep a diary of all liquid and solid food intake; must buy postage scales for weighing meat, fish, and seafoods; must undergo tests for cholesterol, uric acid, and glucose tolerance; and must pay regular weekly visits to the medical center to discuss progress and review diary and weight records.

Beyond that, no smoking is allowed. Any would-be participant who is a smoker must agree to give up smoking before being admitted. Not all heavy smokers live up to their vows, but three-fourths of them have done so. Backsliders are dropped. Dr. Heyden believes smoking is a greater health hazard than obesity and fears that smokers would increase cigarette consumption under the stress of dieting.

Not only have weights come down. A number of diabetic patients have returned to normal blood sugar levels. Several patients with gout have been free of pain since weight returned to normal. In patients with high cholesterol levels, the levels have dropped to normal. Without exception, every hypertensive patient has reduced elevated blood pressure to normal. For example, in a forty-three-year-old man who lost 60 pounds, blood pressure has come down from a previous 190/110 to 132/90; in a forty-one-year-old woman who lost 49 pounds, blood pressure has been lowered from 215/130 to 144/80.

We cite this program here as an example of innovative methods being developed by medical men to combat the vast problem of overweight. Obviously, no reader should undertake such a stringent program on his or her own.

PILLS AS PROPS

Are medications of any value in weight reduction? In some individual cases, physicians may feel that an antiappetite agent may have some use as a temporary aid and will prescribe one for trial. In most cases, however, they believe that patients can, if sufficiently motivated, achieve weight reduction without such a crutch.

In the past, medicines for weight reduction generally were based on Benzedrine, which so stimulated patients that physicians were reluctant to use them. Now a number of appetite-reducing agents, almost free of the side effect of overstimulation, are available. These apparently safer agents can be obtained only on prescription.

Over-the-counter, no-prescription-required, reducing preparations are big business. At worst, they can be risky because of possible side effects; at best, the money is foolishly spent because in and of themselves the medicines are not to be relied upon for effective permanent weight reduction.

Not long ago, one physician suggested that if there were to be an ideal drug for treating obesity it would have to be one that would kill the appetite, be nonaddictive, not put the patient to sleep or make him feel too euphoric, and at the same time energize him. As an editorial in a medical journal observed: "One can imagine the pharmacologist contemplating such an assignment. He will doubtless shake his head sadly, observing that no combination of known drugs can do all of these things for a patient at one and the same time, without resulting in an explosion!"

The problem with even the best of presently available reducing aid agents is that they are only supports, crutches, that at best help temporarily. It makes more sense, considering the real objective of reducing, to regulate diet by a healthy change in eating habits which, once desired weight reduction is achieved, can be continued with some upward shift in calorie intake to maintain proper weight permanently.

DIET CLUBS

In recent years, many people have turned to weight-reducing clubs where they can join with others wishing to reduce. The clubs are helpful in providing motivation and even some emotional support. But physicians have reservations about the medical supervision provided by some of the organizations.

The clubs vary in their programs but all emphasize diet coupled with lectures, literature, and experience-sharing. Some prescribe particular exercises. Many require an initial medical certificate for membership but not all have continuing medical supervision. Physicians have reported that, because of the lack of medical supervision in some clubs, the conditions of their heart and diabetic patients in particular have worsened as a result of diet advice given.

If you consider joining a diet club, the best policy is to check with your physician about that particular club and its standing and whether he thinks it is suitable for you.

6

"Bunions on the Seat Instead of the Feet":
The Whole Exercise Story

In his novel *Anna Karenina,* Tolstoy describes how the noble-man Levin works hard at physical labor, mowing hay along with the peasants. When his brother comments on how well he looks, Levin says, "You can't imagine what an effectual remedy it is for every sort of foolishness. I want to enrich medicine with a new word: *Arbeitskur"* (work cure).

By every account—on the basis of striking findings of Israeli studies added to a vast number of significant, often ingenious investigations in the United States and throughout much of the world—physical work or exercise can be a major beneficial factor for much of what ails us, including coronary heart disease.

Some years ago, an American physician, noting a tremen-dous rise in United States coronary heart disease deaths be-tween 1930 and 1960, observed, "It was during this same thirty years that we started to drive rather than walk, that suburban communities were laid out without sidewalks, that a man walking down the street became a subject of investigation by the police, that the only exercise in golf was extracted by invention of the electric golf cart. Even in Atlantic City, the roller chairs are now electrically powered, so the pushers can ride."

More recently, another American physician wrote that man "has moved from the jungles of trees, where he fought against flesh and blood, to the jungles of concrete and steel, where he wrestles with frustration, anxiety, and repressed hostility in a never-ending stream. His brain has risen to ascendancy, and he now has bunions on his seat rather than on his feet. . . . Man, originally the muscled meathead, has traded one chief adversary for another as he has become man, the mental mannequin. First, it was saber-toothed tigers; next, plague and pestilence; and now it is degenerative disease, of which cardiovascular disease is chief."

There are many factors involved in atherosclerosis and coronary heart disease and physical activity—or, more precisely, the lack of it—is only one; nevertheless it would seem that the values of physical activity are multiple for atherosclerosis. There is, as we will see, a body of strong evidence now that activity has beneficial effects on most of the major risk factors associated with the disease.

Upon their arrival in Israel, the Yemenites were remarkable for their low weights and their capacity for hard physical work. Indeed, those weights (despite some persistence of a myth to the contrary in this country) could only be possible with considerable physical activity added to dietary control.

Other Israelis with low heart attack rates are all active people. The kibbutz-dweller's mode of life is based on the philosophy that the Jew should return to the soil and become a man who takes pride in working with his hands. Visit a kibbutz and you can find a member of parliament taking his turn over a weekend doing physical work. In a kibbutz people often walk, jog, or run to work. In the inner settled area of a kibbutz one of us happens to know best, there are no roads, and vehicles are used only for long hauls or very heavy goods.

It is of interest, too, that of the many games that might have been chosen in this kibbutz, the one that is the favorite, basketball, calls for almost constant activity.

In recent years, with diversification in the kibbutzim and the addition of industry to agriculture, a portion of the settlements' population has had to take on sedentary occupations. And while cardiovascular death rates of the kibbutz dwellers as a whole still are only one-third those for residents of Tel Aviv–Jaffa, the rates within the kibbutzim for the nonsedentary workers are only one-third as high as for the sedentary.

At the University of Texas Medical School at Dallas, doctors have been using such tools as the phonocardiogram, a sensitive device that records delicate heart sounds, and other sophisticated gadgetry to monitor the changing physical state of some 100 sedentary males sweating off their flab.

A classic case of poor heart conditioning among the first volunteers tested as part of the program is a thirty-five-year-old government clerk who works entirely behind a desk. His only exercise was walking to his parked car. At home, he was also chairbound—watching TV. He did no yardwork, didn't walk a dog. In school he played in the band and never took part in athletics.

In a pre-exercise examination, the man showed a high and erratic pulse rate while resting, 80 to 100 beats a minute (a well-trained athlete's heart beats steadily at about 50). Just a moderate level of bike-pedaling sent his heart pounding to 150. On a "tilt" bed slanted on circular rockers at a 70-degree angle, the young man turned pale and became dizzy; his pulse climbed to 120 and his blood pressure dropped, even though he was inert. These responses indicated, among other things, poor return of blood to the heart and poor blood vessel tone. The man's ability to withstand any stress to his heart was dangerously low.

With slowly accelerating exercise, marked changes have been noted, including a striking increase in the ability of the once-sluggish heart to pump blood efficiently. There have been other rewarding physical—and psychological—changes as a result of the training.

The exercise story is a considerable story. It should not be oversimplified, as it too often has been. It is, in fact, an enlarging story. We propose to give it a hard look, examining common myths and misconceptions—plus the mounting evidence of the valuable role that exercise can play in lowering elevated blood pressure, favorably influencing the course of diabetes, decreasing blood levels of the fats relating to atherosclerosis, assisting in weight control and preventing obesity, helping those who want to curtail smoking, relieving emotional stress, and in affecting for the good other factors linked to coronary heart disease.

EXERCISE AND WEIGHT

Old myths die hard, and the myth that exercise is a negligible factor in avoiding or overcoming excessive weight has particular staying power.

It may stem in part from a misunderstanding of the significance of some commonly quoted statistics. For example, all of us have heard or read repeatedly that it takes five hours of chopping wood to lose a pound or still more walking to accomplish the same result. And the implication seems to be that no mentally sound person would chop wood or walk for so many hours to accomplish so little.

If these figures are accurate as far as they go, it is necessary to go a step further. To lose a pound of excess weight requires burning up 3,500 calories. But it is not necessary to use exercise to burn it all up at one time. If you increase caloric intake by ingesting one extra pat of butter a day, you will gain eight pounds in a year. Or add one piece of pie per week and you can expect to gain more than three pounds in a year. Similarly, if you increase physical activity enough to use an additional

TABLE 5

CALORIES—IN AND OUT

Weight loss requires burning up more calories than the number taken in as food. The extra calories come from fat stored in the body. The chart below shows the caloric content of typical foods and how long in *minutes* various activities must be pursued to burn the calories. For example, you would have to sleep 300 minutes, or 5 hours, to burn up the 350 calories supplied by a hamburger—or bowl 80 minutes. Figures in the chart are for a 150-pound person.

Food	Calories per Serving	Sleeping	Walking	Bowling	Golf	Tennis	Bicycling	Swimming	Running
Raw carrot	42	36	8	10	8	6	5	4	2
Boiled egg	77	66	15	17	15	11	9	7	4
Fried egg	110	94	21	25	22	15	13	10	6
Bread/butter	78	67	15	18	16	11	10	7	4
Bacon (2 strips)	96	82	18	22	19	14	12	9	5
Apple (large)	101	87	19	23	20	14	12	9	5
Beer (glass)	114	98	22	26	23	16	14	10	6

TABLE 5 (Continued)

Food	Calories per Serving	Sleeping	Walking	Bowling	Golf	Tennis	Bicycling	Swimming	Running
Orange juice (glass)	120	103	23	27	24	17	15	11	6
Milk (glass)	166	142	32	38	33	23	20	15	9
Pancake/syrup	124	106	24	28	25	17	15	11	6
Cheese pizza	180	154	35	41	36	25	22	16	9
½ breast, fried chicken	232	199	45	53	46	33	28	21	12
T-bone steak	235	201	45	53	47	33	29	21	12
Hamburger	350	300	67	80	70	49	43	31	18
Tuna fish salad sandwich	278	238	53	63	56	39	34	25	14
Ice cream soda	255	219	49	58	51	36	31	23	13
⅙ apple pie	377	323	73	86	75	53	46	34	19
Spaghetti	396	339	76	90	79	56	48	35	20
Strawberry shortcake	400	343	77	91	80	56	49	36	21

200 calories a day, this would equal 73,000 calories at the end of a year, enough to get rid of 20 excess pounds.

For most people, using up an extra 200 calories a day would mean, for example, a daily walk of less than one hour. The calories expended during walking depend both upon the speed and the weight of the individual. At three miles an hour, a 150-pound person, for instance, will use up 120 calories in half an hour, and if he walks no more than that and at that pace—which is hardly inordinate—he can expect to lose more than 12 pounds in a year.

Exercise and weight are inseparably linked, and this has been shown repeatedly in scientific studies. In one, for example, a group of college men were offered payment if, during the course of the study, they could keep their weight constant. First, the students were put on a low-calorie diet, much lower than they had been accustomed to. They soon found that they had to limit their activity to avoid weight loss. Then the diet was increased to 6,000 calories a day. Now they had to exercise almost frantically—running, rowing, doing calisthenics—to keep their weight constant.

Why is such a large proportion of the American population obese? Is it because of heavy eating? Certainly not just that. In fact, there is some evidence that many of us eat less than our forefathers did. As one distinguished nutritionist puts it: "The sight of an old-time wedding menu is enough to demonstrate this point. But, in order to get to the wedding, grandpa had to walk or ride horseback for long distances even in the dead of winter. Old-fashioned wedding dancing, too, was generally more strenuous than the modern variety. By the time our grandparents were home, they had expended a large part of the surplus calories they had accumulated."

We don't really appreciate how sedentary contemporary living in the Western world is. Even farmers now ride tractors where once they walked. The housewife no longer scrubs floors or washes clothes at an energy expense of 250 calories per hour; she uses modern devices including washing machines and vacuum cleaners at an output of 120 calories per hour.

Writes a British physiologist: "Even young military cadets spend 17¾ hours a day either lying, sitting, or standing; the corresponding figure for coal miners is 18¾ hours a day; for colliery clerks, 20 hours a day. Military cadets and miners have two of the most physically active occupations, and yet about three-quarters of their life is sedentary. The daily physical activity of many thousands of light workers may be below the threshold needed for appetite to function normally. For this reason they may overeat and become obese."

There is a widespread misconception that exercise is useless for weight reduction because it increases appetite.

In a normal person, it is true that an increase in appetite occurs with an increase in activity. This is why the weight of most people is relatively constant. But a fat person does not react the same way. Only when he exercises to excess does he experience an appetite increase. He has large stores of fat and moderate exercise in his case is not likely to stimulate appetite. The difference between the response to exercise of fat and thin people is an important one.

Obesity is very largely a disease of modern civilization— perhaps to some extent related to rich diet but to a very great extent related to lessened routine opportunity for physical activity. We grow fat over periods of months and years, failing to make use of the small daily means of caloric output. Suddenly, one day, we take a good look in the mirror or step onto a scale and discover with some dismay how much overweight we are. Then we go on a crash diet, which works temporarily. But soon the pounds are back on again. The solution, obvious and sensible, is to use exercise both to help trim off and keep off excess weight.

This makes sense not only in terms of arriving and staying at desirable weight for esthetic reasons and to overcome undesirable effects of excess weight on the heart, but also because of the other desirable effects on heart health that exercise can have.

ACTIVITY AND CHD

Every large population that has been found to have a low incidence of coronary heart disease also indulges in far more physical activity than Western populations.

Although physical activity has been considered by many since early Grecian times to be essential for health, no sizable data from studies specifically examining the possible relationship to heart disease were reported until just the last two decades.

An early study by Dr. J. N. Morris and his associates in Great Britain established that the drivers of London double-decker buses had half again as many heart attacks as did the conductors. Quite possibly personality factors could be involved, not just the greater activity of the conductors on the job; perhaps a different type of man chooses to be a driver than does the man who chooses to be a conductor. Possibly, too, drivers are exposed to more stress in the form of traffic snarls. But Dr. Morris and his fellow investigators felt that the most likely explanation was the difference in activity, with conductors running up and down steps to collect fares.

Studies of American workers also have shown fewer heart attacks among the physically active. One which covered 120,000 railroad employes revealed a heart attack incidence among sedentary office workers almost twice that for men working in the yards. Another, of 2,000 postal workers in the District of Columbia, found excess risk of coronary heart disease for the clerks was 1.4 to 1.9 times that of the carriers.

Among 355 Harvard football lettermen who were followed over an extended period, 34 developed coronary heart disease.

But no man who had maintained a heavy exercise program since leaving college had become a CHD victim.

Longshoremen, of course, are manual workers, but even within that occupation there are degrees of physical expenditure. A recent study covering 3,263 longshoremen over a 16-year period found that 291 deaths from coronary heart disease occurred during that time. Men with the less vigorous jobs expended 925 fewer calories per work day and sustained coronary death rates one-third higher than the others.

In England, after the original driver-conductor study, Dr. Morris and his team went on to do a national autopsy survey in hospitals in Scotland, England, and Wales. They found additional evidence to support the theory that men in physically active jobs have a lower incidence of coronary heart disease. Approximately 5,000 autopsy reports were analyzed and each was correlated with the physical activity of the subject. Job activity was classified as light (for example, a schoolteacher), active (a postman), heavy (a laborer). Not only did the men in physically active and heavy-work jobs have less coronary heart disease, but when the disease developed, it was less severe. Also, it developed later than in men in sedentary work.

One study which has become almost a classic was made by Harvard scientists who decided to compare 700 Bostonians of Irish descent with their brothers who had remained in Ireland. The men were in the thirty- to sixty-year age range. Coronary heart disease deaths in the Boston group turned out to be twice as great as in the Ireland group. The men in Ireland ate more eggs, more butter, and more of other saturated fats, yet had lower blood cholesterol levels. They consumed 400 calories more per day on the average than their Boston brothers but weighed 10 percent less. They were getting more exercise, and their lower cholesterol levels showed that physical activity does more than just burn off calories.

In fact, the idea that exercise is good medicine for the heart is based upon studies showing that physical activity has a considerable number of significantly beneficial influences.

THE EFFECT ON CHOLESTEROL

As the study comparing the Boston men with their brothers in Ireland indicated, exercise can lower cholesterol levels as well as burn off calories. Other studies demonstrate the same thing.

Rabbits, for example, have been fed diets rich in cholesterol and have been divided into two groups, one group being vigorously exercised, the other not. Upon examination, the exercised animals had lower cholesterol values and were found to be free of atherosclerosis while the others had developed the disease process.

At Camp Lejune, North Carolina, a group of more than 100 marines in rigorous training were fed at least 4,500 calories a day in a diet deliberately made rich with saturated fat. At the end of six months of heavy eating and continuous hard work, their weights and blood fats were unchanged.

With three medical students as his volunteers, Dr. G. V. Mann at Harvard carried out a diet-exercise study, starting with a doubling of the men's caloric intake while they exercised vigorously. As long as they were physically active, there was neither a gain in weight nor in blood fat levels. But when the exercising was stopped and the same high caloric intake continued, both weight and blood fat levels shot up. In another study with medical students, 45 extra grams of fat a day were deliberately introduced into the diet, but with the men exercising more vigorously than before the study, there was no increase in blood cholesterol.

At Kent State University, Dr. Lawrence A. Golding carried out a study with 42 men, aged twenty-nine to sixty-three, all in sedentary jobs. For an hour a day, five days a week, for nine months, they took part in an intensive physical-fitness program. In every man, blood cholesterol declined, with the greatest drop occurring in men who had had the highest levels at the outset.

When they checked on the residents of a Swiss Alpine village, Dr. Jean Mayer of Harvard and Dr. Daniella Gsell of Basel found a rather remarkable example of the influence of exercise on cholesterol. The village, Blattendorf, is in a remote valley in the southern Swiss Alps. All inhabitants are farmers. Farms and pastures spread over steep slopes at altitudes ranging from 4,000 to 8,000 feet. Because the village is several miles from the nearest road, all distances have to be walked. People carry hay, wood, milk, and building materials on their backs. Men often carry loads of as much as 100 pounds and even elderly women carry 50- and 60-pound loads up and down mountain paths.

The cholesterol levels of the men in the village ranged from 164 in the thirty- to thirty-nine-year-old group to 200 for those fifty to fifty-nine. Women in the same age groups showed levels of 160 to 190. In all cases, the levels were markedly below those of working-class men and women of similar ancestry who were studied in the city of Basel.

When the two doctors carried out a two-week dietary survey in the village, they found an average per capita consumption of 3,643 calories, of which 34 percent came from fats. Animal fats made up 27 percent of the total intake. Dairy products, bread, and potatoes were consumed in quantity.

In contrast, the people in Basel consumed only 2,643 calories, of which a similar percentage came from fat, with the proportion of animal fats and saturated and unsaturated fatty acids essentially similar to those in the villagers' diet. Considering the villagers' higher total caloric intake, this meant that the intake of fat was about 30 percent greater. Yet cholesterol levels among the villagers were much lower—and their mortality from cardiovascular disease was much lower. Drs. Mayer and Gsell could only attribute this to the greater level of physical activity.

But if all this is impressive, it should be noted that not all studies have found tremendously great differences in cholesterol levels between physically active and sedentary individuals. It is a fact that the physically active Navajo Indians and the physically active Trappist brothers as well have average blood cholesterol levels just barely significantly lower than those for the general American male population—but they have a coronary heart disease incidence dramatically less than that of American men in general.

Thus, physical activity, beyond what it does for controlling cholesterol levels and weight, may serve to protect the heart in other ways.

THE EFFECT ON TENSION

It has been said that action absorbs anxiety and tension. The role of mental and emotional stress in heart disease may be a substantial one and is the subject of the next chapter. But here we can examine briefly the effect of activity on stress.

Anxiety and tension seem to be almost inescapable in modern society. We are under constant bombardment by the environment. We are under pressure on the job to achieve more. We are beset by worries over the seemingly increasingly complex business of getting to and from work, educating our children, maintaining healthy family structures.

Tension appears to be the rule, not the exception. And though we are aware of the general debilitating effects, let alone what tension may do to the heart, we are also aware that we cannot simply tell ourselves to relax. Our keyed-up nerves do not respond to commands. They seem, at least temporarily, to respond somewhat to drugs—witness the inordinate sales of tranquilizers and sleeping pills. But drugging the mind can hardly be considered the ideal way to deal with tension. There are too many penalties in undesirable side effects and habituation possibilities.

The way to relax the mind is not to relax the body. Vigorous physical activity is the best antidote for mental and emotional tension. It is difficult, if not impossible, to remain tense during vigorous physical activity. Who can long remain tense in mind while swatting a tennis ball or stroking a golf ball or even taking a brisk walk!

Aside from such everyday observation of the value of activity for promoting relaxation, there is a considerable body of knowledge now about the physiological basis for the relaxing effects.

Under tension and stress, the adrenal glands atop the kidneys increase their hormone secretions. It is a function of these glands to ready you for action in an emergency situation, to prepare you to fight or flee. Our ancient ancestors became tense and anxious usually in situations of physical emergency —for example, when confronted with a fierce animal or storm of nature. They had to react quickly to live, react by combating the danger or running away from it. The increased adrenal gland secretions permitted the sudden mustering of extra energy they needed.

We have inherited the mechanism but not the same type of emergencies. Our anxieties and tensions arise from pressures and problems that rarely permit a reaction as simple and direct as doing physical battle or running away. We sit and stew. Where our ancestors immediately used up the extra energy mobilized by their increased adrenal gland secretions, we do not. And there is evidence that one of the significant effects of the adrenal gland outpouring is an increase in the level of blood fats. The hormones mobilize them from body stores for energy. The fats are not used. High levels of them circulate in the blood stream, and this may lead to fat deposition in the artery walls.

If we sit and stew, the tension within us mounts. The extra energy potential goes round and round inside since it has nowhere else to go. With exercise, we release it, externalize it, and nicely use up, too, the excess of fats in the blood that otherwise may nest in the artery walls.

THE EFFECT ON HYPERTENSION

High blood pressure is a prime risk factor for coronary heart disease and strokes. We will consider it more thoroughly in Chapter 9, but we can mention briefly here the role of exercise in controlling blood pressure.

Many studies have demonstrated the ability of physical activity to keep blood pressure at healthy levels. Recently, for example, researchers examined 61 former champion endurance runners or cross-country skiers forty to seventy-nine years of age and a comparison group of 54 nonathletes of the same ages. The mean blood-pressure values for the nonathletes were above normal limits; those for the athletes were nicely within the normal range.

Studies not only in this country but elsewhere around the world indicate that long participation in sports tends to lower blood pressure. Fifty percent of endurance athletes among Soviet "Masters of Sport" are reported to have systolic pressures below 99, far below what is considered the upper limit of normal, 140.

In one of the most recent studies in this country, Drs. John L. Boyer and Fred W. Kasch of the San Diego State College Exercise Laboratory worked with 23 hypertensive men, placing them on a moderate exercise program. The program consisted of 15 to 20 minutes of warm-up calisthenics and no more than 30 to 35 minutes of walking-jogging twice a week. Before the program, mean blood pressure for the men was 159/105. After six months of exercising, it was 146/93.

THE EFFECT ON CORONARY BLOOD FLOW

The two great coronary arteries and their large branches which feed the heart muscle do so, as we have observed earlier, by breaking up into smaller tributary vessels, forming a large and complex system of coronary blood flow. It's an adaptable system. When a heart attack occurs because of blockage of a coronary vessel, the coronary system tries to establish new vessels to transport blood to the heart area deprived of normal nourishment by the blockage. This collateral circulation, as it is called, is an important element in successful recovery from a heart attack.

The opening up of collateral circulation during a heart attack is, in effect, a response to sudden stress. There is evidence that exercise, providing a kind of controlled stress over an extended period of time, can lead to the development of collateral circulation, a desirable result indeed.

There have been many studies to show this, including experimental work in animals. With dogs, for example, investigators have been able to demonstrate that exercise promotes collateral vessel growth. It does so, too, in animals who already have mild narrowing of the coronary arteries. And the growth produced by exercise is much greater than that produced when, to duplicate the conditions of a heart attack, the arteries of underexercised dogs are constricted.

If collateral circulation is sufficiently developed, it may help to prevent a heart attack. With enough spare vessels available to take over instantly when a coronary artery becomes blocked, there may be virtually no interruption of blood flow to the heart muscle, no damage to it, and therefore no actual heart attack.

Collateral circulation also helps to explain why some people, despite severe atherosclerosis, do not suffer from angina pectoris, the chest pain stemming from reduced blood supply to the heart muscle. In their case, collateral circulation has kept pace with the atherosclerosis. While there has been progressive diminution of blood flow through the vessels affected by atherosclerosis, new pathways have formed through which blood can move, counterbalancing the diminished flow through the original vessels.

In the Framingham study, investigators found that sedentary people had greater mortality from coronary heart disease and were especially prone to sudden death. Their findings suggested that the greater protection enjoyed by the physically active could be due in large part to the promotion of collaterals even when the coronary circulation had already been impaired.

It may seem almost paradoxical to prescribe exercise for a patient already experiencing angina, wincing with pain at slight effort. Yet some physicians have long had the impression that a carefully guided program of activity for the angina patient could be helpful. If begun slowly and built up gradually—always stopping short of the point of provoking an angina attack—exercise could, they believed, stimulate collateral development.

Recently, there have been numerous studies aimed at measuring objectively the results of carefully designed exercise programs in just such patients. They do, indeed, indicate that many patients benefit with reduced anginal symptoms and increased exercise tolerance.

Moreover, investigators have been finding that physical exercise is of value in reconditioning patients who have suffered heart attacks. Dr. Brunner, for example, carried out a comparison study. Three months after they had had a first heart attack, 64 patients agreed to participate in an exercise program and continued at it for at least a year. In that time, there were 2 fatalities and 4 recurrent heart attacks in the group; no patient complained of severe angina. On the other hand, among 65 comparable patients who did not receive active reconditioning, there were 7 fatalities, 9 recurrent heart attacks, and 30 complained of angina.

The Trained Heart

Exercise can materially increase the efficiency of the heart itself. One indication of this is the slow heart beat at rest of the individual accustomed to vigorous exercise.

A good example is Roger Bannister, now a physician, who was the first man in history to run the four-minute mile. Before he began training for that feat, Bannister had a heart rate when he was sitting still or was otherwise at rest in the mid-seventies, just about average. By the time he had improved his physical condition to the point of being able to run the then-record four-minute mile, Bannister's resting heart rate was 40 beats a minute.

How does this happen and what is its significance?

One adaptation made by the heart of a trained athlete is to enlarge. The muscle fibers gradually lengthen. But this is not the kind of lengthening that occurs in a diseased and failing heart. A failing heart also enlarges; the muscle fibers over-stretch because of weakness. In the trained heart, however, the fibers lengthen in healthy fashion and have greater strength. As a result of the lengthening and enlargement, the ventricles of the heart can hold and pump more blood.

At rest, the trained heart is fully dilated and empties only partially with each beat. Between beats, it serves as a reservoir for blood. Because of the trained heart's increased development of tiny blood vessels, capillaries (through which oxygen exchange takes place), the heart muscle is able to extract oxygen from its blood supply more effectively. This is equally true of muscles throughout the body which, during training, also develop more of the tiny blood vessels.

Thus, when the body is at rest, thanks to the increased efficiency of oxygen extraction both by the heart muscle and the skeletal muscles, the heart rate may be halved as compared with the rate for an unfit individual. There just isn't the need for the greater rate of contraction. As a result, the workload of the heart is decreased when the body is at rest. The heart also gets more rest because there is a longer period between contractions.

During activity, the trained heart responds easily because it has larger capacity. It responds by pumping out more blood with each beat. Where the untrained heart must meet increased workloads chiefly by increasing its beat rate, the trained heart can meet some or much of the extra demand by increasing its stroke volume, achieving the same amount of blood flow with fewer beats.

Mild exercise may not significantly increase the rate of a well-trained heart. And even after a period of heavy exercise, when the beat rate does go up, the recovery period—the interval during which the heart rate slows to the normal resting level—is fairly short compared to the recovery period for the unfit person.

Recently, heart specialists, and psychiatrists as well, have become fascinated by the tribe of Tarahumara Indians of Mexico. As the result of training from childhood, men and women participants in the tribe's popular game of kick-ball can run continuously for over 100 miles at a speed of six to seven miles an hour while kicking and pursuing a wooden ball. Equally amazing is the psychological adjustment of these Indians. In the past 25 years, there have been no suicides and only one homicide among the 50,000 tribesmen.

Physicians made an intensive study of eight men runners, eighteen to forty-eight years old. At the midpoint of a long kick-ball race, they checked the blood pressures of the men and found that they had decreased considerably from what they had been at the start of the race. At the same time, pulse rates had risen to levels of 120 to 155. Weight loss during the race averaged five pounds. Extensive tests after the race showed no abnormal changes of any kind. None of the Indians could remember a single instance when a runner had dropped out of a race because of chest pain or shortness of breath.

Dr. Dale Groom, one of the physician-investigators, who is professor of medicine and associate dean of the University of Oklahoma Medical Center, tells us: "These marathon demonstrations of really phenomenal endurance are convincing evidence that most of us, brought up in our comfortable and sedentary civilizations, actually develop and use only a fraction of our potential cardiac reserve."

OTHER BENEFITS

While exercise can hardly be considered a panacea, in itself capable of assuring complete freedom from atherosclerosis and heart attack, it does contribute in many ways beyond those already mentioned to heart and circulatory health and to general health as well.

Diabetes is a risk factor for coronary disease (see Chapter 9). Exercise is often of considerable value in the control of diabetes.

Of considerable importance, recent studies indicate, are the changes in the blood brought about by exercise. With physical activity, there is an increase in the tendency for blood to clot. At the same time, however, there is a marked increase in the production of fibrinolysin, an agent that dissolves clots.

Do these two opposing changes seem paradoxical? There is sound reason for them. An active person—in the jungles of old, the jungles of modern war, in a gym, or anywhere—stands some chance of injury. The injury could possibly lead to bleeding. But the physical activity causes biochemical changes that make it possible for blood to clot more readily, thus minimizing the likelihood of bleeding to death. At the same time, fibrinolysin is produced so it is available to dissolve the clot when danger has passed. As an extra dividend, the fibrinolysin may conceivably dissolve old clots that are present, including clots that have lodged in critical areas such as the coronary arteries and which, with further enlargement, might lead to heart attack.

Increased ability to dissolve clots has actually been measured by many investigators during exercise. They have found it to be proportional to the amount and intensity of exercise. In one study, clot-dissolving ability produced by maximal exercise was found to be seven times as great as that produced by moderate exercise. The effect has been found to be transient and can only be maintained by daily exercise.

Valuable for toning the heart muscle, exercise is no less so for body muscles. With regular physical activity, muscles that may have been weak and sagging become stronger, better toned. Along with an increase in muscular strength and endurance, there may also be an increase in coordination and in joint flexibility leading to a marked reduction of minor aches and pains. Postural defects, too, may be corrected and there is likely to be an improvement in general appearance. Feelings of listlessness and fatigue are likely to be replaced by sensations of alertness and energy.

The human body, it has been reported, is capable of generating 14 horsepower with maximum effort. It generates only 0.1 horsepower at rest. In many of us who lead sedentary lives, there is some muscular atrophy, or wasting away. We become undermuscled for our weight and we may lack the strength and endurance needed even for sedentary work. In addition, it has been suggested that the unused horsepower, so to speak, may go into building up tension, with the tension then becoming a factor in producing fatigue and, sometimes, other complaints as well.

Sometimes, it is possible to obtain new or added insights into the value of something by depriving people of it. Recently, Dr. Frederick Baekeland of the State University of New York Downstate Medical Center, Brooklyn, carried out one such deprivation study. He investigated the sleep of 14 normal college students accustomed to regular exercise on two nights when they exercised and on four nights during a one-month period when all exercise was prohibited. Not only did the subjects complain that they didn't sleep as well during the month without exercise, but on the four nights when their sleep was actually monitored with sensitive electrical equipment in the laboratory, there were clear changes in the pattern of sleep indicating increased anxiety. Dr. Baekeland also notes that during the month without exercise, the students experienced increased sexual tension.

It has been aptly observed that if man, sociologically speaking, has become a pushbutton modernist, he remains, physiologically speaking, a cave man. For maximal health, he needs exercise; his whole body is keyed to it.

And for Women

No less than men, women need exercise. They need it as a help in combating atherosclerosis and coronary heart disease to which, if somewhat later than men, they are nevertheless subject.

Studies of women, including those in the Israeli kibbutzim, as we will see later, show that those who are physically active have considerably lower rates of angina and heart attacks than those who are sedentary.

And women need exercise for other than heart health reasons.

"The tired, complaining, cross female companion, date, wife, daughter, or friend is no joy to anyone. If her problem is based on disability and medical incapacity, hopefully she can be cured. If, however, no diagnosed clinical condition exists, and she appears 'normal,' then we must, as physicians, develop a higher index of suspicion about her physical fitness."

Those words come from a woman physician, Dr. Evalyn S.

Gendel of the Kansas State Department of Health. Dr. Gendel has placed some of the blame on the medical profession for perpetuating myths about menstrual discomfort, chronic back disability, and other complaints and for legitimizing excuses from physical activity because of them—thereby contributing, Dr. Gendel believes, to the unfitness of American women.

Dr. Gendel reached these conclusions through studies of chronic fatigue, backache, menstrual discomfort, and other vague symptoms in relation to actual medical conditions and physical fitness of young women.

In one study, she worked with 67 college women between seventeen and twenty-five years of age, 55 of them single and 12 married with one child. Each woman was thoroughly interviewed about her health history, current and past physical activity, and medical complaints. Each underwent a physical and orthopedic examination and a series of physical fitness tests.

Most of the women had been exposed to only 1.3 years of physical education in high school. Even those who had been or were fairly active physically did not engage in activity taxing the heart and blood vessel system.

The most common complaint was menstrual difficulty but abnormal findings on thorough examination were rare. The next most common complaints were allergies and colds, and finally fatigue and headache. There were also some backache and digestive complaints.

It was notable that even though not one of the women could be rated as being extremely active, those who were fairly active and scored highest in physical fitness had the fewest complaints about colds, allergies, digestive disorders, and fatigue. Those who scored lowest in fitness had the highest incidence of backache complaints.

Dr. Gendel also found that the women who had borne children after a lifetime of relative inactivity suffered the greatest amount of decreased abdominal muscle tone, backache, and fatigue—and she predicts that, if their lack of adequate physical activity is allowed to persist, the stress of pregnancy could make the remaining women candidates for similar problems.

Dr. Gendel concludes that educators and physicians must provide motivation to overcome the burdens of physical inactivity on women. Programs for children in early school years should help them explore their physical abilities and enjoy strenuous activity. Girls' and women's competitive programs should become part of the regular school environment, she believes, and should not be limited to track and swimming. And physicians who recognize the preventive value of fitness and the medical relationships between fitness and health will have to become "more vocal about it," in Dr. Gendel's words. "Conditioning for life 'workloads,' " she emphasizes, "should become as important as the conditioning we insist upon for our trained athletes and for the commercial ventures of professional athletics and for Olympic competition."

It would, indeed, be a good thing—for extending life, helping to reduce the toll coronary heart disease takes among women, as well as for minimizing the nonfatal but spoiling minor disturbances so common among women.

Nor is there any reason why most if not all women (just as most if not all men) at any age cannot begin to get the value of exercise.

EXERCISE AT ANY AGE

That even elderly people, men in their seventies for example, can regain much of the vigor and physical function of men in their forties through well-planned activity has been demonstrated in many studies.

Dr. Brunner reports that Israeli men who have had heart attacks and have entered a program of activity—gradually intensified until it becomes vigorous and includes long jogs along the Mediterranean Sea—now are often more fit than before their heart attacks, and more fit than nontrained people of their age who have not had coronary heart disease.

In a study carried out at the University of Southern California, 69 men aged fifty to eighty-seven worked out for an hour three times a week. Their carefully prescribed and closely supervised regimen included calisthenics, stretching, swimming, and jogging. At the end of a year, these were the results, expressed in group averages: Blood pressure improved by 6 percent; body fat decreased by 4.8 percent; oxygen consumption increased by 9.2 percent; arm strength increased by 7.2 percent; and nervous tension was reduced by 14 percent.

It would be an invitation to disaster for older people—and, for that matter, for younger people—to rush into vigorous activity after long years of sedentary living without a thorough medical checkup first, followed by a thoughtfully worked out program emphasizing a slow start and gradual progression toward more and more vigorous exercises and sports. But there is growing evidence now that, at any age, suitable activity can help prolong the active years and help to retard and possibly avoid some of the degenerative diseases, including coronary heart disease.

What motivates people to take part in exercise programs? Data from pilot studies at Pennsylvania State University, the University of Minnesota, the University of Wisconsin, and the National Aeronautics and Space Administration show that "health enhancement" is the number one reason, but also a desire for a "change in routine" sends some men to the gym. Interestingly, the data show that the reasons men stay in such programs are not necessarily the same ones that impelled them to enter in the first place. Once in, they cite "a feeling of well-being," "physical accomplishment," "social aspects," "fitness," and "competition" as benefits they derive. How the exercisers' wives felt about the programs also had a part to play. Many of the exercisers found that the beneficial effects of exercise extended to other parts of their lives and that exercise improved their attitude toward work.

If the benefits of exercise for adults are many, as indeed they are, there can also be some spillover for children. The poor physical condition of American youngsters is of growing concern. Children should be encouraged to be more than spectators. They should be encouraged to respect their bodies and the needs of their bodies; to be active; to engage in sports not only for the sake of becoming athletes but for the sake of their health; to learn to be skillful; and to take pleasure not just in team sports but in more individualized sport activities they can use throughout life. They can be encouraged all the more if adults set the example.

When Exercise Can Be Dangerous

Unless it is done sensibly, exercise can be dangerous; it can even be lethal.

Jogging, for example, is among the most accessible and effective exercises for developing heart and lung stamina. But, when it is done improperly, it has fatal possibilities we are told by Dr. Richard L. Bohannon, president of the National Jogging Association, Washington, D.C., which has received notices of a worrisome number of deaths during or immediately after jogging.

Dr. Bohannon, certainly an outstanding expert on this particular activity, advises that any sedentary person over thirty who wants to jog should first be examined by a physician and then, if all is well, make a slow start. A good way to begin: 20 minutes of just walking daily. By the time you work up to two brisk 20-minute walking sessions a day, Dr. Bohannon notes, you may well find yourself occasionally breaking into a brief jog "just because you feel like doing so. Have patience. Let time work for you. Never push exertion beyond the dictates of common sense and prudence."

What makes crash exercise programs dangerous? Animal studies indicate that when there is extensive coronary artery disease already present, exercise that suddenly and greatly exceeds the usual level of activity can put so much demand on the heart muscle, far enough exceeding the ability of the blood supply to match it, that there may be damage to the heart muscle like that produced by a heart attack.

Autopsies of young World War II soldiers who died suddenly of heart attacks during strenuous physical activity often showed the presence of coronary artery disease, suggesting that blood supply to part of the heart muscle had already been compromised. They might have survived if there had been no sudden great demand so far exceeding the ability of the coronary artery system to supply it that the heart muscle was damaged. They might have survived, too, if they had been exposed to gradually increased exercise levels to provide training for the heart and to allow stimulation of collateral vessel development.

Deaths from exercise do not indict exercise—only the improper use of exercise.

We shall have more to say about exercise and its proper use in later pages.

7

Does Stress Trigger Heart Attacks?

"A motor car doesn't suddenly cease running because of old age. It stops because of failure of some part that has worn out. It is the same with people. Under continuous stress—either physical or mental—some vital body part gives way, leading to a variety of illnesses, and eventually to death."

So declares Dr. Hans Selye, director of the Institute of Experimental Medicine and Surgery at the University of Montreal, and the man responsible for the development of the stress theory, which may rank as one of the most significant of twentieth century research achievements.

In arriving at the theory, Selye subjected laboratory animals to many types of stresses: noise, zero temperatures, overwhelming fatigue produced by motor-driven cages that kept the animals in constant motion, and frustration produced by tying the animals, spread-eagled, to a board.

No matter what form the stress took, when it had to be endured for prolonged periods it wreaked internal havoc. Blood pressure climbed sharply. At autopsy, the animals were found to have peptic ulcers, enlarged adrenal glands, and disturbances in other glands.

Selye's research led to this picture of what happens under stressful conditions: Upon first being presented with a stress, the body swings into action to deal with it. Whether it is a physical stress such as heat or cold or an emotional one such as nervous tension, the body's glands provide extra hormones to deal with the situation. And this, the first response, occurs in what is called the *alarm* stage.

All is well for a while. The extra hormones keep the body working at the high pitch needed under the conditions of stress. This is called the *resistance* stage.

Eventually, if the supercharged rate of living is maintained, the extra hormones begin to impair the functioning of various body organs. This is the *exhaustion* stage. Now the body is no longer able to live with the stress.

"Depending upon the intensity of the stressor agent and the predisposition of the individual, a heart attack can occur at any point along this road," Dr. Selye says.

Selye's concept of stress was first presented in 1950. Since then, evidence that stress—particularly emotional stress—may play an important role in coronary heart disease has been accumulating. Let's examine a sampling of the evidence.

THE HEARTBEATS OF INTERNS

At nine o'clock one morning, Dr. Arthur J. Moss, associate professor of medicine at the University of Rochester School of Medicine and Dentistry, attached a portable electrocardiographic tape recorder to the chest of a twenty-six year-old medical intern at Strong Memorial Hospital in Rochester.

At 10:30, grand rounds began. The young doctor's heart rate before grand rounds had been 75 beats a minute. But during grand rounds, as he was called upon to present a case—

in effect, to demonstrate his medical acuity by detailing the findings he had made about the patient, and his diagnosis and plan for treatment—his heart rate reached 187 beats a minute. This lasted for only a minute and as the young intern continued to talk, his heart rate dropped. By the end of his five-minute presentation, his heart rate was approaching 75 beats a minute again.

This was no isolated case of heart speed-up because of "stage fright." Dr. Moss recorded the heart rates of ten house officers who presented cases and found that their average rates increased from 73 to 154 beats a minute.

As Dr. Moss tells us, "This tremendous tachycardia (increased heart rate) is an example of how nonphysical stress can affect the heart. The rates recorded are generally greater than those obtained in skiers during vigorous cross-country competition. After grand rounds we had the young house officers run up six flights of steps, and we couldn't produce as high a heart rate as they experienced during their case presentations."

In addition to increased heart rate, studies have shown that blood pressure rises during stress. And this represents an increased workload for the heart which must expend more energy, contracting harder to push out blood against the increased pressure in the arteries.

THE EFFECT ON BLOOD FATS

Stress can elevate blood cholesterol level. In students preparing for final examinations, blood cholesterol levels have been found to fluctuate wildly within short periods of time. Income tax accountants have been found to have higher cholesterol levels during their heavy stress period just prior to income tax filing time than at other times.

Investigators have established that cholesterol levels are

higher among air force men under stress, with the levels coming down during rest periods or when their type of work has been changed.

In studies at the University of Oklahoma in which diet, exercise, and other factors were held constant, with only emotional stress changing, marked cholesterol level increases were measured when stress increased.

Recently, researchers at the Columbia University College of Physicians and Surgeons developed a technique for electrically stimulating mental activity in conscious dogs and cats one to two hours after a fat-rich feeding. Through implanted electrodes, they excited the amygdaloid nucleus, an area of the brain that influences emotional activities such as rage and fear. During such excitation, lasting no longer than four minutes, the animals' blood plasma turned milky because of an increase in the concentration of triglycerides. The way in which these fatty increases are brought about is still not entirely understood. In part, however, it may be because the imposed emotional activity impedes the action of a fat-clearing agent, called heparin.

JOB STRESS

Not all stress is bad. Joy is a stress; so is a game of tennis or watching a motion picture or television suspense thriller. Stress is part of life and makes us live. Trouble, however, comes when excessive stress is applied too long.

Some years ago, Dr. Henry I. Russek of New York City made a study of 100 young coronary patients and found that at the time of their heart attacks 91 of these men were holding down two jobs, working more than 60 hours a week, or experiencing unusual fear, insecurity, discontent, frustration, restlessness, or feelings of inadequacy in connection with their work.

Prompted by this finding, Dr. Russek sent questionnaires to

more than 12,000 professional persons in 14 occupational groups. He compared the prevalence of coronary disease in various job categories in which differences with respect to tensions created by routine demands on the job could be defined. Among those surveyed were physicians, dentists, and lawyers in general practice and in various specialties.

Coronary heart disease turned out to be three times more frequent among general medical practitioners, for example, than among specialists such as dermatologists, who presumably have more regular hours and by the nature of their practice encounter less stressful situations. Trial lawyers were more prone to coronary heart disease than patent attorneys whose practices may be less stressful.

Classifying jobs on the basis of their stressfulness is no simple matter. The higher the position, it might seem, the greater the stress. The stereotype of the business executive is a hard-driving, pressure-ridden man subject to ulcers and early heart attack. But this isn't the case.

Dr. Lawrence Hinkle, Jr., and associates studied 270,000 men employed by the Bell System operating companies— people of different occupations, levels of achievement, and education. The study failed to demonstrate that men with great responsibility had any more risk of heart attack than those with lesser responsibility. Actually, the study found that men with college educations and men successful in achieving their goals had fewer heart attacks than less educated or less successful men.

Another study in industry revealed that initial heart attacks occurred more often among lower-salaried employees than among those in higher brackets. In fact, men receiving the highest salaries had the lowest heart attack rate, half that for the men in the lowest-salaried group. It may be that men who reach the top get there because they are well adjusted and more capable of handling stresses.

It is possible to draw that same conclusion from one recent

study which found that men listed in *Who's Who in America* live longer than unlisted men. As the life insurance statisticians who made the study noted, the findings "contradict the belief in some quarters that the mercilessness with which men may drive themselves during their forties to outstanding positions in their careers is reflected in broken health when they are in their fifties." Age for age, eminent men enjoyed more favorable life expectancies than men in the general population.

(Although *Who's Who* men lived longer than men not listed, there were wide differences in mortality among various vocational groups. Scientists had the lowest mortality rate; correspondents, journalists, authors, editors, and critics had the highest; church officials, clergymen, educators, and military men had lower than average rates; physicians and surgeons and government officials had higher than average rates; for business executives, judges, lawyers, engineers, artists, illustrators, and sculptors rates were about average.)

Rapid movement of people to new places and modes of living and rapid movement within occupations can produce a type of stress that appears to predispose to heart attacks. A National Heart Institute study conducted in North Dakota covered coronary patients and healthy men. It delved into the occupations of the men's fathers, the men's own occupations, job changes, and movements from place to place. It turned out that the low-risk group was composed of farm and blue-collar workers who had not moved about geographically and had had little or no occupational change. The high-risk men, with coronary rates six times higher than the others, consisted of white-collar workers who had come from rural backgrounds and had had marked occupational changes.

Another study of rural mountaineers who went to work in textile factories in North Carolina produced similar findings, substantiating the concept that a rapid change in way of life may be unduly stressful and increase the risk of coronary heart disease.

Nazareth, Pa., is a community of some 6,000 people which has been undergoing change and recently became the subject of an investigation of the effect of change on heart disease rates. It has been a "Pennsylvania Dutch" community, its economy largely dependent upon manufacturing, with most men employed as craftsmen, foremen, or operative or service workers in some 26 industries. But the major industry, cement, has been declining in importance, and other opportunities for employment are limited to skilled manual labor now. In addition, the historic ethnic and religious exclusiveness of the community has been disappearing as individuals from other ethnic and religious groups have moved in.

For the study, investigators set up a free medical clinic, offering physical and laboratory examinations to all adult Nazareth residents. A total of 1,549 people were examined. Those with coronary heart disease were matched against others free of the disease. Sociological interviews were carried out.

The findings were largely what the investigators expected they might be. CHD patients tended to be relative newcomers to the community. Significantly more of them worked at two or more jobs than did those without CHD. They proved to be much more anxious than the healthy. Altogether, the findings indicated that, as a group, the coronary patients had been having a difficult time adapting to environmental and social change in a community to which they had migrated relatively recently, one that traditionally had not accepted outsiders and offered limited occupational alternatives.

HEART-REMARKABLE ROSETO

When they discovered the town of Roseto, Pa., University of Oklahoma scientists found a community with an unusually low incidence of deaths from heart attacks. But what made Roseto all the more remarkable was that the low incidence prevailed despite the weights and eating habits of the towns-people.

Roseto, population 1,630, was settled in 1882 by immigrants from Roseto in the province of Foggia, Italy. More than 95 percent of the people in the Pennsylvania town are of Italian descent.

In a survey covering a seven-year period, investigators found no deaths at all from heart attacks in either men or women under the age of forty-seven. And in groups older than that, the coronary heart disease death rate was much lower than in neighboring towns.

Bangor, for example, only one mile away, a town of 5,766 people, was originally settled by Welsh quarriers who worked the nearby slate deposits. It now contains a mixture of ethnic groups including many people of German and Italian origin who serve surrounding farmers as merchants and tradesmen and work in nearby construction and steel industries. Roseto has half the CHD death rate of Bangor and the figure is all the more impressive because substantially the same physicians care for the populations of both towns and use the same neighboring hospitals.

There is much to make the Roseto experience even more striking. Rosetans work in small factories that produce shirts and blouses, in nearby steel mills, and in electrical industries. Vigorous and fun-loving, they eat heartily and drink considerable alcohol, mainly in the form of wine. A favorite dish, prosciutto, a pressed ham delicacy, has a rim of fat more than an inch thick and Rosetans eat it whole, without discarding the fat. Most families cook with lard rather than olive oil as the principal shortening. Another favorite dish is fried peppers, and nearly all Rosetans eat the peppers often and most dip their bread in the lard gravy.

Fat consumption, the study indicated, is at least equal to that of the average United States family. Indeed, investigators came away with the impression that Rosetans eat substantially more calories and substantially more fat than the average American. Men and women over age twenty-one, almost without exception, were found to be overweight.

What, then, accounts for the low coronary heart disease death rate if Rosetans eat so much, include so much fat in their diet, and are overweight?

The most striking feature of Roseto noted by the investigators was the way in which the people seemed to enjoy life. In their report the University of Oklahoma scientists note: "They were gay, boisterous, and unpretentious. The wealthy dressed and behaved in a way similar to their more impecunious neighbors. The visitor's impression of the community was of a one-class, peasant-type society made up of simple, warm, and very hospitable people. They were found to be mutually trusting (there is no crime in Roseto) and mutually supporting. There is poverty but no real want since neighbors provide for the needy, especially the recent immigrants who still continue to arrive in small numbers from Italy."

Maintaining a scientific attitude, the scientists went on to report: "The reason for the relatively salubrious conditions of the Rosetans is not clear at the present moment. Whether or not their sensible way of life contributes to their good health is still to be determined. Genetic and ethnic factors may be important, although it is noteworthy that deaths from myocardial infarction (heart attack) at a relatively young age have been documented among men born in Roseto who lived most of their lives in neighboring parts of Pennsylvania, New York, or New Jersey."

In Israel, the healthier heart condition of kibbutz dwellers vis-a-vis the rest of the general Israeli population could be due in no small part to the relative absence of certain types of stress, to the greater physical activity, and to the value of such activity in helping to relieve stress.

People in a kibbutz generally have a deep sense of belonging to the community. A kibbutz member has security in many ways; he or she is taken care of for life as are spouse and children, and even parents may be brought in from anywhere to live with a kibbutz member.

Stress is not absent in a kibbutz. Wherever there are interpersonal relations, Dr. Brunner points out, some stress must develop. But the stress in a kibbutz is a different kind of stress from what he calls "income tax stress," his label for the type of stress to be found in modern highly industrialized urban societies.

One of the countries in which coronary heart disease has had a reportedly low frequency is Yugoslavia. After World War II, when Yugoslavia was in difficulty, the United States made surplus food available. The food was sold but under an agreement by which the United States was credited in local currency. Since dinars are not negotiable in international exchange, they cannot be used outside Yugoslavia. Recently, by agreement between the United States and Yugoslavia, it became possible to use the funds for research considered beneficial to both countries.

One research project has been concerned with determining if the reported low rate of CHD for Yugoslavia was in fact correct and if so to what it might be attributed. Sponsored by the National Heart Institute and carried out cooperatively by Yugoslav and American physicans, the study covered two communities and found that, indeed, the heart attack death rate was only one-third that for comparable United States population groups.

In addition to having low serum cholesterol levels, the Yugoslavs are, on the average, thinner and accustomed to harder work and more vigorous exercise than Americans. Their blood pressure levels, however, are similar and their cigarette consumption no less.

Summing up the findings, Dr. Thomas R. Dawber of Boston

University School of Medicine, who served as a consultant for the study, recently had this to say:

It is difficult to escape the conclusion that diets low in animal fat, a high energy output through vigorous work and exercise, and resultant lack of obesity are important factors in the relative absence of coronary heart disease in this Balkan country. Those who wish to attribute good health to psychosocial factors might point to some of the characteristics of the Yugoslavs as responsible for their low rates of coronary heart disease. By and large, they are hard working, conscientious citizens but also possessed of a reasonably good sense of humor and an ability to enjoy themselves in spite of their lack of the affluence to which Americans have become accustomed.

They have a strong sense of independence and a feeling of nationalism which appears to be the result of Marshal Tito's ability to unify the former independent kingdoms. Once, while traveling through the country during the fruit harvest time, our party came upon a farmer distilling the ferment from purple plums (sliva). This plum brandy (slivovic) is the national drink and is highly regarded. When I told the farmer that such a "still" called for a jail sentence in the United States, he remarked that if such action was an example of the "freedom" the United States boasted about, he was staying in Yugoslavia.

STRESS AND OTHER RISK FACTORS

The coronary-prone individual has been compared by Dr. Stewart G. Wolf with the mythological Sisyphus who passed the time in Hades pushing a large rock up a steep hill and never quite getting it there. The coronary disease candidate, Dr. Wolf asserts, is a person who not only meets a challenge by putting out extra effort, but who takes little satisfaction from his accomplishments.

Dr. Henry I. Russek has found that the most characteristic trait of the young coronary patient is his restlessness during leisure hours and his sense of guilt during periods of "relaxation." Because of this, such a man rarely takes vacations and what leisure time he has is often regimented by obligatory participation in assorted social, civic, or educational activities. Emotional stress is an inevitable by-product of such compulsive behavior. Some investigators have tended to consider emotional stress of little significance. They point to racial groups in various areas—Korea, China, Japan, Yemen—who live on low-fat diets and have a distinct immunity to coronary heart disease despite obvious emotional stress in their patterns of life. But they lose the immunity when high-fat diets are used.

Dr. Russek, however, argues that while the lethal effect of emotional stress is strongly mitigated and perhaps even nullified by a low-fat diet, there is good evidence to indicate that the deadliness of a high-fat diet in Western society is greatly compounded by the influence of stressful living.

He points to the fact that Benedictine monks live in rural areas, removed from urban life stresses, and in monastic environments free from economic and family problems. They eat well; their blood fat levels are not low. It appears significant, Dr. Russek believes, that "although the 'unstressed' Benedictine monk eats as much fat as the greatly harassed general practitioner of medicine, he suffers only about one-fifth as frequently from clinical coronary disease. Of the many variables which undoubtedly participate, none appears more decisive than psychic stress."

Dr. Russek also points to Somali camel herdsmen who are free of symptoms suggestive of atherosclerosis although they live on a high-fat diet derived from about five quarts of camel's milk a day. While many theories might conceivably be advanced to explain this paradoxical immunity, a major factor, Dr. Russek is convinced, is the relative freedom from serious psychological stress of these people whose pastoral way of life has remained unchanged for centuries.

Investigators who believe stress important have noted with

considerable interest a phenomenon among mammals and birds in the Philadelphia zoo. Although their diet has been constant, there has been a tenfold increase in coronary atherosclerosis among these animals in a ten-year period. What has changed, however, has been the population density in the zoo. Increased crowding could be a stress factor for animals and could possibly help to explain why in man the coronary heart disease death rates are higher in metropolitan areas than in rural ones.

Even if it were to have no direct effects, stress has enough indirect ones, many investigators believe, to make it of prime importance in the development of coronary heart disease.

As Dr. Russek puts it: "It is well recognized that emotional tension may result in compulsive eating, drinking, and smoking in many persons as compensation for anxiety. Moreover, it does frequently contribute to the failure to achieve daily exercise by promoting fatigue, creating a sense of time urgency, and decreasing motivation. Nervous strain of occupational, cultural, social, or domestic origin is known to elevate blood pressure, to increase the tendency to obesity, to contribute to excessive smoking, to participate in hypercholesterolemia (high cholesterol levels), and to aggravate diabetes."

Another major coronary heart disease researcher, Dr. Jeremiah Stamler, also argues that while it may be difficult to assess such complex things as stress, tension, behavior, and pace of life, nevertheless evidence keeps mounting that they play a significant role in producing premature atherosclerotic disease.

He emphasizes that there is no good scientific reason to deal with the many factors influencing coronary heart disease in "one-versus-the-other fashion" as if they were mutually exclusive. The real need is to assess the relative contribution of each of the major factors and the interplay among them.

Dr. Stamler tells us: "The findings in the populations of the economically underdeveloped countries are relevant in this regard. At the present juncture in world affairs it is certainly unnecessary to belabor the point that many of these peoples lead lives that are stressful in many ways. Nevertheless, they are remarkably free of premature atherosclerotic disease. Perhaps . . . the specific types of stress they are subjected to are [not atherosclerosis-producing]. A more likely explanation is that [the rich diet] is lacking and therefore stress and tension cannot exert their contributory effect."

BEHAVIOR PATTERN A

Perhaps some of the most provocative and potentially useful work on the role of stress in coronary heart disease has been done by Dr. Meyer Friedman and Dr. Ray Rosenman over more than a dozen years at the Harold Brunn Institute of the Mt. Zion Hospital and Medical Center in San Francisco.

That work indicates there is an emotional façade, a behavior pattern, that is characteristic of people prone to CHD— and the pattern imposes great and continuing stress. The victims are victims of stress which, not knowingly, they make for themselves.

There had been suggestions before that personality might well play a part in producing coronary heart disease. As early as 1936, Drs. Karl and William Menninger of the Menninger Clinic in Topeka, Kansas, were among the first psychiatrists to become interested in studying the personalities of patients suffering from CHD. They concluded that such people sometimes exhibited strongly aggressive tendencies which they usually managed to suppress.

In 1943, Dr. H. F. Dunbar had examined a large group of coronary patients and had found them to be hard-driving individuals with single-direction personalities seeking refuge in work. She also had concluded that they had less interest in sports, more illnesses, more constipation, and less sexual tranquility than noncoronary subjects.

In 1945, Dr. J. A. Arlow found that his coronary patients seemed to share an inner insecurity, a belief that they were shams; and because their real accomplishments failed to assuage that belief, they had an incessant need to go after new successes. About the same time, Dr. C. Kemple was describing people with the "coronary personality" thus: "They manifest a persistent pattern of aggressiveness and drive to dominate which distinguishes them. They are usually very ambitious and strive compulsively to achieve goals incorporating power and prestige."

These early studies produced a strikingly similar picture of the coronary patient but little attention was paid to it. One reason may be that the language of psychiatrists sometimes grates on the ears of other physicians. They also publish their findings in journals not often read by other physicians. It is a fact, too, that the early psychiatric studies concentrated on personality of coronary patients and suggested that here was the reason for their disease. Although CHD incidence was increasing at an epidemic rate, they failed to consider that it might be due to something other than an intrinsic fault of personality.

Arnold Toynbee, the historian, may have been the first to sense that "something other" when, in his *A Study of History*, he wrote, "At the earliest moment at which we catch our first glimpse of Man on Earth, we find him not only on the move but already moving at an *accelerating* pace. This crescendo of acceleration is continuing today. In our generation, it is perhaps the most difficult and dangerous of all the current problems of the human race."

As Dr. Friedman notes, perhaps this most difficult and dangerous problem might have been taken into account by psychiatrists and others concerned about coronary heart disease "if they themselves could have felt its shuddering impact as immigrants to a Western country . . . first experienced this 'hot breath of haste and speed.' " But they like all the rest of us had lived so long with the constantly speeding-up pace of Western living that its hazards were not clear.

At any rate, little attention was paid to it—despite hints to be found in the rise in coronary heart disease rates in Japanese immigrants moving to Los Angeles or Boston and in Irishmen moving to America. Moreover, as Dr. Friedman puts it, "Not even the relatively low incidence of coronary disease in groups such as the Navajo Indians and Trappist monks—who while living in Western society, nevertheless remain relatively isolated from the society's pace of living—had aroused sufficient suspicion in most research quarters that the etiology of coronary disease could not be explained solely in terms of diet, physical activity, heredity, or any combination of these factors."

About 1955, Dr. Friedman and Dr. Rosenman began to note the presence of certain traits in almost every one of their middle-aged and younger coronary patients, which they did not see nearly so often in patients with noncardiac disorders.

And then they did a simple thing which brought a jolting response. They questioned about 200 business executives and about 75 physicians who were treating heart patients. What, in their opinion, caused heart attacks in friends and patients? Three-fourths of both the doctors and the executives incriminated the same thing: excessive drive and deadline-meeting. And they distinguished sharply between anxiety or worry and excessive drive and deadline-meeting.

It was then that Dr. Friedman and his colleagues decided to investigate thoroughly the possible relationship of behavior pattern and coronary heart disease.

A Description of the Pattern

Out of their work since 1955 has come the definition of a behavior pattern, called type A, which seems to be present in most people with CHD.

"If an individual with behavior pattern A were forced to display or wear a heraldic emblem consonant with his personality," Dr. Friedman has written, "a most appropriate symbol might well be a clenched fist holding a stopwatch."

Virtually all people wish to succeed and are obliged to meet at least some deadlines. Pattern-A people, however, take the wish and obligation to excess. They engage themselves in what Dr. Friedman calls a relatively *chronic struggle* to get an *unlimited* number of things, usually *poorly defined* things, from their environment in the *shortest* period of time.

There are degrees of intensity for the pattern. Not all who have it display it to the same extent. And, in fact, because the pattern actually depends not on particular personality facets alone but on the interaction when these facets are challenged by a specific environment, an afflicted person may not exhibit the pattern at all if he happens to be in an environment that carries no challenge for him.

For example, let a minor illness make it necessary to hospitalize an unusually hard-driving, time-conscious, aggressive, competitive man and he may well shed all those traits and appear to be tranquil and passive.

While hostility and aggressive tendencies are often apparent in people with pattern A, it is not so easy to establish whether they suffer from any more insecurity than the more tranquil, relatively slow-moving people who exhibit type-B behavior pattern. Whatever their psychiatric characteristics, Dr. Friedman finds, pattern-A people almost never show any overt signs of anxiety and "it is not overt worry, fear, hysteria, or anxiety that initiates, sustains, or characterizes behavior pattern A."

How many people have pattern A is not known. Since its development depends upon interaction of personality with environment, the latter plays a great part in determining incidence. It would be expected, for example, that the Boston Irishmen studied by Harvard investigators and previously mentioned would have a higher incidence of pattern A than their brothers remaining in Ireland because the Boston milieu probably favors emergence of the pattern more than does rural Ireland. But it is also possible that the Irishmen who moved to Boston had a more aggressive drive than their brothers.

In their studies, Friedman and his colleagues checked on more than 3,000 men in the San Francisco Bay area, aged thirty-nine to fifty-nine, and found about half showing behavior pattern A. Most of the men worked in clerical or executive jobs. But the A pattern isn't limited to such men, belonging to the middle and upper portions of the middle class, as indicated by the fact that in one of the companies studied a large fraction of subjects consisted of blue-collar workers and here again the incidence of A was about half. While men in certain jobs, such as sales managers and public relations officers, seemed to have the pattern more often, no definite correlation yet has been found between job and type-A behavior pattern.

Nor was the pattern equally intense in all the men who had it. No more than 15 percent had what might be called fully developed pattern A—and only about the same percentage had fully developed pattern B, in which there appears to be almost no sense of time urgency and the individual exhibits no significant drive, ambition, or eagerness to compete.

How to Detect Pattern A

Many years ago, the distinguished physician Sir William Osler characterized the patient suffering from angina pectoris as "not the delicate, neurotic person, but the robust, the vigorous in mind and body, the keen and ambitious man, the indicator of whose engine is always at 'full speed ahead.' "

The San Francisco studies suggest that Osler's characterization is well suited to the person with fully developed pattern A.

Most subjects with A behavior have an appearance of brisk self-confidence; they are decisive in the way they speak, move, even sit. They have a resolute, determined look; their jaw muscles are often partially tensed and are rarely fully relaxed.

In his actions, an A person, although he may exhibit no undue haste, never dawdles. If he drops something, he picks it up briskly, lights a cigarette the same way. He is likely to use his hands forefully when speaking about something of concern to him.

Rarely does a person with A pattern speak in a weak or monotonous manner; instead he uses various words of his sentences as "battering rams" in his effort to communicate. He usually uses upper rather than lower chest breathing. He is apt to sigh—not the long, inspiratory sigh of a person with anxiety but rather a sigh that comes at the end of the exhaling phase of breathing.

When it comes to drive and ambition, it is often characteristic of an A person to be involved in multiple jobs, many community and civic activities, and to be relatively dissatisfied and impatient with his present or past economic achievement. And if a subject's wife has often told him to slow down, take it easy, or quit rushing about, suggests Dr. Friedman, the chances are good that he has pattern A.

What of competitive, aggressive and hostile feelings? They can be detected by questions dealing with a subject's attitudes about (a) playing games (he always plays to win even if he is playing with his children); (b) competing with fellow workers (he loves to compete); (c) gaining his associates' respect, admiration, or affection (he wants respect more than affection); (d) motorists driving in his lane too slowly to suit him (he will usually answer the question with an outbreak of pure hostility); and (e) people who he believes needlessly or thoughtlessly delay his activities (often his voice or face will betray his hostility).

But it is a sense of time urgency that most distinguishes

pattern A people. Very much conscious of the limits of time, they try to squeeze more and more events in. They may go to extreme limits for the squeezing. Says Dr. Friedman: "For example, some subjects like to evacuate their bowels, read the financial section of the newspaper, and shave with an electric razor, all at the same time. One subject admitted that he had already purchased ten different electric razors in his efforts to find one that would shave faster than all others, and another subject liked to use two electric razors at the same time so that he could cut his shaving time in half."

The sense of time urgency often can be uncovered with a few questions about a subject's (a) punctuality (he is always on time); (b) attitude about waiting for a table in a restaurant (he will never wait if he can possibly avoid doing so); and (c) attitude toward persons who take a long time to get to the point in a conversation (he will try to move them quickly to the point or will begin to think of something else of interest to him).

But the simplest way to detect the sense of time urgency, Dr. Friedman has found, is for an interviewer to begin to ask some question whose answer is apparent to the interviewee even before the question is completed, then to stutter before finishing the question. Invariably, the subject will burst in and answer the question without waiting for it to be completed.

Pattern A and CHD

To determine the association of pattern A with coronary heart disease, Dr. Friedman and Dr. Rosenman first asked a group of laymen to select from among friends and associates those who seemed most obviously to have pattern A behavior. The names of 83 men were furnished. Union executives then were asked to choose from among members of their organizations 83 individuals who exhibited most obviously just the opposite type of behavior, pattern B. In addition, the investigators studied 46 blind men manifesting chronic anxiety and insecurity.

The dietary intake of total calories, total fats, and animal fats was investigated and found to be essentially the same in all three groups, as was the amount of physical activity. Blood and electrocardiographic studies were made.

The findings: 23 of the 83 type-A men (28 percent) showed evidence of coronary heart disease, while only 3 of the type-B men (4 percent) and 2 of the 46 anxiety cases suffered from the disease. Thus, type-A men had 7 times as much CHD as did type-B men.

These figures do not mean that any large group of type-A people will have 7 times as much CHD as a large group of type-B subjects. For in this study, most of the pattern-A (83 percent) and most of the pattern-B (70 percent) subjects, picked as overtly typical by lay people, were of the fully developed type. There would be a far lower proportion of the fully developed cases in large, unselected groups. But the results do suggest that subjects with pattern-A behavior are relatively prone and those with B relatively immune to early occurrence of coronary heart disease.

The San Francisco researchers went on to study women also chosen by lay people: 125 with pattern-A and 132 with pattern-B behavior. Most of the A women worked in industry or in the professions; most B women were housewives. And the A women turned out to have almost five times as much coronary heart disease as the B women.

But while such studies indicated that among people selected from a general population those with fully developed A behavior already had four to seven times more coronary heart disease than those with B, they did not prove that subjects with pattern A but without existing heart disease would develop the heart disease in the future more frequently than individuals with pattern B.

So in 1960–1961, the Western Collaborative Study Group (WCGS) was set up, enlisting more than 3,500 men, aged thirty-nine to fifty-nine, and apparently free of coronary heart disease. A careful history, detailed information on diet, drinking, and smoking habits, measurements of blood pressure and blood fats and other factors, and an assessment of behavior pattern were obtained for each man.

Four years later, 52 of the 3,500 men had developed their first heart attack and 18 their first attack of angina pectoris. The dietary intake and other factors had been much the same for these men as for the group as a whole. But the incidence of CHD proved to be three times as great in the group originally classified as having pattern A behavior as in those with pattern B.

Other Pattern A Studies

How does behavior pattern A influence the development of coronary heart disease?

To determine whether the pattern—or components of it such as time urgency and working under deadline conditions— might have a direct effect on blood cholesterol, Friedman and his colleagues got the help of a group of accountants who agreed to come in for blood tests twice a month for a six-month period. They were men who showed no well-developed form of either A or B behavior pattern under normal circumstances but by the very nature of their work they would be under considerable time urgency and deadline stress just before the April 15 tax-filing deadline time. Sure enough, early in April, they had significantly higher average serum cholesterol levels than at other times.

Also, during the six-month study, many of the accountants had individual stress-producing situations even more severe, they believed, than tax-return deadlines. When the serum cholesterol of each man obtained at the time he believed himself under greatest stress was compared with values at other times, it proved markedly higher.

The investigators also studied cholesterol levels in young, premenopausal women and found that those with fully developed pattern-A behavior had a significantly higher average blood cholesterol level than those with fully developed pattern B.

Going into the laboratory, the researchers found that cholesterol-fed rats exposed to electrically induced emotional stress developed markedly higher cholesterol levels than similarly fed but unstressed rats. And later, checking on blood triglyceride levels, they found that these doubled in fat-fed rats subjected to stress.

In their studies of people with A and B behavior patterns, Friedman and his associates could make a number of other observations.

They found that while there are about as many cigarette smokers in type-B as in type-A subjects, the fully developed type-A man smokes more than the type B. That was equally true in the case of women. And while neither type A nor B indulges very much in physical activity, the type-A individual usually finds less time and has much less inclination to engage in recreational physical activity.

In Dr. Friedman's view, certainly an overload in the diet of cholesterol, animal fat, and in many cases sugar can lead to excessive blood levels of fats. But it seems to him the excessive loads don't necessarily produce coronary heart disease unless an individual is especially vulnerable.

The vulnerability can come from behavior pattern, inadequate physical activity, or excessive cigarette smoking.

And unfortunately, the individual with pattern A, Dr. Friedman points out, is most vulnerable of all because in addition to having the pattern that itself leads to blood fat elevations, he also eats a diet rich in cholesterol fat, generally avoids exercise, and frequently smokes cigarettes excessively. In a tragic sort of way, he exemplifies most graphically how coronary heart disease is caused by many factors that interact with each other.

A Dramatic Example

One of the most dramatic illustrations of the effects of behavior-induced stress on the heart is to be found in a report of his own heart attack by Dr. Irvine Page to fellow physicians at an American Heart Association meeting not long ago in San Francisco.

A top authority on heart and artery disease, past president of the American Heart Association and until 1966 Research Director of the famed Cleveland Clinic, Dr. Page was working at the clinic as director emeritus in 1967 when he experienced a fire in his chest. "I knew I'd had a heart attack. In the months since then, I've experienced first hand the problems that I had been studying for years."

Since 1930, Dr. Page had been studying high blood pressure; his own excellent reading of 127/78 gave him no warning. Realizing the dangers of overweight, he had kept his 5'10½" frame to 146 pounds. He had been a moderate social drinker, and had limited his smoking to half a pack of cigarettes a day. Although he had not exercised as regularly as he should have, he used stairways rather than elevators whenever possible.

What else had he failed to do? "I came to realize that I had not been living moderately. I worked hard but I was continually dissatisfied, and I always tried to drive myself harder. Although I have told a thousand audiences not to use stimulants, I drank up to ten cups of coffee a day, trying to squeeze the last bit of efficiency out of myself. The competitor never understands when he has had enough. It was this sort of drive in my case."

Since his heart attack, Dr. Page has made changes in his way of life. He takes it much easier at work, has given up smoking, jogs in place beside his bed each morning, takes regular walks. "And walking is becoming increasingly possible because I no longer give a damn whether I get somewhere in a hurry or not."

And analyzing Dr. Page's case, a group of authorities came to this conclusion published in a report called *Executive Health:* "It was not overwork that laid Dr. Page low. It was his pattern-A personality. He had paid little attention to his behavior and its deadly hazard to his heart."

What are Dr. Friedman's recommendations?

"Extraordinarily efficient prevention could be achieved," he is convinced, "if each of these four measures were adopted: (1) drastic elimination of dietary cholesterol and animal fat, (2) avoidance of behavior pattern A, (3) lifetime participation in an extensive degree of physical activity, and (4) exclusion of cigarette smoking." He foresees that adoption of just one or two of the measures could help but would not provide the same degree of protection against atherosclerosis and coronary heart disease as adoption of all four would.

In a personal letter to one of us, Dr. Friedman has written about behavior pattern-A people. "If I were God perhaps I could force these people to cease cramming more and more events into an ever diminishing frame of time; perhaps I could make them see that it is more worthwhile to strive to obtain the things worth *being* rather than the things they believe are worth *having*; perhaps I could substitute love for their so easily aroused hostility; perhaps I could even cajole them into believing that equanimity is more to be desired than status enhancement."

Dr. Friedman thinks it unlikely that in the near future the majority of any population group will adopt all four of the measures he sees as capable of providing effective prevention against coronary heart disease. Perhaps that would require perceptive insights and determination beyond what most people currently have. We would hope that the reader, after finishing this book and reflecting upon all of the facts now available, will opt for adopting many if not most of the measures which can help make for a longer, healthier life.

There are other measures, too, which in specific instances may be of practical value in dealing with stress.

Aids to Mitigating Stress

A stress-free life is an impossibility. Stress is inherent in living. And most stresses, provided they are not applied continuously over prolonged periods, cause no health problems.

Dr. Hans Selye, who has devoted his life to the study of stress, considers that possibly among the worst stresses are hatred, frustration, and anxiety. It would be naive to expect anyone continuously frustrated by job, unpleasant home situation, or failure to achieve success to heed any advice to stop worrying.

But distractions, Selye points out, sometimes are helpful— not likely to entirely eliminate a dangerous stress but may be the realization of how long-continued hatred, frustration, and anxiety can be deadly. Intellectual realization in itself is not likely to entirely eliminate a dangerous stress but may temper it, and that is so much gained.

It is possible for some people who set their minds to it to learn to shrug off unduly stressful situations. But if a frustrating job, constantly irritating boss, or nagging spouse cannot be shrugged off, it may be wiser to quit the job and find a new one (no matter how wrenching the experience) rather than go on and face incapacitating, even deadly illness—and wiser to get marital counsel or even divorce than continue in a debilitating, potentially destructive marriage.

There are many possible maneuvers that may help ameliorate stress. Selye recalls that "once when I was about six years old I was crying, miserable. What brought it on, I do not remember. My grandmother was sympathetic—and wise. 'Go to the mirror,' she said, 'and smile with your face. Soon you will be smiling all over.' Curiously enough, it worked—and was less stressful than pounding my head against a wall."

Fatigue stress seems to be common today, but the stress is not from true fatigue resulting from overworked muscles and the temporary pile-up of waste products in them. More often now, fatigue stems from monotony, from the boring repetitiveness of many tasks. A possible answer is to do something different, to intersperse relaxation or a different activity—to take a coffee break, to pause and get up from a desk job and walk about, or to pull out a book or magazine and read, however briefly. Actually, lessening the stress of monotony is good for both health and increased efficiency of performance.

Day-long emotional turmoil is bad enough; taking the turmoil to bed at night is to compound the penalty. For years physicians have known that exercise can do much to release tensions and distract from and even markedly reduce turmoil. Use exercise during the day whenever possible. Put it to work, in the form of a brisk walk or any other vigorously tiring activity, before getting into bed.

There are environmental stresses that often can be combated at least to some degree. Heat can increase the workload of the heart as well as make for general discomfort; an air conditioner is a good investment. Undue noise is a stress. We have anti-noise statutes which need stricter enforcement, and we can argue and vote for such enforcement. We can choose dwellings with some attention to the use in them of sound-absorbent materials, and many of us can landscape the space about our homes to provide tree and bush barriers to noise.

The pressure of population, of city congestion, of crowds in public transportation and at lunch counters—all this is stressful. There are some who consider it a mark of wisdom to get up earlier to ride to work in an uncrowded bus, subway, or train and to take an odd lunch hour or bring a sandwich from home to avoid noon-hour rush and clamor.

8

Smoking

The relationship between smoking and heart disease is not a simple one, certainly not in comparison with that between smoking and lung cancer.

Cigarette smoking is held to be responsible for most of the deaths from lung cancer. But we know that such factors as diet, overweight, lack of physical activity, and high blood pressure contribute to coronary heart disease.

The heavy smoker's risk of dying of lung cancer appears from many studies to be about 20 times that of a nonsmoker while the risk of a heavy smoker dying of coronary heart disease is about 3 times that of a nonsmoker. If comparatively less, the smoking-induced risk for heart disease nevertheless is worrisome, and all the more so in view of the fact that there are so many more deaths from coronary heart disease than from lung cancer (more than 10 times as many). It has been estimated that the total number of coronary heart disease deaths attributable at least in part to smoking is 2½ to 3 times the number of lung cancer deaths from smoking.

It is true that coronary heart disease is the commonest cause of death among nonsmokers—and no doubt would continue to be the leading lethal disease if smoking were discontinued completely. It is also a fact that many individuals among even the relatively CHD-immune groups in Israel are heavy smokers.

So cigarette smoking can hardly be considered a sole cause. Perhaps if every other factor influencing heart health were way over on the good side, smoking might have relatively little detrimental effect on the heart. But this is uncommonly the case.

The case against cigarette smoking as a heart disease pro-voker, long overshadowed by the case against it as a cancer factor, has been building up rapidly, particularly in just the last half dozen years.

A BIT OF HISTORY

In the late fifteenth century, Columbus, who had sailed from Spain with the hope of returning with the riches of India, brought back tobacco instead. Until then, Western civilization, as one writer has put it, had never known the joys of tobacco-stained teeth, of breath and clothing impregnated with the odor of tobacco.

The American Indian had made limited use of tobacco, smoking it ceremonially in pipes. Before long, however, the white man was chewing it, snuffing it, putting it in pipes, and then in little white papers.

Cigarette smoking seems to have been born in Spain in the seventeenth century. From Spain, cigarettes spread to Turkey and Russia and then, introduced by soldiers serving in Eastern Europe during the Crimean War, into France and England. Some Americans began to smoke cigarettes before the Civil War but it was the invention of the cigarette-rolling machine in the 1880's that started the rise to wide popularity in this country.

Gradually, the use of tobacco became almost universal. It penetrated even remote, undeveloped regions of Asia, Africa, and South America. The widespread distribution was an amazing phenomenon. Anthropologists working in Colombia, South America, found that almost every native—man, woman, and child—even in primitive tribes in remote mountainous areas smoked.

Accompanying widespread distribution, individual consumption mounted. By 1900, the average American fifteen years of age and over smoked a total of 49 cigarettes per year; in 1920, 611; in 1940, 1,828; in 1967, 4,003.

THE FIRST ALARMS

As early as 1927, a British physician, F. E. Tylecote, was noting that in almost every case of lung cancer he had seen or known about, the patient was a regular smoker, usually of cigarettes. Nine years later, somewhat more specifically, two Chicago physicians, Aaron Arkin and David H. Wagner, reported that of 135 men with lung cancer they had examined, 90 percent were smokers.

Such reports were suggestive but hardly solid evidence. They did not rule out the possibility that, say, 90 percent of men of the same ages, occupations, and residence in Chicago who did not die of lung cancer might also be chronic smokers.

The next step was the start of controlled retrospective studies in which each lung cancer patient was matched with a person free of lung cancer to determine what might be the significant differences. One such study reported from England in 1950 compared 1,465 lung cancer patients matched on the basis of age and sex with 1,465 hospital patients free of cancer. Only one lung cancer patient in 200 was a nonsmoker compared with one in 22 among the noncancer patients.

Many such retrospective studies were carried out in this country as well. The upshot: no investigation in which lung cancer victims were matched with other (control) subjects ever found that the lung cancer victims smoked less than the controls, or only to the same extent, or only a little more; it was a lot more.

Still more impressive statistical evidence was to come from prospective studies which started in 1954. In prospective studies, investigators work with groups of apparently healthy smokers and nonsmokers and follow them for extended periods to see what happens.

One such study in England followed 40,000 physicians, aged thirty-five and over, for 54 months. It turned out that mild smokers were 7 times as likely to die of lung cancer as non-smokers; moderate smokers, 12 times as likely; immoderate smokers, 24 times as likely.

A larger study in this country, made for the American Cancer Society, followed 187,783 men, aged fifty to sixty-nine, for 44 months, during which time there were 11,870 deaths. The tally showed that the lung cancer death rate per 100,000 men per year for nonsmokers was 12.8, making lung cancer a rare disease among nonsmokers. Among men smoking up to one pack of cigarettes a day, the rate was 107.8; among those smoking one to two packs daily, it was 229.2; and among still heavier smokers, it was 264.2.

Until recently, such statistical studies were the basis for associating lung cancer with smoking. No one, by animal experiments, had been able to show a direct cause-and-effect relationship. The health hazards of drugs, pesticides, and similar materials could be tested well enough by administering them to a wide variety of animals; but rats, mice, guinea pigs, dogs, and other animals do not take readily to smoking. In some experiments, animals had been kept in smoke-filled compartments and had died; but this was not considered hard evidence since there remained a suspicion that they could have died of causes other than entry of smoke into the lungs.

Recently, however, dogs—pedigreed male beagles—have been

trained to smoke with the aid of a tube implanted in the neck and leading to the windpipe. And once trained, they became so habituated that they wagged their tails and whined for cigarettes.

Thirty-eight dogs were placed on a regimen of heavy smoking of nonfilter cigarettes; others were placed on a regimen of light smoking of nonfilter cigarettes; still others on a heavy regimen of filter tips; and eight dogs, for comparison purposes, were kept from smoking. After more than two years, when half the heavy smokers had died, all the remaining dogs were sacrificed and their lungs examined. Tumors were found in 25 percent of the nonsmoking dogs; in 33 percent of those on filter tips; in 58 percent of those lightly smoking nonfilters; and in 79 percent of the heavy smokers.

(In commenting on the results, the American Cancer Society has warned that filter-tip smokers "should not be lulled into a feeling of false security" since the dog study had shown that filter cigarettes "are, at best, only less damaging to lung tissue than nonfilter cigarettes.")

We give you this background on smoking and cancer both because of its inherent importance and also because it may offer some insights helpful in understanding the indictment against smoking in heart disease.

SMOKING AND HEART DISEASE

Actually, as early as 1908, an influence of tobacco on blood vessels was observed in Buerger's disease, a rare but serious disorder which affects the arteries of the extremities, reducing blood flow through them. In advanced cases, gangrene, particularly of the legs, occurs and leads to amputation. It turned out that smoking prohibition was vital in treating the disease. If patients failed to give up smoking or resumed the habit, the disease progressed.

This finding led to some early investigations of how tobacco influenced blood vessels. It soon became evident that nicotine produces contraction or spasm of leg and arm arteries.

There was then some study, too, of individuals with intermittent chest pain whose attacks seemed to be precipitated by smoking. There were relatively few such individuals studied; and they were considered to have a special sensitivity of some kind to tobacco, causing what was called tobacco angina.

In 1940, a study of 2,400 electrocardiograms of seemingly healthy men revealed abnormal tracings in some—and 50 percent more such abnormalities in smokers than in nonsmokers, suggesting an association between cigarette smoking and heart damage. In 1952, investigators compared the smoking habits of patients with coronary disease with those of patients without the disease and found that the coronary disease incidence was one and a half times as high among heavy smokers (more than 20 cigarettes a day) as among moderate, light and nonsmokers.

But a major alert to the effect of smoking on heart health came with the big prospective studies, including the American Cancer Society study already mentioned. Not only did this study of more than 187,000 men reveal the influence of smoking on lung cancer; it showed a clear association between smoking and heart disease.

Death rates from coronary heart disease proved to be more than twice as high for smokers of a pack or more of cigarettes daily than for nonsmokers. Death rates were found to increase with the number of cigarettes smoked, the degree of inhalation, and the age at which smoking began (they were one-third higher for those who started before fifteen than for those who started after twenty-five).

Another study by Drs. Joseph T. Doyle and Thomas R. Dawber covered 1,838 male civil servants aged thirty to fifty-five in Albany, New York, and 2,282 men residents of Framingham, Mass., aged thirty to sixty-two. All the men were thoroughly examined for coronary heart disease at the begin-

ning of the study and found free of it. They were then periodically re-examined over the next six to eight years. The heavy
cigarette smokers experienced three times as many heart attacks in that time as the nonsmokers.

There have been numerous other studies. Dr. Oglesby Paul
and associates in Chicago found that among middle-aged men
in an industrial firm cigarette smoking contributed significantly
to risk of heart attack. In a study of employees of a Chicago
utility company, Dr. Jeremiah Stamler and colleagues found
a significantly greater five-year death rate from heart attacks,
and from all causes, in smokers of a pack of cigarettes a day
compared with all other middle-aged men in the company.
Dr. David Spain of New York found that heavy smoking in
men with coronary heart disease was associated with sudden
death at a younger age. Men smoking a pack or more daily
died 16 years sooner on the average than nonsmokers. At the
time of death, the average age of heavy smokers was only 47.4
years (with a range of from 35 to 62) contrasted with an
average age of 63.2 (with a range of 61 to 69) for nonsmokers.

According to the American Heart Association, some 125,000
preventable deaths from cardiovascular disease in the United
States each year are associated with cigarette smoking.

All studies agree that cigar and pipe smokers do better than
cigarette users possibly because they do not inhale, as do the
latter. Generally, little extra risk of premature death from heart
disease has been found among pipe and cigar smokers.

INTERPLAY

That smoke of cigarette tobacco has varying effects on
coronary heart disease incidence in different population groups
has been shown by many studies.

In Finland, for example, 1,925 cigarettes per adult per year
are smoked; in Japan, not many fewer, 1,667. Yet the coronary
heart disease death rate in Finland is nine times greater than

that in Japan. While there appears to be no significant difference in physical activity between the populations of the two countries, there is a possibility that behavior pattern differences could be significant. There is no doubt that the average fat intake in Japan is much less than in Finland. It is therefore possible that excessive smoking becomes a significant risk factor when indulged in by people eating a high-fat diet.

A study by the Health Insurance Plan of Greater New York involving 110,000 men and women found that male smokers as a whole are twice as likely to suffer heart attacks as non-smokers—and that physically inactive smokers are three times as likely as physically active smokers to suffer heart attacks. Also, if a smoker has a heart attack his chances of surviving are twice as good if he has been physically active. The study suggests that to avoid heart attacks it is best to be a nonsmoker who is at least moderately active; such an individual is nine times less likely to have a fatal heart attack than his inactive smoking counterpart.

In a North Dakota study, farmers were found to have half the incidence of heart attacks of other men less physically active. In farmers, smoking appeared to have relatively little effect on the incidence of heart attacks but in the other less-active men, heart attacks occurred twice as often among smokers as nonsmokers.

In the Israeli experience, smoking has been found deleterious generally in terms of coronary heart disease. Yet some Israeli groups—Bedouins, for example—smoke as much as or more than the general Israeli population and still are virtually immune to coronary heart disease. So other factors (notably diet and activity) in the Bedouins appear to help counterbalance the effects of smoking.

CIGARETTES, CIGARS, PIPES

The fact that even heavy cigar and pipe smokers have no greater incidence of coronary heart disease than nonsmokers suggests to some investigators that there must be something more than the smoke of cigarettes that is responsible for the association between cigarette smoking and CHD.

Recent studies indicate that pipe and cigar smokers, even though they may not inhale, nevertheless absorb considerable amounts of nicotine.

It has been no simple matter to determine just how much nicotine absorption occurs during any type of smoking. Many factors affect the amount absorbed by a cigarette smoker: how fast he draws in the smoke, how much he deliberately inhales, how much of the cigarette he smokes (the last third contains much more nicotine because of the absorption of nicotine from the smoke passing through the butt). For a pipe smoker the amount absorbed is affected by the size of the pipe bowl, the density of the tobacco in the bowl, the speed of drawing in the smoke, the amount of deliberate or inadvertent inhalation, and how long the smoke is kept in the mouth before being exhaled. There are similar variables for cigar smokers.

It has been estimated that on the average a smoker retains about 1 milligram of nicotine from one cigarette and 1.65 milligrams of nicotine from one pipeful even if he does not deliberately inhale. A recent study in which nicotine content of the urine of subjects who smoked the same quantity of tobacco either as cigarettes, cigars, or in pipes found that noninhaling pipe smokers absorbed one-third the amount of nicotine absorbed by inhaling cigarette smokers. Cigar smokers may absorb as much or even more nicotine than heavy cigarette smokers. Some studies indicate that the nicotine absorbed from 6 cigars equals the amount absorbed from inhaling 30 cigarettes.

Even if pipe smokers absorb much less nicotine, it would seem that they should show some effects, especially in view of the fact that the death rate from coronary heart disease varies directly with the number of cigarettes smoked.

It could, of course, be that cigarette paper has something to do with this, that the paper helps to account for the heart harmfulness of cigarette smoking. But it could also be that personality enters the picture. Men with behavior pattern A, Dr. Friedman's studies indicate, smoke more cigarettes than other men; they rarely have the patience to smoke a pipe.

There have been studies showing that most heavy cigarette smokers consume many more cigarettes during periods of mental stress. When, in 1964, the Advisory Committee to the Surgeon General issued its now-famed report on smoking and health, it noted that ". . . the relationship between smoking behavior and coronary heart disease may reflect the influence of stress factors and/or personality mechanisms."

What Happens When You Smoke

Tobacco smoke is made up of gases, vapors, and other materials of which the best known is nicotine. Ninety percent of the nicotine (and probably other substances in smoke) is absorbed into the body when smoke is inhaled; as little as 10 percent is absorbed when smoke is puffed without inhaling.

One of the potentially harmful gases in cigarette smoke is hydrogen cyanide, a poisonous substance. Another is carbon monoxide. Carbon monoxide combines with hemoglobin, a part of the red blood cells that serves to transport oxygen from the lungs to body tissues. When carbon monoxide combines with hemoglobin, it is usurping oxygen's ride.

Carbon monoxide is of increasing concern today as an environmental pollutant from many sources, including automobile exhausts. Yet the air of our cities rarely contains more than 30 parts of carbon monoxide per million parts of air.

Cigarette smoke streams have been found to contain from 400 to 40,000 parts per million of carbon monoxide.

The human body itself produces some carbon monoxide—about a teaspoonful worth a day. This small amount combines with about eight-tenths of one percent of the hemoglobin. By contrast, a light cigarette smoker loads about 3 percent of his hemoglobin with carbon monoxide, a heavy smoker about 8 percent. Pipe and cigar smokers rarely achieve such loadings.

When carbon monoxide steals oxygen's place and reduces the amount of oxygen that can be transported in the blood, one result is shortness of breath on exertion. Animal studies indicate that long-term excessive exposure to carbon monoxide may cause an increase in the deposits of cholesterol on blood vessel walls.

Very recent research suggests that the red blood cells of smokers may haul around an unwelcome hitchhiker, a material other than carbon monoxide from cigarette smoke which reduces the attraction of hemoglobin for oxygen. Obtaining hemoglobin from smokers, investigators cleared it of carbon monoxide by thorough degassing in a vacuum system. They found that, even with the carbon monoxide removed, the hemoglobin's affinity for oxygen was reduced enough to suggest that up to 20 percent of the blood pumped around by the heart of a smoker is not working insofar as transport of oxygen is concerned. "Since the heart has the highest of all oxygen requirements per unit of weight of any tissue, any alteration in the supply of oxygen should first affect the heart," notes one of the investigators, Dr. Robert S. Eliot of Gainesville, Fla., "and this may account for the increased risk of myocardial infarction [heart attack] in the smoker." The investigators also found that blood taken from smokers for transfusion has an impaired ability to transport oxygen to the tissues of the transfusion recipient.

Also contained in each cubic centimeter of smoke are

millions of tiny particles called particulate matter which, upon condensation, form the brown mass called tar. In addition to nicotine, tar contains more than a dozen chemicals known to trigger cancer when applied to the skin or breathing passages of laboratory animals. For example, one of them, benzpyrene, has been diluted 1,000 times and placed in paraffin pellets implanted in the cheek pouches of hamsters; 90 percent of the animals developed mouth cancer within 25 weeks.

Nicotine, which is a colorless compound occurring in cigarettes in a range of ½ to 2 milligrams, is a potent poison in concentrated form. If injected, 70 milligrams (one drop) will kill an average man.

A person just beginning to smoke experiences symptoms of mild nicotine poisoning: rapid pulse, faintness, dizziness, nausea, clammy skin. Even long-experienced smokers sometimes develop one or more of the symptoms.

Among other chemicals in cigarette smoke are phenols, which interfere with the action of the cilia, the hairlike projections lining the respiratory tract to sweep up debris. Also included among the chemicals are irritants contributing to cigarette cough and some believed to be involved in the gradual deterioration of the lungs in the disease emphysema.

IMMEDIATE SMOKING EFFECTS

Smoking tends to reduce appetite. There is also a dulling of taste and smell and, because of the tar, the breath tends to become odorous.

Because of the nicotine, smoking produces an immediate feeling of "lift" followed by depression. This happens as nicotine first causes the adrenal glands to discharge a hormone, epinephrine, which stimulates the nervous system and also produces release of some sugar from the liver. The result is a kind of "kick" and some relief of fatigue, followed shortly by return of fatigue and a sense of depression as the nervous system quickly becomes depressed again.

With smoking, there is an increase in heart rate; occasionally, the heartbeat may become irregular. Blood pressure usually rises somewhat. Smoking also tends to constrict smaller arteries, reducing blood flow and lowering skin temperature. An average drop of about 5 degrees Fahrenheit occurs in finger and toe temperature after one cigarette is smoked.

OTHER EFFECTS

It is well known that excessive smoking causes coughing, hoarseness, and bronchitis, all of which usually disappear when smoking is abandoned. Physicians have little difficulty identifying a smoker by one look at the inflamed mucous membranes of the nose and throat.

The mucous membranes secrete a sticky fluid which traps dust and other particles in inhaled air. The cilia lining the passages, through a continuous whiplike motion, carry the sticky fluid and its trapped material upward so it can be swallowed or expectorated, keeping the lungs clean. Cigarette smoking has been shown to impair cilia action and if continued long enough may destroy the cilia. Carefully controlled studies—in boarding schools, for example, where observations could be carried out over extended periods—have shown that regular smokers have nine times as high an incidence of severe respiratory infections as do nonsmokers.

With cigarette smoking, there is a brisk release of free fatty acids into the blood stream. This may have an effect on how cholesterol is handled since heavy smokers tend to have higher blood cholesterol concentrations than nonsmokers.

There has been some evidence that increased sugar consumption may be a factor in coronary heart disease. Recent studies in England indicate that there may be an association between increased sugar intake and cigarette smoking. Among almost 6,000 men checked, the cigarette smokers were found to take in much more sugar daily in hot drinks than other men—and the greater the quantity of cigarettes smoked, the greater the amount of drinks. Smoking tends to dry the mouth, suggest the researchers, so that smokers tend to drink more hot beverages than other men; and they may load the beverages with more sugar because smoking has adversely affected their ability to taste.

There have been investigations indicating that cigarette smoking may accelerate blood clotting, which can be dangerous when arteries are narrowed so that a clot may become lodged, obstructing blood flow. Microscopic studies have revealed rupturing and thickening of walls of the air sacs in the lungs of smokers, and thickening of the walls of small arteries in the lungs. It has been suggested that these tissue changes add to the work of the heart.

The exact way in which cigarette smoking accelerates atherosclerosis is not definitively established. It is possible that smoking may damage the inner lining of the coronary arteries or possibly interfere with normal transport of fats from the blood through the artery walls and out to the lymphatic drainage system. Either mechanism could favor atherosclerosis.

Much also remains to be learned about the direct influences of cigarette smoking on the heart muscle. One recent animal study suggests that smoking adds to the risk of ventricular fibrillation—wild, useless, often fatal beating of the heart. Should this be confirmed, it would explain the frequency of sudden deaths in heavy smokers.

Since the first Surgeon General's report on smoking in 1964, there have been regular annual reports, each linking smoking more and more tightly not only with lung cancer and coronary heart disease but with other diseases as well.

The latest report notes that cigarette smoking, in addition

to other ways it may contribute to coronary heart disease, can do so by increasing the adhesiveness of certain elements in the blood called platelets, thus furthering clot formation. Beyond diminishing the availability of oxygen to the heart muscle through the combination of carbon monoxide from smoke with hemoglobin in the red cells, smoking may diminish it still more by its impairment of lung function. And, at the same time that it reduces the oxygen supply, smoking has been found to cause the release of certain chemicals, called catecholamines, which increase the tension of the heart wall, adding to the work of the heart and thus to the need for more oxygen.

The latest report also calls smoking "the most important cause of chronic obstructive bronchopulmonary disease in the United States"—a disease category including chronic bronchitis and emphysema, the lung disorders that have been causing a rapidly increasing number of deaths.

No small part of the report is devoted to evidence that smoking by women during pregnancy retards the baby's growth and contributes to a significantly higher number of unsuccessful pregnancies due to stillbirths and deaths shortly after birth.

WOMEN AND SMOKING

Women generally outlive men. Over the past 50 years, they have been favored more and more in terms of life expectancy. Fifty years ago, while they could expect to live somewhat longer than men, the extra years at most numbered three. More recently, in the United States and most Western countries, their extra life expectancy has moved up to six years.

To many investigators, a factor that seems to account for the phenomenon is that in every country where data are available, the per capita consumption of cigarettes for women has been markedly lower than for men.

But the smoking picture has been changing. A comparison of smoking habits in the United States in 1955 and 1966 by the National Center for Health Statistics showed a drop in cigarette consumption in men under fifty-five. Among women, however, in that eleven-year period, every age group showed an increase. In 1955, a little more than one-fourth of women over age eighteen smoked; in 1966, the figure had risen to nearly one-third. Moreover, among the women smokers, there were substantial increases in those smoking more than half a pack a day. There was a 40 percent increase in those smoking 10 to 20 cigarettes daily, more than a 100 percent increase in those smoking 21 to 40, and a tripling of those smoking more than 40.

Recently, when British investigators studied groups of men and women smokers, they made a disturbing finding. In both sexes, smoking increased blood fat levels, but the increase was much greater in women heavy smokers than in men heavy smokers. These were young men and women, in their twenties. The mean value of blood cholesterol, for example, was 184 in the men heavy smokers; it was 239 in the women.

As the investigators who made the study note, the marked increase in blood fats in women heavy smokers suggests that smoking may result in women below the age of fifty years losing some of their natural immunity to coronary heart disease.

THE REWARDS OF STOPPING

For many if not most people, breaking the cigarette habit is no easy matter. Yet the U.S. Public Health Service estimates that 21 million Americans have given up cigarette smoking.

Of all men who have ever smoked, one fourth recently have stopped. Of all physicians who have ever smoked, more than half have quit.

According to many surveys, most smokers now would like to break the habit. One survey found this true of 86 percent of all smokers.

The rewards, taken all together, provide powerful motivation.

Go beyond heart disease—in which, as we have seen, cigarette smoking, though only one of many culprits, is clearly one it would be desirable to eliminate.

What of lung cancer? Recent studies indicate that if smoking is stopped before lung cancer has actually started, damaged lung tissue tends to heal itself. Even for those who have been long-time heavy smokers, the lung cancer risk begins to decrease about one year after the habit is abandoned, and then continues to decline progressively until after ten years it is very little higher than for people who have never smoked regularly.

In a recent study, British investigators compared the lung cancer death rate among physicians, many of whom had stopped smoking, with that of the population in general. The physicians' death rate from the decrease was declining by 30 percent while the rate for British men in general was actually increasing by 25 percent.

In chronic bronchitis and emphysema, elimination of smoking is vital for treatment. And elimination of smoking before these diseases become full-blown can go far toward preventing their ever becoming serious problems. In advanced stages, they are diseases of great significance. Emphysema, which affects the air sacs within the lungs, now ranks in the United States as the biggest single cause of disability of lung origin. It makes breathing difficult—too often to the point of invalidism and death. In addition to being a cause of death in itself, it is often a contributing factor to deaths from coronary heart disease because of the added strain it imposes on the heart. Within a few weeks after smoking is stopped, cough is reduced and other symptoms of chronic bronchitis and emphsyema improve. While lung tissue damaged by emphysema is not replaced, usually the progress of the disease is slowed and may even be arrested.

There are many other rewards: a better taste in the mouth, reduced fatigue and shortness of breath, relief of cough and nasal stuffiness, fewer headaches.

Very much worth noting is an extra benefit for the heart. Few people now are unaware of at least some of the dangers of cigarette smoking. Few can escape worry, conscious or unconscious, when they continue to smoke. The heart, as we have seen earlier, can be affected by mental stress. And the heart must benefit from the reduced stress, the conscious and unconscious relief the ex-smoker feels when he realizes that by giving up the habit, he has minimized his chances of contracting lung cancer and emphysema.

Once it could be argued that for many people smoking promoted relaxation, and the relaxation had some value for the heart. With today's knowledge of what smoking can lead to, there can be no relaxed smoker—with the possible exception of the rare person able to restrict himself to three or four cigarettes a day.

ECONOMIC REWARDS

Perhaps the economic rewards of giving up cigarette smoking have not been stressed enough in personal terms.

It may be important but it is not enough merely to observe that Americans spend $8.8 billion annually for tobacco—which is more than they spend for personal care ($8.2 billion), more than they spend for all the electricity they use ($7.7 billion), more than they spend for medical expenses ($6.7 billion).

Consider a husband and wife, each smoking about a pack of cigarettes a day. They spend on the order of $300 a year for tobacco. For the family that goes in heavily for smoking, the bills can be very high, e.g., if the husband smokes two packs a day, the wife one and a half packs, and two teenagers each smoke one and a half packs, the family spends about $1,000 a year on tobacco (and how much on cough drops and throat lozenges!).

But even a $300 annual expenditure for smoking can be a high percentage of the real, free, unencumbered money a family can accumulate in a year. In some cases, families actually, aware of it or not, are borrowing money to feed the cigarette habit.

In addition to direct benefits of no-smoking on the heart, the cash savings can have good effects on the heart in secondary ways: cash available for more complete medical checkups, for relaxing weekends or vacations, for savings toward retirement or education or emergency situations—savings that provide a certain amount of peace of mind, which is good for arteries and heart.

Recently, the American Heart Association reported on a computer program developed to help convince cigarette smokers of the cash value of quitting. An example: John Doe, age twenty-six, started smoking at seventeen. He smokes 21 cigarettes a day, 7,665 a year, spends $153 yearly for smokes, and is likely, the computer figures, to spend $287 a year for them in the future. He has lost 6.25 years of estimated life thus far from his smoking. But there is hope for John Doe, the computer indicates. If he quits today, he will regain the lost years of estimated life by age thirty-six. If he quits today and invests his cigarette money in average stocks, he will accumulate $86,861 by age sixty-five.

BREAKING THE HABIT

If you decide you wish to break the cigarette habit, you may find the quitting process relatively easy; many do not but some do. It would be a mistake to believe that if you have made unsuccessful efforts in the past to quit, you are doomed to go on smoking. If you have failed before, that does not mean you are hopelessly weak-willed. Along with determination, you need strong motivation and insight.

Perhaps it would not be out of order to relate here how one of us, after many years of smoking and repeated abortive efforts to stop, finally managed to do so.

There was to be a lecture for physicians on how to help their patients stop smoking. We had planned to attend but then found it impossible to do so. So instead, we gave the lecture we would have liked to have heard—and addressed it to our children. And when we spoke of the various effects, the pathologic lesions, that could result from smoking, we tried to imagine vividly each such lesion in our body—a cancer of the lung, the damage of emphysema, the dead tissue in the heart after a heart attack. Also, we tried to feel the symptoms that would accompany each such lesion, and the pain and disfigurement of surgery. Then we assumed that each lesion could be fatal—and tried as dramatically as possible to live through the death from each one.

Whether it was this or something completely outside of consciousness that led to success we may never know; but we do know that we have finally stopped smoking cigarettes and seem to have the determination and power to kick the habit permanently.

If you wish to quit smoking, there are now many valuable aids. You will find more and more physicians interested in helping patients to break the habit. Many have done so themselves; in effect, they "know the ropes" from personal experience. In addition to providing suggestions that may be helpful to you, they help by offering support during the early days and whenever needed.

Hypnosis seems to help some, though not all, people to give up smoking. Some physicians now make use of hypnosis as a means of aiding some patients.

In many communities today, group sessions are conducted

by various organizations. The Seventh Day Adventists, for example, have sponsored programs in many areas—usually intensive programs carried out during five consecutive evening sessions.

Dr. Donald Frederickson of the New York City Health Department has developed a program of group sessions, with encouraging results in many hundreds of people. The program starts with a lecture to convince the smoker he has the capacity to permanently free himself of the habit and that withdrawal can be a rewarding experience. He is asked to develop a list of reasons for quitting, to build his motivation. He is also asked to keep a daily smoking record, noting time, activities, and feeling states associated with each cigarette as a means of developing insights into factors associated with his smoking habit and to help break into the unconscious reflex aspects of the habit.

Smokers are placed in groups of 15 which meet twice a week for four weeks, then once a week for another four weeks. The meetings last about 90 minutes and an ex-smoker serves the group as a discussion leader.

Smokers have a choice of sudden or gradual withdrawal. In the group sessions, they help each other build strong motivation, discuss each other's attitudes during withdrawal, and mutually support each other.

After withdrawal has been achieved, groups meet at less frequent intervals as a means of maintaining freedom from smoking.

Some smokers are able to break the habit on their own. They find a few or all of many techniques helpful in doing so. They may start with reading a book or booklet on the subject (a chapter such as this one could serve the purpose). To help break unconscious routines, they may place their cigarettes in unusual, out-of-the-way places. They may nibble on fruit, hard candy, bits of ginger, or chew gum. Frequent water drinking and also intervals of deep breathing are found valuable by some.

Many people recently have been finding that exercise is a great aid to breaking the smoking habit. It is a familiar observation that when people exercise more, they smoke less. Report after report from jogging programs now show that considerable numbers of members, especially men, give up smoking when they become involved in regular jogging activity.

Many smokers seeking on their own to abandon the cigarette habit pick a day on which they stop cold. Others reduce gradually, using some definite schedule such as no smoking between eight and nine, ten and eleven, and certain other periods. They then gradually lengthen the nonsmoking periods.

One technique many people find helpful is to promise themselves only that they will stop for one day at a time. When the day is successfully concluded, they promise themselves another day of freedom from cigarettes. Because of the limited promise, they can, without feeling guilty, resume smoking at the end of any 24-hour period. Many never smoke again.

The American Cancer Society has performed a valuable service in rounding up helpful suggestions from many experimental stop-smoking projects and from leading medical and health authorities and psychologists. These it has published in a pamphlet called "If You Want to Give Up Cigarettes." With the cooperation of the American Cancer Society, the contents of the pamphlet, full of specific advice and details, are published in Appendix V.

IF YOU CAN'T QUIT ENTIRELY

If you must smoke cigarettes, you can take some steps to at least reduce somewhat the risk involved. Smoke those containing less tar and nicotine. Never smoke a cigarette all the way down; leave at least the last third unsmoked—it yields twice as much tar and nicotine as the first third. Take fewer puffs on each cigarette. Smoke fewer cigarettes a day. Reduce inhaling; make a conscious effort to do this.

If you possibly can, try to wean yourself to use of pipe or cigars. While there is still some risk of mouth cancer from smoking a pipe or cigars, overall mortality of cigar and pipe smokers is only a little higher than for nonsmokers if the smoke is not inhaled.

9

The Often-Hidden Diseases
That Increase Risk of Heart Attacks

Certain diseases greatly increase the tendency toward heart attacks. They act to accelerate the atherosclerotic disease process in the coronary arteries.

The two most important—hypertension and diabetes—are extremely common, affecting between them well over 20 million Americans. Very often, they are unrecognized because of their subtle nature. Very often, too, even when recognized, hypertension in particular has been inadequately treated or even completely neglected because until quite recently the importance of anything but the most severe form was not fully recognized.

HYPERTENSION AND ITS INFLUENCE

The body's system for regulating blood pressure is a remarkable one—so finely tuned that it can accommodate instantly to the shifting demands for blood of all organs and tissues as we lie down, stand up, work, play, eat, or are affected by fear and anger. But the system can become impaired, resulting in

171

chronic high blood pressure or hypertension. And it does become impaired often enough to make the recognition and treatment of hypertension critical.

Without question, hypertension now must rank as one of the gravest of all disorders because it is a major contributor to coronary heart disease and heart attacks, and to strokes as well.

Almost 40 years ago, one physician noted that 60 percent of his 145 patients with heart attacks had been hypertensive. In a 1948 study of young soldiers, there were more than four times as many coronary deaths among those with elevated pressure as among those with normal.

The Framingham study also shows that in men forty to fifty-five years of age, hypertension increases the risk of coronary disease almost threefold. The findings of many other studies corroborate this.

Many estimates have been made about the prevalence of hypertension, ranging from the lowest figure, of 10 percent of the population, to the highest, 42.4 percent. The latter comes from a study by Dr. Caroline B. Thomas and her associates at Johns Hopkins University who followed 1,130 male medical students for 8 to 22 years after they were first examined at a mean age of twenty-three. In that time, 42.4 percent developed hypertension.

Another long-range study by Dr. F. A. Mathewson on young, healthy men who had met physical requirements for Royal Canadian Air Force pilot training during World War II showed that 21 percent developed hypertension in a 15- to 20-year follow-up period. Other investigations have arrived at various figures, all uncomfortably high: the United States health survey for 1960–62 found hypertension affecting 29 percent of the population and the Greenbrier survey of 1962 arrived at a figure of 33.9 percent.

The prevalence of hypertension in such studies varies depending on population groups studied, age, sex composition, and also the criteria used. Some investigators have defined hypertension as anything above 160/95. Many now believe that the definition should include any reading over 140/90.

No matter how it is defined, the hypertension problem is huge. And what is most appalling is the little being done to combat it.

According to Dr. Jeremiah Stamler of the Chicago Health Research Foundation, not only are about one-half of the country's many millions of hypertensives undetected, "half of those that are detected, go untreated, and only about half of those receiving treatment have had their blood pressures brought down to levels of less than 90 diastolic and less than 140 systolic."

Dr. Edward D. Freis of the Washington, D.C., Veterans Administration Hospital, who has been chairing a coast-to-coast long-term study of the benefits of treating even very mild hypertension, says that only about 12 percent of people with hypertension are receiving the treatment they need.

And Dr. Oglesby Paul, former American Heart Association president and now professor of medicine at Northwestern University, tells us: "It is not too much to say that the diagnosis, study, and treatment of mild hypertension in young and middle-aged adults constitutes one of our greatest health challenges today."

The Stealth of Hypertension

Blood pressure is simply the force against the walls of arteries. Each time the heart beats, the pressure increases; each time the heart relaxes between beats, the pressure goes down. And when a physician measures pressure, he makes two readings and writes them in the form of a fraction, such as 130/80. The first and larger figure is the systolic pressure (when the heart pumps); the second is diastolic pressure (when the heart rests).

It is quite normal for pressure to fluctuate, decreasing during sleep, increasing during physical exertion or emotional excitement. And there is a wide range of normal. At rest, a systolic pressure in the 100–140 range and a diastolic in the 60–90 range is considered normal. Nor does any one isolated reading above 140/90 indicate abnormal pressure. But when there is continuous elevation, a person is considered to have hypertension.

Not that he will usually know it—unless informed by his physician. Hypertension is stealthy. It often produces no symptoms at all. Even when it does produce some, such as headache, dizziness, fatigue, or weakness, they may not be recognized for what they are since they are common to many other disorders.

But, with or without symptoms, hypertension can be doing its deadly work. Excessive pressure burdens the heart which must pump harder because of the pressure elevation. To accommodate to the task, the heart may enlarge. Eventually, however, the enlarged heart may weaken. Abnormalities of heartbeat may develop. Each year, about 50,000 Americans have been dying of such hypertensive heart disease.

Serious enough, the problem of hypertensive heart disease is overshadowed by coronary heart disease, and the heart attacks that strike as many as 7,000 times a day and prove fatal for more than 600,000 Americans a year.

Just as excessive water pressure in a garden hose may damage the hose after a time, excessive pressure in the coronary arteries may damage the internal walls, providing nesting places for any excess fats in the blood. Some investigators believe that high pressure may even help force the fats into the walls to start the buildup of artery-narrowing deposits.

Not only have there been the many studies—the Framingham and others—indicating a far higher incidence of coronary heart disease and heart attacks in hypertensive people, but others have found that hypertension increases the deadliness of a heart attack when it comes.

The Health Insurance Plan of Greater New York, in a recent investigation, determined that among men with hypertension before a first heart attack the number dead within a month after the attack is twice the number among men with normal pressure before the attack. Moreover, compared with men with normal pressure who survive a first attack, hypertensive men who survive have twice the risk of recurrence and more than five times the risk of heart death during the next four and a half years.

Recently, too, has come evidence of the role of hypertension in stroke. That devastating disease—the term stroke was coined centuries ago in the belief that a victim was struck down by God—most commonly is the result of atherosclerosis of brain arteries. It is even more of a killer and crippler than has been supposed. There are now two million Americans living with stroke-caused disabilities: paralysis, loss of sensation, loss of balance, loss of vision, or loss of speech. The death toll in this country has been believed to be 200,000 yearly. But Dr. Alice J. Gifford of Johns Hopkins University recently has reported that a critical re-examination of death certificates to find the basic cause of death might well show the death toll from stroke to be 400,000 annually.

Many studies now indicate that hypertension plays a major role in stroke. The Framingham study, for example, has found that the risk of stroke is five times higher among people with even moderately elevated (160/95) blood pressure levels than among those with normal pressures. And in terms of stroke as well as coronary heart disease, women do not tolerate hypertension any better than men.

The Value of Treatment

It has been known for years that controlling very severe hypertension—malignant hypertension—has dramatic effects. Malignant hypertension, a rapidly progressive type, once killed 80 percent of its victims within a year. Now, thanks to a wide array of antihypertensive medications, most patients with malignant hypertension can look forward to useful lives.

For a long time there was some doubt about the value of treating moderate and mild hypertension. Then, beginning in 1963, the Veterans Administration Cooperative Study Group, chaired by Dr. Edward D. Freis, undertook a long-term study, first in moderately hypertensive patients. Eighteen V.A. hospitals across the country participated.

The patients ranged upward in age from thirty, with 115 to 129 diastolic pressures, at least 25 points above the 90 considered normal. Some received active treatment with antihypertensive medication; others, for comparison, received placebo, or inactive pills. There were no deaths in the actively treated group, 4 in the other group. There were 27 serious events—heart attacks, strokes, heart failure—among the placebo patients, only 2 among the treated. The study was stopped much earlier than planned so the placebo group could be switched to active treatment to reduce their risk.

More recently, the V.A. Cooperative Study Group carried out a five-year trial with patients having only mild hypertension—with diastolic pressures of 90 to 114, just above the 90 level considered top normal. Again there were two groups, actively treated and placebo. And the study showed a two-thirds reduction among the treated of the risk of developing a heart attack or stroke. Even within the five-year period of the study, more than 10 percent of the men in the placebo group went on to develop severe hypertension; no man in the treated group did.

Causes and Treatments

What causes hypertension? In only 10 to 15 percent of all cases can some definite physical cause be found. It may be a narrowing (coarctation) of the aorta, the great artery emerging from the heart; this type is curable by an operation that eliminates the narrowing.

An adrenal gland tumor, called a pheochromocytoma, is usually benign but produces large quantities of hormones that elevate pressure; it, too, is curable by surgery. Obstruction to normal blood flow in a kidney artery may lead to high blood pressure and the hypertension can be cured by bypassing or otherwise correcting the obstruction surgically.

But 85 to 90 percent of hypertension cases are classified as essential, meaning that the basic cause remains unknown. Often such cases are related to obesity. Very commonly, particularly in mild and moderate cases, hypertension yields remarkably well to weight reduction. In people who may be taking excessive salt in the diet, moderation of salt intake alone, or in combination with medication, brings pressure back toward normal value.

When drugs are needed, the physician now has available a wide variety. They range from mild to very potent. Some act as calmatives in the central nervous system, reducing the flow of exciting impulses that can raise pressure. Some act by blocking certain nerve pathways that tend to carry excessive messages which constrict small blood vessels and, in so doing, raise pressure. Other medications help by increasing the body's excretion of salt.

The physician can choose a medication likely to be suitable for the individual patient, combine it with another when necessary, and adjust dosage until a regimen is arrived at that controls pressure effectively and produces minimal or no side effects.

The ideal is to bring pressure to normal and keep it there. Many physicians now find that a big help in this is to have patients take their own blood pressure readings at home. Such readings may give a truer picture of the blood pressure than measurements in the doctor's office which sometimes tend to make the patient anxious. And home readings simplify treatment, make fewer visits to the physician necessary. Although some have supposed that home measurements might make patients anxious, this, in the experience of physicians using the technique, is rarely if ever the case.

The Neglect Problem

Today, physicians are taking even the mildest form of hypertension seriously. But a major problem is to get patients to take blood pressure elevation seriously.

Most people with hypertension have no symptoms; for early diagnosis, therefore, there must be regular medical checkups. Typically, as the American Heart Association reports, at one large industry in Michigan a screening program uncovered 919 employees with hypertension, but 78 percent did not know they had it.

In addition to the many who fail to get checkups that could reveal their hypertension, there are the many who know they have hypertension, start treatment, then discontinue because they have no symptoms. In a special program in Baldwin County, Georgia, public health nurses made house-to-house calls on 3,000 persons and found 630 with high blood pressure. Only 55 percent were aware of their condition. Even among those who were aware, there was self-neglect. Most had stopped taking their medicine within three months.

Of some concern has been the recent finding that hypertension is not limited to adults; not infrequently it occurs in adolescents. At Duke University Medical Center, physicians studied fifty teen-agers with elevated pressures, often only slightly elevated. Thirty of the fifty could be followed up seven years later when twelve were found to have normal pressure. But five had greater elevation, six had already developed major complications (which led to deaths in two), and seven had the original elevation. The major factor in those who continued to have the same or more severe elevations and the complications was weight gain. It would seem wise to treat any weight-gaining adolescent who has even mild pressure elevation with a strict weight-reduction program.

There have been recent reports that in some women contraceptive pills have a hypertensive effect. How often this occurs is not known but in one recent study a rise in blood pressure was found in 11 of 62 women. The pressure may rise weeks to months after start of use of the pill; it usually falls within four weeks after use is discontinued. It would seem wise—and some medical journal editorials have been calling for it—for every woman using the pill to have at least an occasional measurement of blood pressure.

Considering its wide prevalence and its established importance even in mild form as a factor in atherosclerosis, heart attacks, and strokes, hypertension is a prime public health problem. It has been estimated in medical testimony before a Senate subcommittee that keeping blood pressure down could reduce heart failure by four-fifths, strokes by one-half, and heart attacks by one-fourth.

What can you do about hypertension?

If you already know you have it, no matter how mild, and have done nothing about it, see your physician now, find out what your pressure currently is, get his advice on bringing it down.

If hypertension has never been diagnosed, recognize that no one is immune, pressure may go up at any time without warning symptoms. Regular medical checks can detect elevation early. And you owe it to yourself to have such checks for many reasons, including keeping on top of diabetes.

DIABETES: ANOTHER STEALTHY RISK

Like hypertension, diabetes mellitus is a disorder that almost every heart researcher believes accelerates the course of coronary atherosclerosis. Like hypertension, it is much more wide-spread than often supposed—and although it is an eminently treatable disease, very often quite simply treatable, it is often allowed to go undetected and untreated.

Anybody can become diabetic, without any history of the disorder in the family. Right now, there are 2,300,000 known diabetics in the country and at least another 1,600,000 who would be diagnosed as definitely diabetic if given the necessary tests. And, beyond this, as Dr. Glen McDonald of the U.S. Public Health Service has pointed out: "There is an even greater total of suspects who are progressing into diabetes. In one large Public Health Service screening program, 10 per-cent of an unselected adult population were found positive."

Recently, Chicago hospitals, which have made it a rule to test all patients for diabetes no matter what the reason for hospitalization, have been uncovering large numbers with the disease. Jackson Park Hospital, for example, has reported find-ing outright diabetes in 6 percent of newly admitted patients, with another 27 percent of patients showing borderline re-sponses to testing, indicating they are diabetic or on the verge of becoming diabetic.

Dutifully, to help get a statewide diabetes-detection pro-gram under way, 265 New Hampshire legislators took a test themselves, and 84—one in five—were astounded when they had to be referred to their physicians as suffering from dia-betes.

Although diabetes may develop at any time of life, four out of five times it makes its first appearance in adulthood.

Diabetes and Coronary Heart Disease

The link between diabetes and CHD is now well docu-mented.

One of the most eye-opening studies started back in 1956, when Dr. Thomas Francis, Jr., and a University of Michigan research team persuaded 8,600 residents of Tecumseh, Michigan, nine-tenths of the community, to undergo complete physical examinations and blood and other tests. The objective was to check on various factors influencing health.

Not only did the study find a high frequency of coronary heart disease among the known diabetics in the community, but for the first time on record, the study found that people with heart disease tended to have diabetes. It appeared that a high blood-sugar level in an individual—whether a known diabetic or not—might well be a most important factor predicting the probability of heart disease and even of a heart attack.

There have been many other studies. In one, 12 percent of a group of 314 patients with CHD also had diabetes. In another with patients with proven CHD, 41 percent had elevated blood sugar when very carefully tested for diabetes. In still another, sensitive testing showed that 66 percent of CHD patients had diabetic blood sugar patterns.

Similarly, studies have demonstrated that the incidence of CHD is high in patients with diabetes. At the Joslin Clinic in Boston 46.5 percent of deaths in diabetics has been reported due to atherosclerotic heart disease. Autopsy studies show significant coronary disease present in 75 to 98 percent of diabetics. A significant feature of these studies is that CHD is as common in diabetic women as in diabetic men.

Some studies indicate that the occurrence rate of coronary heart disease is twice as high in diabetics as nondiabetics. The Framingham study has found that among men aged thirty to fifty-nine initially free of CHD, diabetics develop 1.4 times the amount of CHD as nondiabetics—and the incidence in diabetic women is 2.5 times greater. The risk of death from CHD is 2.3 times higher in diabetic men and 5.7 times higher in diabetic women.

Researchers have found that cholesterol levels are higher in diabetics than in nondiabetics, that hypertension is nearly twice as frequent, and that four of every five newly discovered diabetics are overweight.

Diabetes Symptoms

Diabetes can be a very subtle disease. It doesn't necessarily signal its presence.

In diabetes, the body cannot properly handle sugar. Normally, all carbohydrate foods—starches and sugars—are converted to a type of sugar called glucose. Ultimately, too, about 60 percent of all protein food is turned into glucose. This normal sugar travels by way of the blood to all tissues to be used to produce energy.

In severe diabetes, the body's inability to handle and burn up sugar properly leads to great accumulations of glucose in the blood. Upon reaching a sufficiently high level—about 180 or more milligrams of glucose for every 100 millilitres of blood— the glucose begins to spill into the urine, taking water with it, and large amounts of urine are passed, making the patient complain of great thirst. If the diabetes is not controlled, the body, unable to use sugar, uses fats, and the breakdown of large amounts of fats leads to accumulation of acid products in the blood, causing the victim to gasp for breath. If the condition still is not corrected, consciousness clouds, and shock and death may follow.

But with mild diabetes, there may be few if any symptoms. Some people may recognize that they feel tired and listless; others recognize no symptoms at all. Sometimes the symptoms are so mild that, unless there are routine checks to discover diabetes, advanced complications (boils in the skin, vision difficulties, and coronary heart disease) develop as the first symptoms.

Causes

Insulin is the sugar-regulating hormone produced by the islets of Langerhans in the pancreas. It promotes the entry of sugar from the blood into cells. Insufficient insulin production may lead to diabetes—or the body may be resistant to the effects of insulin.

It is now known that there are two quite different types of diabetes. One, the juvenile type, starts in the early years and involves a definite lack of insulin secretion. The other, maturity onset, occurs later in life and involves no shortage of insulin. Insulin is produced in plenty but the body does not respond to it properly. And this, many investigators believe, may be due to blockage of the usual routes of insulin to the cells or, since obesity is so common in adult-onset diabetes, to the resistance of fat-laden cells to the action of insulin.

Treatment

While insulin is the mainstay of treatment for juvenile diabetes, in the far more common adult-onset type, weight reduction alone is often all that is needed to bring blood sugar levels back to normal. When necessary, the weight reduction may be supplemented by oral antidiabetes medication.

In one study at Pennsylvania Hospital, Philadelphia, careful testing showed that 51 percent of 800 obese men and women were diabetic although they hadn't known it. When many went on reducing diets, they not only lost weight but they tested normal instead of diabetic. No antidiabetic medication was required.

Detecting Diabetes

Diabetes tests are becoming increasingly refined.

The old test of a urine sample for sugar content missed 80 to 90 percent of early diabetes cases.

One now commonly used screening test is for sugar in a blood sample drawn two hours after eating. In addition, there are more sensitive tests that can be used to confirm diabetes suggested by the simple blood test and to check in doubtful cases when the blood test fails to indicate diabetes.

One is the glucose-tolerance test. In this, blood sugar is first determined after several hours of fasting and then again at intervals after the patient is given three and a half ounces of glucose solution to drink. By studying the curve drawn between the measurements at various times, the physician can detect a diabetic tendency.

Another sensitive test is the oral cortisone–glucose-tolerance procedure in which cortisone is taken by mouth eight and a half hours and again two hours before proceeding with the glucose-tolerance test.

Recently, too, investigators have made another discovery about testing. Traditionally, glucose-tolerance studies have been done in the morning. But at Virginia Mason Research Center, Seattle, investigators have found that performing the test in the afternoon can lead to identification of a substantial number of patients with incipient diabetes who otherwise would be missed. Among 1,429 patients tested at the center, 45 percent were found to have "afternoon diabetes," though they tested normal in the morning.

It is now possible to detect diabetes very early, in very mild form. And its detection during regular medical checkups— with prompt treatment, very often calling for only weight reduction—can do much to keep this potentially serious risk factor for coronary heart disease from actually becoming one.

GOUT (OBVIOUS AND NOT) AND CHD

People who have gout—whether or not it is the obvious kind—have a greater tendency to atherosclerosis of the coronary arteries than people who are free of this disorder.

Gout can, indeed, be a fooler.

In its classical form, it affects a great toe, and an attack of agonizingly painful gouty toe can be easy enough to recognize for what it is. The quick response of the attack to a medicine, colchicine, virtually clinches the diagnosis for colchicine has no other recognized use except for relieving a gout attack.

But gout can attack almost any joint in the body, and many cases are found in which the victim for a long time has suffered needlessly from attacks that he has mistakenly considered to be bursitis or arthritis manifestations.

Moreover, not everyone with gout gets painful joint attacks; by far the great majority of cases are without symptoms.

With or without symptoms, gout is an inherited ailment, very largely but not entirely confined to men, in which uric acid levels in the blood are elevated. In gout, there is an inability to properly handle certain important compounds, called purines, in food. As a result of the abnormal handling or metabolism, uric acid, which is a breakdown product of purines, builds up in the blood. Sometimes excess uric acid may be deposited in joints, causing an inflammatory reaction that leads to severe pain, swelling, and stiffness.

Whether or not inflammatory reactions occur, elevated levels of uric acid in the blood have been found to be a factor of some importance in coronary heart disease. As far back as 1951, some investigators were able to document an association between elevated uric acid levels and patients with heart attacks. And more recently the Framingham study has produced evidence that there is a 1.6 times increase in risk of coronary heart disease associated with such elevated levels. The reason is not clear. There is one theory that the higher concentrations of uric acid in the blood somehow sensitize the delicate inner walls of the coronary arteries to damage by cholesterol.

Fortunately, a relatively simple blood test can determine when uric acid levels are increased beyond normal range. And highly effective medications are available for control.

Several of the medications act to promote excretion of the uric acid via the kidneys. Interestingly, one of them, probenecid, had its first use during World War II, shortly after the discovery of penicillin when the antibiotic was scarce. It turned out that probenecid was a penicillin extender; it could make a little of the bacteria-fighting agent go a long way. Not long afterward, it was to turn out to be an agent that changed the whole picture for gout sufferers. When taken regularly, it minimized the number of gout attacks and in some cases avoided them entirely.

A recent addition to the treatment of gout may make even probenecid obsolete. Called allopurinol, it blocks the enzyme that is otherwise active in producing uric acid. Therefore, no uric acid is formed. Allopurinol also stimulates the breakdown and excretion of uric acid deposits that may already have accumulated.

Thus, all three of the major conspiratorial diseases, the often-hidden ailments that can contribute greatly to risk of coronary heart disease, today are getting the serious medical attention that is their due. They can be detected readily enough during medical checkups and they can be curbed or completely eliminated as risk factors by treatment that is very often simple.

10

Preface to the Israeli Story

Where else can you use water skis to follow in the footsteps of Jesus, or lunch on the same kind of fish as those caught by St. Peter? Where else can you find horseback riding, submarine and underwater archeology, sophisticated discotheques and restaurants, and wild and rare game hunting in one country? Where else golf courses on which, if you fail to keep your head down, you'll not only top the ball, but you'll see remnants of Roman aqueducts and Byzantine mosaics?

So one United States magazine recently introduced a travel report on the state of Israel. Remarkable in such ways, the tiny state is remarkable in other ways that make it of unusual interest to medical scientists, especially those concerned with heart disease.

Since its founding in 1948, more than a million people have migrated to Israel from diverse corners of the world. The varied peoples making the migration and the different modes of life they took up upon arrival, coupled with the modes of life of other people long resident before the establishment of the state, have provided an unparalleled opportunity for investigations of some of the most basic questions related to coronary heart disease: the influence of genetic factors, the influence of many distinct environmental factors, how genetic and environmental factors interact, how the influence of certain beneficial environmental factors may counter or cancel out the influence of detrimental environmental factors.

Among the immigrants have been Ashkenazi Jews of Europe, with heart disease rates in their countries of origin no different than those in the United States and elsewhere in the Western world. But after settling in Israel, there have been striking differences in rates between those taking up residence in the cities and those going to the kibbutzim.

Of tremendous interest among the ethnic groups are the Yemenite Jews, coming from a kind of life little changed from that of Biblical times, virtually free upon arrival of coronary heart disease and risk of coronary heart disease. But what happened to the Yemenites after 8, 10, 15 years in Israel is a remarkable demonstration of what happens to many of us, and why.

The Bedouins in the Negev desert of Israel, virtually immune to heart trouble except for a handful—the sheikhs taking up Western ways—form another scientifically rewarding group.

Scientific inquiry seeks to go beyond mere impressions, to probe a problem, pick at its pieces, test, and measure. If something conceivably could be a cause of disease, then the scientific effort must be to test whether it really is the cause by manipulating it while keeping other conditions steady, unchanged. If manipulating the one factor—diminishing it, increasing it—significantly influences disease incidence or severity, there is a valid basis for indicting it as causative. If it shows no significant influence, that, too, constitutes progress: that factor now can be dismissed and others investigated until finally valid insights into the disease are built up.

Not by design but because of its distinctive population groups and their varied ways of life, Israel has provided un-usual opportunity for scientific investigations of coronary heart disease. It is a brave, young, growing nation. It is also a laboratory of a nation.

Happily, too, it is a nation with scientific strength.

With a population of 2.8 million, 1/1,400 of the total world population, Israel produces 1/200 of the scientific papers, more than all of Latin America or Africa.

Small as it is, Israel has seven main centers of education and research, unquestionably big-league institutions in terms of size, equipment, quality of personnel, and scope of studies. Israel's version of our own Massachusetts Institute of Technology, for example, is the Technion of Haifa, with 45 buildings on a 300-acre site on Mount Carmel, overlooking the port city of Haifa, housing an academic staff of more than 1,000, some 4,000 undergraduate students, nearly 1,700 master and doctoral degree candidates. Hebrew University of Jerusalem is a huge, modern, highly diversified institution, with a current enrollment of 15,000. Tel Aviv University, founded only in 1956 as a municipal college, now has 1,700 faculty members and 10,000 students, and is expected to have 20,000 within ten years. The Weizmann Institute, a world-famed center of research, has a staff of 1,600, a budget of $12 million annually, Dr. Albert Sabin of polio vaccine fame as its new president, and plans for major expansion.

The ties between the Israeli and American scientific communities are strong. When, for example, the Weizmann Institute recently sought an outside review of its research programs, the committee that provided the review was headed by two of the most distinguished men of American science, Nobel Laureate I. I. Rabi and Dr. Jerome Weisner, White House scientific adviser under President John F. Kennedy and now president of M.I.T. Israel is on the American "sabbatical circuit"; during their customary year for travel and research away from their own home universities, many American scientists do research at Israeli institutions. And to no small extent, scientific work in Israel—particularly work in the area of medical research and especially heart research— has been sponsored by angencies of the U.S. Government such as the National Institutes of Health and the National Science Foundation.

If Israel is a unique laboratory, Daniel Brunner, M.D., is an unusual man. Of the many distinguished investigators in Israel, Brunner is one of the foremost concerned with coronary heart disease. He is recognized as a world authority and his frequent reports of research results at American medical meetings are eagerly studied.

He was born in Vienna, attended the University of Vienna, and received his Doctor of Medicine degree there. He was one of the last Jews to receive this degree in Nazi-influenced Austria. As he remarks wryly: "They gave me the diploma; they did not give me the hand." That was in 1939.

The next year, Brunner migrated to Israel. He hadn't prac- ticed medicine in Austria; he did not plan to practice it in Israel. He was a member of the Zionist Youth Movement in Vienna. The Movement had been opposed to any higher studies for its members. The need was for agricultural workers; members went to farms in Austria to prepare themselves for migration to Palestine. Brunner was one of the few in the Movement granted special permission to study.

Upon arrival in Israel, he went to a kibbutz—as an agricul- tural worker. He spent two years as an agricultural worker, years he describes as "the best of my life." (A description of kibbutz life presented later may help to explain why.)

Dan Brunner doesn't talk about it but the two years were interrupted by a mission to deal with Hitler's man, Eichmann, seeking to buy the lives of Jews scheduled to die in the ovens. It was a dangerous assignment.

Finally, much as he loved kibbutz life, Brunner faced the fact that he loved medicine. He needed more medical training and experience. He got both first with the Sick Fund of Israel, then at one of the only two hospitals in Palestine, the Beilinson Hospital, where he stayed from 1942 to 1948. When he left Beilinson as chief of a department, it was to go to the first military hospital of the Jewish Armed Forces established in a kibbutz in Galilee.

In the novel *Exodus* there is the story of a beleaguered kibbutz in a valley and of children being rescued from the hills by the people of the kibbutz who had to cross enemy territory to get to them. Brunner was the doctor of the story who helped retrieve the children and calm their anxieties.

Brunner had a yearning for research as well as clinical practice. The desire to do research had begun to build up as early as 1946 when he was still at Beilinson. He was an internist and had become fascinated by the problem of coronary heart disease. As he recalls: "If you are head of a medical department and make daily rounds, and 30 to 40 percent of all patients are there because of a heart problem; if you see Jews from Germany, Jews from Poland, Jews from almost everywhere with heart trouble but virtually never see a Jew from Yemen with it, you become intrigued."

Medical research in Israel has to be selective. "If you're going to do research in Israel," Brunner says, "your project, ideally, should fill three requirements. It should be something special that can be done in Israel and possibly nowhere else— not in the United States, for example, where there are much greater research facilities. Secondly, it should be concerned with a problem that exists in sufficient numbers in Israel. If you were to pick a relatively rare problem—for example, tumor of the spleen—there would not be enough cases in a small country like Israel to permit adequate study. And, thirdly, whatever the project, it must be concerned with something of general interest."

It seemed to him that the investigation of why Yemenites are relatively free of coronary heart disease might provide valuable clues as to the causes of the disease. And the project certainly fulfilled all three criteria.

So he began his studies on his own. After the first results were in, he received the support of the U.S. National Institutes of Health. As he continued the investigations of the Yemenites, he also went back to the kibbutzim for other studies that provided valuable insights.

He was not alone. He had colleagues to help in the work. Meanwhile, too, other Israeli investigators working independently began to turn up valuable information that fitted into the coronary heart disease puzzle.

11

Israel: A Whole Nation as a Revealing Laboratory

PEOPLE FROM THE PAST

The Yemenite Jews have a long history. For more than 2,000 years they lived in isolation in the southern part of the Arabian peninsula, maintaining their religion, traditions, and way of life virtually unchanged from what they had been at the time of the temple in Jerusalem. Most probably, the Jews came to Yemen after destruction of the first temple by the Babylonian King Nebuchadnezzar in 586 B.C.

They speak the Hebrew of the Bible. Their children, in the years in Yemen, learned to read and write by age three or four. In the dark world of the Middle Ages, there were no illiterates among the Yemenite Jews. There is the seemingly apocryphal but true story of the Yemenite children who, upon arrival in Israel, caused astonishment by their ability to read Hebrew upside down, a result of the fact that books were so scarce in Yemen that for their lessons many children had to sit in a circle reading from a single book.

Most Jews in Yemen were not farmers but artisans, particu-

larly goldsmiths. They were kept separated from the surrounding Islamic population, suffering severe discrimination.
The first Yemenite Jews came to Palestine at the beginning of
the twentieth century and in somewhat greater numbers in
the 1920's. Life was to become more difficult for Jews in
Yemen with the Arab-Jewish conflict over efforts to establish
the State of Israel.

With the founding of Israel, the Yemenite Jews almost
literally believed that the days of the Messiah had arrived. It
was written in the Bible that when the Messiah came he would
bring his people on the wings of a great bird to the Holy
Country—and the Yemenites, indeed, were to be carried on the
wings of great birds to Israel. Thousands upon thousands, the
Yemenites began a long hike through the desert to reach the
port of Aden on the Red Sea and from there they were
brought, in an action called "Flying Carpet," by plane to
Israel. At the beginning of 1948, there had been 50,000 Jews in
Yemen; in 1951, only 200 remained.

The migration of this ethnic group of honest, industrious
people is a unique example of the miraculous transfer of a
whole community, as described in fairy tales, from the desert
and the most primitive of economic conditions to a modern,
dynamic, democratic society. It was not only a change of place
but a jump of many hundreds of years directly into the
twentieth century.

When the Yemenite Jews arrived in Israel they were a
small, thin people, afflicted with parasitic and infectious
diseases, especially tuberculosis. They were in a state of malnutrition. One survey found an average adult weight of 56
kilograms, or 123 pounds, and a height of 164 centimeters, or
5'4". But the Yemenites did not suffer from degenerative
atherosclerotic diseases.

The Yemenites adapted themselves to the new environment.
Tuberculosis, typhoid, malaria, and other infectious diseases
disappeared. The Yemenites learned to live with electricity,

radios, refrigerators, and television as well as with agricultural machinery. Their sons and daughters went to school and later served in the army (in Israel, girls serve in the army for 20 months). The adults became members of trade unions and political parties. And in addition to sociological changes, there were biological ones as well.

The Yemenite Jews who arrived in Israel in the years 1948 to 1950 had unusually low serum cholesterol values. The average in adult men was about 150 mg percent, but many had values as low as 110 to 120. Nutritional surveys performed by various research teams showed a surprisingly low total caloric intake. For men, the average daily intake was only 2,057 calories, 60 percent of them derived from carbohydrates, 26 percent from fats, and 14 percent from proteins.

How small this is can be realized by comparison with the diet of American and Canadian agricultural workers which provides more than 4,000 calories daily. And the Yemenites surveyed included hard-toiling agricultural workers.

Dr. Brunner recalls being so astonished at the ability of the Yemenites to live on such little input while working hard in the fields that he consulted a nutrition expert at Jerusalem University. The equally astonished expert at first concluded that it was impossible but then, after careful calculations, decided that it was possible: a 2,000- to 2,100-calorie intake could be a bare borderline intake allowing hard work and survival.

Nor, as Brunner determined, was the low intake traceable to want. Even the poorest of the Yemenites had food available. They ate little out of custom, not poverty.

But with time the custom brought from Yemen was moderated in Israel. Investigators determined that there were noticeable differences between the late-arrived Yemenites, those who had come to Israel in 1948 to 1950, and the early-arrived who had migrated to Palestine in the twenties and thirties.

One study comparing 188 early-arrived with 124 late-arrived Yemenites showed the former to be taller, heavier, with higher blood pressure and higher serum cholesterol. Nor were the early-arrived heavier simply because they were taller. When a ponderal index—a formula to relate body weight to height—was employed, it demonstrated that the extra weight was greater than what could be attributed to increased height. The increase in height among young people in the early-arrived group is no isolated phenomenon. Among many populations throughout the world, sons are taller than fathers and daughters taller than mothers, and the height increase from generation to generation appears to depend upon better nutrition in the early period of life.

The Changes

Beginning in 1953, Dr. M. Toor and associates of Beilinson Hospital, and other investigators as well, began to make intensive dietary surveys and other studies of the Yemenites.

They found that recent Yemenite immigrants consumed mainly a type of flat, yeastless bread called "pita," large quantities of vegetables, very little meat (once weekly), and very little fat (mostly in the form of "samme," or boiled butter with a spice, "hilbe"). Even after five years in Israel, their caloric intake remained low and their serum cholesterol levels were far below those of any other group.

As the years went by, and the investigators restudied the Yemenites, they found that by the tenth year in Israel, there was a 43 percent increase in caloric intake and a 7 percent increase in the percentage of calories derived from fats. In men aged forty-five to sixty-four, there was a significant increase in serum cholesterol.

Taking a hard look at the changes in the composition of the diet, investigators found that in Yemen fats had been mainly of animal origin, samme, milk, mutton, beef; very few eggs had been eaten; vegetable oil had been rarely used. In Israel, the amount of fat from animal sources remained about the same but there was some increase in oil consumption. In

Yemen, carbohydrates had been mainly starch; almost no sugar was used. In Israel, there was a striking increase in sugar consumption. It seemed to some researchers that along with increased fat and increased total caloric intake, increased sugar consumption might have a role in the somewhat increased blood fat levels and atherosclerosis in Yemenites living for many years in Israel.

When physicians at Hebrew University–Hadassah Medical School, Jerusalem, performed autopsy studies—required in Israel in all cases of accidental or sudden death—on 59 Yemenite Jews aged twenty years and older, they found that those fifty years old and older who had resided for more than ten years in Israel had significantly greater atherosclerosis of the coronary arteries than more recent immigrants from Yemen of the same age group. Since recently arrived Yemenites and those long resident in Israel belonged to the same genetic group, the difference had to be attributed to differences in diet.

Clearly, there were changes occurring in the heart health of Yemenites the longer they lived in Israel. But they were slow changes because Yemenites clung to many of their old dietary customs.

In one interesting investigation, researchers studied 220 aged Yemenites and 260 aged European Jews, all over seventy, in a village for the aged. The village is made up of a number of homes, each organized as a separate unit with its own kitchen and common dining room. The Yemenites studied belonged to one of these homes, the European Jews to another.

The Europeans consumed mainly the food supplied to them through their common kitchen and dining room. In contrast, most of the Yemenites cultivated small tracts of land where they raised maize, sunflower seeds, red pepper, and onions, as well as various spices which they used for food they were served in the common dining room.

Even after ten years in Israel, there was a marked difference in dietary habits of Yemenites and Europeans. The Yemenites still loved their traditional spicy food, consumed great quantities of bread, and ate less animal proteins and fats than did the Europeans.

Compared with the Europeans, most of the aged Yemenites had slender body builds. Cholesterol values were significantly lower in Yemenite men and women—176 and 205 respectively—than in European men and women—211 and 244.

Electrocardiographic studies showed no signs of old heart attacks among Yemenite men and women, as compared with an incidence of 3.7 and 3.4 percent among European men and women. The incidence of heart rhythm disturbances was two to three times higher in Europeans than in Yemenites. Other evidence, including x-ray studies, indicated a lower incidence of atherosclerosis in aged Yemenites than in aged Europeans.

The investigators concluded that, since both groups had lived for the last ten years under the same environmental conditions, the difference in incidence and severity of atherosclerosis had to be attributed mainly to the dietary factor.

Three and one-half years later, the investigators repeated the study of the same groups. In the interim, some had died: 23.2 percent of the original European men, 10.3 percent of the Yemenite men; 10.7 percent of the European women, 8.1 percent of the Yemenite women.

Once again, Yemenite men and women had significantly lower serum cholesterol levels (170 and 195 respectively) compared to European men and women (227 and 259). No electrocardiographic indications of heart attacks were found among Yemenite men and women compared with 7.7 percent for European men and 4.6 percent for European women.

More and more, as many investigators studied Yemenites resident in Israel for varying lengths of time and obtained corresponding data for 5,000 men and women of the general Israeli population, they found significant differences in weight, height, ponderal index, blood pressure, and cholesterol values.

They could establish a gradient, with late-arrived Yemenites at the bottom, early-arrived Yemenites in the middle, and the general Israeli population at the top.

That didn't mean that the early-arrived Yemenites had abnormal blood pressures or unusually high cholesterol values. In fact, their average values never passed the limits of normal. But clearly the direction of development in a primitive population exposed to a modern society was toward biological values considered to be risk factors for coronary heart disease. Such a process may spread over a period of many years. But it can be speeded up, as Dr. Brunner and his colleagues were able to show.

A Speed-Up Trial

In a special nutritional study, a kitchen and a dining room were set up in the center of a Yemenite village in Israel, and 29 Yemenite Jews, agricultural workers, were placed on a high-fat, high-caloric, Western diet for seven months.

Their average daily food intake was 4,685 calories, more than twice the original Yemenite dietary intake. Fats made up 49 percent of the calories, proteins 18 percent. The meals were cooked by Yemenite women of the village in order to retain the special spicy taste of the Yemenite cuisine. The "eaters" did their eating under observation in the dining room and were not allowed to take any food home. There were no other changes in the routine of daily life. The participants continued with their daily work and lived at home with their families.

At the beginning of the study, the average cholesterol was 152 mg percent. Only five months were needed to turn the Yemenite Jews into European Jews in regard to cholesterol levels. In that short time, the average cholesterol level increased to 203 mg percent. After seven months, the participants returned to their usual food at home for three months and the cholesterol levels fell to an average of 160.

Afterward, the trial was resumed again for another two months, and now the increase was quicker and steeper. There were no exceptions; the slope of cholesterol increase was similar in all the participants, regardless of age or initial cholesterol level.

It was an impressive demonstration of the effect of an environmental factor on one of the major risk factors for coronary heart disease.

And No "Age" Effect

In the United States, investigators had started with a group of 2,000 males aged 17 in Minnesota and, following them closely, had found an average increase per year of age of 2.2 in cholesterol level. A study in New York had shown that the mean cholesterol level in 18- to 22-year-old men was 185.2 but in men 48 to 52 it was 238.8. Danish studies had shown a tendency toward increasing blood fat levels with age. And Dr. Ancel Keys, who had directed the Minnesota study, made another in Southern Italy and found that from the age of 20 to the early thirties average cholesterol levels rose about 3 mg a year.

But is a rise in blood fat levels inevitable with age? Does age really influence the levels at all?

To try to answer these questions, Dr. Brunner and his colleagues checked on 41 young Yemenite Jews, aged 18 to 20; 35 adult Yemenites, aged 30 to 50; 45 young European Jews, aged 18 to 20; and more than 100 adult European Jews, aged 30 to 55.

Contrary to any view that cholesterol levels must rise with age, no such trend was found in the Yemenites. The young Yemenites had an average cholesterol level of 160—and the level for the adult Yemenites was virtually the same. On the other hand, the young European Jews started out with a higher level, 198 on the average, and the level increased to an average of 217 for the adults.

It would seem, therefore, that a cholesterol level rise with age is not inevitable, not a physiological phenomenon. When there are environmental factors leading to an increase in cholesterol, the increase keeps on over a period of time. It is not age that is involved but a detrimental factor given more and more time to express itself. Something in the mode of life of European Jews in Israel—and of Americans, Danes, and Italians studied—accounts for the cholesterol rise with time, something not present in the mode of life of the Yemenites, and it would seem to be diet.

The Diabetes Phenomenon

Studies of Yemenite Jews in Israel have produced another striking finding.

As noted in an earlier chapter, diabetes is one of the major risk factors for coronary heart disease. Both the incidence of coronary disease among diabetics and the incidence of diabetes among coronary patients are high.

Diabetes clinics in Boston and Cleveland have reported that as many as half of all diabetic patients over a period of years develop atherosclerotic disease involving leg, coronary, or cerebral arteries. The dread of eventually developing serious blood vessel disease, leading to gangrene of a leg and amputation, disturbance of vision, stroke or heart attack is one that haunts diabetics almost everywhere. But not Yemenite diabetics.

Diabetes occurs in Yemenites. It is detectable in about 0.55 percent of the Yemenite population, a prevalence rate one-half that for the entire Israeli population. But blood vessel disease complications among Yemenite diabetics are rare.

Dr. Brunner and his co-workers examined a group of 76 Yemenite diabetics, including 34 with diabetes for at least five years and 13 for at least ten years. In only one elderly man was there evidence of an old myocardial infarction, or heart attack. Otherwise, in no case was there electrocardiographic evidence of heart damage, and in no case could evidence be found of disease of brain or leg arteries. A comparison study of 76 non-Yemenite Israeli diabetics of comparable age, sex, and duration of diabetes showed that 26 percent had had myocardial infarction or had signs of heart muscle damage and 13 percent had indications of leg artery disease.

What could account for the strikingly low incidence of blood vessel disease in the Yemenite diabetics?

Brunner and his group concluded that a likely reason could be adherence to the Yemenite diet, low in fats and calories. They found that cholesterol values in diabetic Yemenites were lower than in other diabetics. They found that while there is some elevation of cholesterol levels in diabetic Yemenites as compared with healthy Yemenites, still the levels in the diabetics were certainly not elevated by Western standards.

It is worth noting here that similar findings have been reported by investigators studying Japanese diabetics. The levels of cholesterol in the diabetics were higher than for the general Japanese population. Nevertheless, in Japanese diabetics atherosclerotic complications were unusual. And the investigators related the relative absence of such complications to the low-fat diet characteristic of the Japanese population.

The high incidence of blood vessel complications in diabetes, Dr. Brunner points out, is found in Western countries—in obese, physically inactive people with high cholesterol. And it may be, he suggests, that if diabetics will avoid overeating and will indulge in physical activity, they will improve both their diabetes and their chances for avoiding coronary heart disease.

THE BEDOUINS

Except for some new Jewish settlements and towns, the Negev Desert, which covers the greater part of southern Israel, is mainly inhabited by 18,000 seminomadic Bedouins. To some extent their way of life has been influenced by the Israeli society but in many if not most respects it is much as it was thousands of years ago.

Here, it seemed to Israeli investigators, was an opportunity to study nutrition and its effect on certain bodily functions and the prevalence of certain diseases and, by comparisons, shed new light on some aspects of nutrition and diseases in Western countries.

The Bedouins in the Negev are part of the large Bedouin population stretching over the whole of the desert from Egypt through the Sinai Peninsula, Iraq, and Trans-Jordan into Saudi Arabia. Those in the Israeli Negev are divided into 18 tribes, each under a feudal ruler or sheikh.

The economy is agricultural. Most food comes from wheat and barley grown in areas that are more or less in the possession of each tribe; some food comes from cattle. No food is raised for the cattle; instead, to find enough wild pasture land for the herds, part of the tribe moves through the desert, sometimes for considerable distances, while the others stay behind at the sown fields.

The Bedouin diet is monotonous. The main food—eaten for breakfast and at the midday and evening meals (in poor families, often without anything else)—is an unleavened bread called "rarif," which is like a thick pancake. Dough for it is made by combining flour and water with a little salt but no yeast. A handful of the dough is flattened like a pancake, swung around, then tossed onto a metal plate which is heated over a small open fire. The bread has advantages: it is simple to prepare; it can be folded up and put into a pocket for later consumption. There is little doubt that rarif is the prototype of the matzo eaten by the Jewish people when they were still nomads.

Even in prosperous families, rarif constitutes the bulk of the food. A consumption of 500 to 600 grams of flour, or slightly more than a pound, per day is normal for an adult man. Sometimes kuskusu, a kind of porridge made of flour, is eaten. Another favorite dish is burgul made from crushed wheat. Barley is produced and eaten but less often.

Some milk is obtained from sheep, goats, camels, and occasionally from asses. Milk from camels is considered especially nutritious by the Bedouins but less prosperous families have only sheep or goat milk for their children. Lentils are eaten occasionally. The more prosperous eat fresh or dried tomatoes all year round. Other vegetables—cabbage, fresh green beans, cucumbers, radishes, potatoes—are only occasional treats.

Meat is a rarity. It is usually used only on special occasions when there are visitors. A family may then slaughter a sheep or lamb and, because there is no way to preserve the meat, a whole animal is consumed in one day.

In their patient research, Dr. J. J. Groen, professor of medicine at Hebrew University–Hadassah Medical School, Jerusalem, and his colleagues overcame many difficulties, including the Oriental habit of trying to impress guests with the abundance of food the host is capable of bestowing. They found that less than 10 percent of families eat meat once a week or more; that meat eating once a month is nearer to the average. Chicken is eaten somewhat more often; fish is practically never used.

In general, little fat, butter, or oil is used; because the Bedouins do not fry food, the need is small.

The investigators found that caloric intake ranged from 1,360 in a poor family to as much as 3,900 in some well-to-do families. Generally, it is lower than that of Westerners. About 75 percent of the calories are derived from carbohydrates, 13 percent from fats, 12 percent from protein (thanks to the high protein content of whole wheat flour). Also because of the high content in the flour, B vitamins are adequate. Vitamin D is practically absent and the Bedouins rely for it on sunshine.

Obesity is rare, occurring only among some elderly well-to-do who rarely walk. Checking on 800 Bedouins, thirty years of age and over, the researchers found that most men weighed between 55 and 64 kilograms (121 and 141 pounds) and were between 160 and 174 centimeters (5'3" and 5'9") tall. Most Bedouins of both sexes have body weights low by Western standards.

Dr. Groen observed that the thin layer of subcutaneous fat in the Bedouins has advantages for desert life where temperatures are high by day, cold by night. For heat regulation, the Bedouins seem to depend less upon constant insulation by subcutaneous fat and more on variable protection by clothing. The Bedouin clothes are wide and spacious. During the day, they wear them wrapped loosely around the body so there is no interference with heat dissipation by conduction and evaporation. At night, the clothes are wrapped tightly around the body and protect against heat loss.

When blood samples were obtained from 733 Bedouins— 477 men and 256 women—the cholesterol values proved to be considerably below those considered normal in Western countries. More than half of the group had levels under 150. Less than 10 percent had levels above 200.

There was no significant increase in the cholesterol levels of men over age thirty. Here again, as with the Yemenites, was evidence that such an increase is not a physiological phenomenon connected with aging but is related to way of life, particularly dietary habits.

And Groen's study showed that myocardial infarction is conspicuously rare among the Bedouins, only a single case— in a seventy-year-old man—being found among 510 men thirty years of age and older.

Other investigators studying the Bedouins have made similar findings: caloric intake is low, in the range of 1,500 to 2,000 daily; cholesterol levels not only of young and middle-aged but of elderly Bedouins are significantly lower than those of comparable normal Europeans. They have found that while

Bedouins do not drink since alcohol is forbidden by their religion, they do smoke—almost as heavily as European Jews with coronary heart disease.

And they have found, too, that the incidence of coronary heart disease in Bedouins is low. In one survey of 500 consecutive admissions of Bedouins to the Beersheba Hospital, for example, there was not a single admission for coronary heart disease.

Of late, there are exceptions to this normal Bedouin pattern of life: the sheikhs and their families who eat a much richer diet, and some of the young men now employed as semiskilled laborers and thus better off economically.

And so investigators are beginning to note exceptions in terms of coronary heart disease—for example, a man of fifty-six, with high blood pressure, heart disease, and a serum cholesterol level elevated to 271. He is a sheikh habituated, unlike his subjects, to a rich Western type of diet.

Taken in conjunction with the Yemenite studies, the investigations of the Bedouins serve to emphasize the importance of diet and caloric intake in the regulation of fats in the blood. They add to the evidence for a positive relationship between abnormal fat levels and coronary heart disease. And they point to the fact that regardless of ethnic origin, a change in dietary habits toward high caloric intake and the rich foods of the Western type is a change in the direction of lost immunity to coronary heart disease.

THE KIBBUTZ PEOPLE

Perhaps nowhere else in the world is there such opportunity for rigorous study of the factors involved in coronary heart disease as in a social experiment unique to Israel.

Throughout Israel there are settlements that cannot be described as towns or villages. In them, the living quarters cluster in crescents, with lawns, flower beds, and avenues of trees between. In the center are larger buildings surrounded by lawns—and not far away there is usually a block of farm buildings, including cowsheds, granaries, poultry runs. All around, as far as the eye can see, are fields of grain, citrus groves, vineyards, plantations, orchards, and fishponds. In addition, there are workshops and large or small factories.

Collectively, the settlements are known as kibbutzim. Each is called a kibbutz. There are more than 250 kibbutzim in Israel with a population of more than 80,000.

Life in a kibbutz differs from every other form of social life. Each kibbutz is an independent legal entity and is owned by its settlers collectively; individuals own nothing. Three elements form the basis for kibbutz life: work, equality, equal partnership. And the kibbutz law of equality reads: "From everyone according to his capacity; to everyone according to his needs."

All in a kibbutz work—but the division of labor is not the usual kind. Men not only work in the fields and factories but also in the kitchen, dining room, and laundry; and women work in the vineyard, cowshed, factory, and in management as well as in the kitchen, dining room, and laundry. While everyone works, some spend most of their time doing physical, others mental, and still others administrative work. As people age, hours of work required of them are reduced gradually.

The kibbutz as a whole decides, based upon needs and opportunities, how much of this or that crop should be sown, how many machines bought, how many new products manufactured, how much new furniture installed in members' rooms. A rotating Labor-Arrangement Committee decides upon the work to be done by members.

When a kibbutz member is elected to any function, he receives no special rights, only added obligations. Almost never is there electioneering for an office; an officeholder counts upon being replaced after his appointed term of service; change of people in office once every year or two is established practice and allows equal distribution of burdens.

Every kibbutz member is entitled to suitable housing, parents to more spacious quarters than single people. Children are entitled to education; the backward or difficult are sent to special institutions; the gifted have opportunity for higher study.

Children live from birth in children's homes near the houses of members and are cared for by professionally trained members. Daily, when parents' work is finished, the children come to stay with them until bedtime. The ability to be with their children in the late afternoon hours, undisturbed by other activities, allows parents to devote attention to them. And kibbutzniks, as the members are called, believe that collective education from birth and the whole way of kibbutz life beneficially modifies the father's position. In a private family, a young child grows up primarily in his mother's company with the father away at work. In the kibbutz, both mother and father participate equally in parental tasks.

The communal dining hall is the kibbutz nerve center. Here, at table, members discuss affairs, argue problems, thrash out solutions, arrange meetings. And it is here that notice is given that a young couple have decided to marry.

The idea for communal settlements was formulated by a Conference of Pioneers in Russia in 1911. The Conference called for "communal settlements in the Land of Israel, not as a personal solution for individuals but as a path for the multitude, for tens of thousands who will follow the first comers in order to build up a new people in the Land of Israel."

Among the main points enumerated by the Conference were:

The purpose of setting up communal settlements in the Land of Israel is liberation from twofold servitude, national and social.

Work in the communal settlement is to be agriculture, cattle raising, handicrafts, and industry.

The advantage of communal settlement in the national and social sense is: greater productivity as a result of the unification of agriculture, cattle-raising, and industry; the awareness that you are working without any compulsion, not because of fear but out of honesty of heart, not for some exploiter but for your own benefit.

Today, in a typical long-established kibbutz there are to be found a cultural center containing library, study room, music room and hall for lectures, concerts, films, shows, and performances; a clothing store; a general store; a club where light refreshments are served. There are sports and playing fields. Members are regularly sent off to vocational and agricultural schools, courses, seminaries, Hebrew University, the Hebrew Technical Institute, an academy of music, and to study abroad.

Is there any lack of personal liberty? Here is how an Israeli publication on the kibbutz answers the question:

Well, all members are deprived of the right to idle. They are not permitted to shift from one working-place to another without very good reason. They cannot break group discipline, act against general equality, or acquire property otherwise than through the society. Nor may they evade those tasks which all must share in. Every individual has to give his social group his working strength, the fruit of his capacities and talents, and his full readiness to devote himself when called upon. Yet those who give all these give them of their own free will and gladly. And who is as free as they are among humankind?

Although the kibbutz movement encompasses less than 3 percent of Israel's population, it has had and still has an impact on the character of society out of proportion to its numbers. The kibbutzim produce more than a fourth of the total agricultural yield—54 percent of the grain, 15 percent of the

vegetables, 67 percent of the fruit, 36 percent of the milk—
and are active in the production of chemicals, textiles, plastics,
and other products.

Beyond this, to be born or reared in a kibbutz is as important
to a politician in Israel as to claim a log-cabin background used
to be to an American; those who do not have it are slightly on
the defensive. And a disproportionate number of young men
from kibbutzim are to be found in the most elite branches of
the Israeli armed forces—the officers corps and the air force
pilot corps.

The Healthy-Hearted

When investigators began to study the incidence of coronary heart disease in kibbutzim and compared it with the
incidence for the rest of Israel, they soon became aware of a
marked difference. The heart attack mortality for kibbutzim
members was much less than for Israeli city dwellers.

Where, for example, kibbutz men aged fifty-one to sixty,
during the period from 1949 to 1958 had an annual death rate
of 0.6 per 1,000 from coronary heart disease, the rate among
men of the same ages in the general Israeli population was 3.7;
and, according to World Health Organization data, the rate for
American men of the same ages was 10.8.

What accounted for the kibbutz advantage?

One of the early studies carried out by Dr. Brunner and an
associate, Dr. Gideon Manelis, sought to find out. A thorough
check was made of the incidence of myocardial infarction in
the ten years up to December 31, 1959, in 8,500 kibbutz
dwellers—4,500 men and 4,000 women—who at the end of
1949 had been aged thirty to fifty-five. Each of the 58 settlements in which these people lived was visited. It was a relatively simple matter, because of the comprehensive medical
service in the settlements and the careful record-keeping, to
obtain complete data—case records, electrocardiograms, postmortem reports.

There were 111 heart attacks, all told, among the 8,500 people. Of these, 34 led to death; 77 patients survived. The number of women suffering from heart attacks was very small. There were 2 deaths among the 4,000 women and 7 others survived one or more attacks.

In the communal settlements, 30 percent of all persons in the age group of the sample population under study were engaged in sedentary work and 70 percent in nonsedentary. By contrast, Brunner and Manelis found that among the patients with heart attacks, 19 of the 34 who died were sedentary workers and of the 77 surviving, 42 were engaged in sedentary work.

It turned out that the annual incidence of heart attacks was 1.36 per 1,000 for nonsedentary male workers whereas it was 4.1 for the sedentary—a three times greater incidence in the sedentary. The mortality rate also was three times greater in the sedentary group.

Clearly enough, the figures seemed to emphasize the preventive value of physical activity against heart attacks in a population group for which all other environmental conditions were identical.

With that to go on among the kibbutz dwellers, Brunner, Manelis, and other investigators went back to the Government Hospital Donolo in Tel Aviv–Jaffa to do a study of what might have been the influence of physical activity in 240 men under age sixty-five who had been admitted to the hospital for initial heart attacks in the years 1951–1955. They were able to follow up 187 patients, 93 percent of all survivors.

The immediate mortality—the 38 deaths that had occurred among the men in the first four weeks after their heart attacks —had been 15.8 percent. The five-year follow-up mortality of the patients who had been able to leave the hospital was 25.2 percent. Thus the total mortality over a five-year period beginning with the acute attack was 38.5 percent.

When Brunner and his co-workers classified the men according to occupations, they found that the immediate mortality of those who were laborers had been 6.1 percent, less than half the 13.8 percent immediate mortality rate for skilled workers. Of 86 merchants and members of professions, 15 had died in hospital, a rate of 17.4 percent. Of 60 office workers, 21.6 percent succumbed in the first four weeks. Thus, the immediate death rate among merchants and members of the professions was about two and a half times and among clerks three times greater than among laborers.

And the five-year death rates also showed striking differences. Mortality rose from 17.4 percent among laborers to 29.5 percent among merchants and professionals.

Thus the total mortality rate—in hospital and later—was 42 percent among merchants and professionals and 41.6 percent among office workers, about twice the 22.4 percent rate for laborers.

Brunner and his colleagues went further. Because modern industrial conditions have led to changes in the nature of working conditions in many occupations, they thought it worthwhile to go beyond classifying the patients by occupations and subdivide them according to whether they did heavy, light, or sedentary work. Now even more pronounced differences in mortality rates appeared.

The immediate mortality rate among heavy manual workers was 5.7 percent, less than a fourth that of the 23 percent for sedentary workers. People in light physical work had an immediate mortality rate of 13 percent, midway between the other two groups.

Similarly, the five-year follow-up mortality rate was 25.7 percent for heavy workers; 46 percent, or nearly twice as great, for sedentary workers; and 32.6 percent, or in between, for light physical workers.

Extending the Kibbutzim Study

Now Brunner and his fellow investigators went back to the kibbutzim for still more studies. This time the group covered consisted of 5,279 men and 5,229 women, aged 40 to 64. The records surveyed were for a 15-year period. And now there were checks for incidence of chest pain (angina) as well as for fatal and nonfatal heart attacks.

For angina among men in the youngest age group, 40 to 44, the annual incidence per 1,000 was 1.2 for the sedentary and 1.1 for the nonsedentary, almost identical. In the 45- to 49-year age range, the incidence for sedentary workers was 2.6 times higher than for nonsedentary. The difference was even more striking in the 50- to 54-year-old men, 4.2 for the sedentary versus 1.1 for the nonsedentary. And in the oldest age groups, the incidence rate was about 3 times greater in the sedentary.

Because fewer women than men suffered from angina, they were subdivided into only two age brackets: 40 to 54 and 55 to 64. In the two groups, annual incidence rates of new cases of angina per 1,000 women were 3.1 and 4.6 times higher for the sedentary than the nonsedentary.

Lumping all age groups together, the annual incidence rate of angina per 1,000 men was 3.2 for sedentary workers, 1.2 for nonsedentary. And for women, the corresponding figures were 1.5 and 0.45.

For nonfatal heart attacks in men, incidence rates in the various age groups ranged from 2.0 to 3.5 times greater for the sedentary than the nonsedentary. And for women, in both age groups, the incidence for the sedentary was about 3 times higher than for the nonsedentary.

As for fatal attacks, because of the relatively small number, men also were subdivided into only two groups—aged 40 to 54 and 55 to 64. The incidence in sedentary men was 1.6 and 3.1 times higher than in the nonsedentary. In women, there were no fatalities under age 54. In women 55 to 64, there were two fatalities among the sedentary, one among the nonsedentary.

About the kibbutzim studies, Dr. Brunner had this to say in

a special report written for a medical book, *Prevention of Ischemic Heart Disease*, edited by a distinguished American heart investigator, Dr. Wilhelm Raab:

In Western society, the differences in socioeconomic status are mainly determined by different occupations and salary levels. This socioeconomic differentiation does not exist in the kibbutz society where the population includes many people of superior intelligence and high educational levels who, because of idealistic motivation, have continued to be manual laborers. In addition, this unique form of life has eliminated many of the emotional and mental factors which are often invoked as causative factors in the increasing incidence of coronary heart disease. On the one hand, such personal problems as stagnation in the salary scale because of inherent inability, or as a result of inequality of previous educational opportunities, have been largely eliminated in the kibbutz society whereas, on the other hand, many more people than in an industrialized private economy have to accept direct responsibility for work and production. Thus the only major differentiating environmental factor in the kibbutz society is the nature of one's work, and it appears justifiable to consider this factor as being responsible for the difference in incidence rates of coronary heart disease in every one of the investigated groups.

The results [of the studies] suggest a favorable influence of physical activity at work on the incidence of coronary heart disease in middle-aged men and women, living under otherwise equal social and environmental conditions.

In the Family?

Another important kibbutzim study has helped to provide new insight into genetic influences on the major coronary heart disease risk factor of high blood fats.

In the past, some investigators have wondered whether there might be an important genetic component in the determination of serum cholesterol levels in healthy persons, so important as to overshadow the influences of environmental factors.

In most societies, there are family eating patterns; parents and children essentially eat "from the same pot"—and this has had a powerful effect in confounding the influences of environment and heredity.

It occurred to Brunner that the kibbutzim offered an unusual opportunity to penetrate the confusion since in the communal settlements there are no family eating patterns. The family does not eat together as a unit; rather, the parents' meals are taken in a communal dining room, as we have seen, the food having been prepared in a single kitchen. The children take their meals with other children.

In five kibbutzim, girls and boys sixteen to eighteen years old and their parents were investigated. A total of 52 boys and 38 girls and their parents were examined for blood fats and uric acid. Sure enough, the study showed a consistent pattern of family similarity for uric acid values, supporting a concept of strong genetic influence for blood uric acid levels. But there was none of the same high degree of correlation between parents and children in terms of blood fat values. The blood fat values for parents spread over a wide range; so did those for children. But when parents had higher or lower values, their children did not necessarily show the same pattern.

Dr. Brunner would like to extend the study to see if any correlation between parental and child blood fat levels appears as the children grow older; but thus far it seems that in normal healthy people, if there is a genetic influence on blood fat levels, it is very small.

12

An Informal Question and Answer Session with Daniel Brunner, M.D.

During the writing of this book, there were long conversations with Dr. Daniel Brunner. Much time was spent on technical matters—details of studies mentioned in the last chapter and of other studies. But some parts of the conversations, all of which were tape-recorded, contain information that we think will be of interest to the reader.

They give a flavor of the man and of Israeli research. They shed added light on the studies already noted and bring in other studies of significance.

A CARDINAL FINDING

Q: Dan, what would you consider to be the most important findings coming out of Israeli research? Take an overview.

DR. BRUNNER: Perhaps most important of all, I'd think, is that environmental factors are so crucial. Certainly there are hereditary influences. There are rare people with genetic backgrounds that make them extremely likely to develop coronary heart disease; there are also the rare ones so resistant that it is almost certain they will never develop it, no matter what. But the overwhelming majority of people—possibly more than 90 percent—have genetic backgrounds such that they will develop the disease given sufficient exposure to disadvantageous environmental conditions. It's not their heredity that makes trouble inevitable for them; the fault lies with environmental influences.

Look at the Yemenites—a beautiful demonstration that environmental influences overwhelm any genetic ones. Here is a people virtually isolated from the world for thousands of years, living the life of Biblical times. Bring them into the Western world, free of coronary heart disease to start with, with none of the biological indications considered risk factors for CHD. Gradually, they begin to develop the risk indications. Their genetics haven't changed, only the environment. You can even speed the process up, make a radical change in a major risk factor—cholesterol level—in just five months by, in effect, force-feeding them a Western type of diet.

Q: And that gives us hope . . .

DR. BRUNNER: It certainly does. If we're not doomed to early CHD trouble by our genes but by environmental influences which we can modify, we're not inevitably doomed at all.

Q: The Bedouin studies help prove the point, too.

DR. BRUNNER: Yes. We need more Bedouin studies. But among the Bedouins, too, CHD is virtually absent, so are the risk factors for it—except among whom? The sheikhs, the wealthy. Not because the sheikhs and the wealthy are genetically different from the common tribesmen. Their wealth and power allow them to indulge themselves in rich fare.

ACTIVITY AND STRESS

Q: While the Yemenite studies demonstrate mainly the influence of diet, the kibbutz studies, wouldn't you say, underscore the importance of physical activity?

Dr. Brunner: The Yemenites, too, are active physically. In the kibbutzim, however, we could, by the very circumstances of life in the settlements, see the influence of activity more sharply.

Q: You mean exactly . . .

Dr. Brunner: That kibbutz members eat food mainly prepared in a single kitchen and served in a communal dining room. Neither their success in nor the importance of any particular job has any bearing on their income or standard of living. They have shared the same environmental conditions; in older kibbutzim, they've shared them for 20 years and more. But their jobs do differ—agriculture, fishing, building, light industry, teaching, accounting, clerking. So, more than in any other society, it's possible to single out the factor of physical activity at work and see its influence on the development of CHD.

Q: And it's clear enough in many ways.

Dr. Brunner: No matter what comparisons you use—angina as an indication of CHD, nonfatal heart attack, fatal heart attack—always the sedentary workers outdo the non-sedentary. For trouble. And this is for large groups of people followed for long periods. And the differences aren't tiny. It's not a matter of a few percentage points—5, 10, 20 percent —more angina, more heart attacks nonfatal and fatal for the sedentary. It's a matter of 200 and 300 percent and more.

Q: You've done other studies relating to physical activity?

Dr. Brunner: Yes. One we did was an autopsy study of 172 men. This was not a kibbutz study. These were men who died unnatural deaths, victims of such things as road and work accidents. We checked on personal documents. We got information from relatives. Ninety-three of the men had led sedentary lives; 79 had been manual workers. Twenty-six men had been thirty to forty years of age; 62 had been sixty-one to seventy; the rest, in between.

Q: And you found?

DR. BRUNNER: We studied the coronary arteries of these men. The severity of the narrowing was surprisingly high in this unselected population. We found the arteries narrowed in some areas by 76 percent or more in one-fourth of the men fifty to sixty years old and in 45 percent of those sixty-one to seventy. We saw up to 20 percent narrowing even in some men in their thirties. And, consistently, in every age group, the greatest narrowing was in the men who had been sedentary.

Q: Going back to the kibbutzim for a moment, would you say that the life in the settlements eliminates stress?

DR. BRUNNER: I don't think you can say that. Stress is everywhere. There can't be life without stress. Wherever people interact with each other there is stress.

Look, we have done a study in a village of Yemenites, a cooperative village. Many people have claimed that the difference between the Yemenites and European Jews lies in the temper of living, in the competition and higher stress in Western society. I think it is an error to believe that in a Yemenite village there is no stress. There is stress there, too. The stress has a different content. It is not income-tax stress— which is a term I sometimes use for the stress of living in a highly industrialized society. But there is a stress of who will be this or that, who will be the chief in the synagogue.

I remember when I was fourteen and fifteen years old and in the Youth Movement, the Zionist Youth Movement. We youngsters didn't have the troubles of our parents and of other adults. But we had stress—the stress of trying to be the best football player, for example, or of being elected this or that.

Q: You don't think stress is important in terms of heart disease.

DR. BRUNNER: No, I would certainly not say that. I think it can be important. But I would not agree with anyone who might argue that it is all-important. Undue stress can be a risk factor, yes. But it is not the whole story.

Look, in Israel, we have a not too small group of Oriental Jews—relatively young, fifty-five to sixty—who are hospitalized with coronary heart disease. You know, men in their fifties, if they come from Iraq or Libya or Egypt or Syria, often stop working. In the Orient men don't consider it to be a virtue to be active, to work hard, to work at all. The idea that work is a virtue was first promulgated about 250 years ago in Geneva by Calvin. Before that nobody believed that work was a good thing.

And if you make rounds in the hospital and you find a Jew from Libya, aged fifty-five, with a heart attack, and you ask him what his work is, he answers that he doesn't work. If you ask him, why not, he will ask: "Why should I work?" And it is difficult to answer him satisfactorily. Because he has a son; the son takes care of him; this is the culture, the concept of the family.

And I think that Oriental Jews in Israel who get heart attacks get them not from stress; they are not unduly stressed at all. They get them, in my opinion, because they stop work. Often, they get them five or six years after they stop being active.

WEIGHT

Q: What of the importance of body weight?

DR. BRUNNER: Well, as you know, there's some controversy about weight. But it's a limited controversy—just over whether or not excess weight, in and of itself, is a direct risk factor for coronary heart disease.

But overweight is often associated with diabetes. It is often associated with high blood pressure. Those links would be enough to make it potentially dangerous.

It's not true, in my experience, that fat people necessarily have high cholesterol levels. Some do; some don't.

But I think obesity is important for another reason. Fat

people are not fit people. Their fatness reflects lack of activity —and that lack is, in my experience, very much involved in CHD.

Q: Obesity is important in diabetes in more than one way.

DR. BRUNNER: Yes. It's true that many if not most people who become diabetic in adulthood are fat. Many investigators think the excess weight is a factor in the development of the diabetes. And often you can treat such diabetes simply by getting rid of the excess weight.

And then there is the matter of the complications. There's a high risk that over an extended period of time diabetics will develop blood vessel disease—and then suffer such things as gangrene of the leg, vision loss, stroke, coronary heart disease. That's often the case even when the diabetes is controlled by medication. But why is it that Yemenite diabetics given the same treatment have so much less of complications? It could be their leanness.

Q: You know, Dan, there is some support for that from a study recently reported here in this country from the Joslin Diabetes Foundation in Boston. It was an investigation of 124 patients free of complications after 25 years of diabetes. What distinguished them from other diabetics? One thing, clearly, was their weight; it was close to ideal for their heights—lower than that for the average American man and woman.

DR. BRUNNER: Ah!

Q: There were also some observations made by Jewish physicians who survived the Nazi concentration camps during the war—observations suggesting the considerable importance of weight in coronary heart disease?

DR. BRUNNER: Yes, they came out with reports that during all the years of their imprisonment they never encountered fellow inmates with heart attacks or with angina, even among those over fifty years of age. Moreover, they noted that people who had previously been their patients before incarceration in the camps, people who were known to them as having had coronary heart disease, became free of any manifestations of the disease after losing considerable weight due to the conditions in the camps.

BLOOD FATS

Q: Dan, you've had considerable experience in the study of cholesterol levels . . .

DR. BRUNNER: And I've been a bit confounded, too. You know, there are peculiar aspects to the cholesterol story.

Recently, I attended an international conference in Yugoslavia where doctors, quite competent ones, from Pakistan made a report on coronary heart disease in Karachi. There is some disease there, but relatively little. The physicians reported a difference in cholesterol levels between healthy people and coronary patients—with the levels averaging 160 for the healthy, 190 for the sick. In the United States, too, there is a difference in the levels—but the average for the healthy is about 230 and for the coronary patients about 260.

It seems that you have in each country a difference between levels for normals and for coronary patients—but what is typical in one country for CHD patients may be typical for healthy people in another country. What does this mean? That the influence of cholesterol on coronary heart disease is geographically dependent? I cannot explain it.

Q: But you do think cholesterol level is important—and that it is environmentally influenced?

DR. BRUNNER: I think it's important and I think it's environmentally influenced.

You know, Ancel Keys* once said to me: "Dr. Brunner, there are such disciplines as cardiology, gastroenterology, dermatology, and the rest. But you're starting a new one called Yemenology."

---

* Dr. Ancel Keys, distinguished American heart investigator.

So let's go back to Yemenology for a minute. When we first began to investigate the Yemenites, we found no differences in cholesterol levels between young boys of eighteen and nineteen and men of forty and fifty. Here was evidence that what is often claimed, that the increase of cholesterol with age is a biological phenomenon, is not true.

Go back and investigate Yemenites now and you find that, just as for the general Israeli population, there is an increase in cholesterol levels with age. In a population exposed to Western society, cholesterol does increase with age. But increasing level is not a geriatric phenomenon, not dependent upon aging—but upon exposure to environmental influences, notably diet, that increase the level. And the longer the exposure, the greater the increase.

Q: Dan, does your "Yemenology" reveal anything special of protective value that the Yemenites eat that maybe we ought to try?

DR. BRUNNER: No. You know, there was a story in Israel that maybe the spices the Yemenites use so much have special virtues. There is some folklore that one spice in particular, hilbe, is capable of healing just about all diseases. But we've investigated hilbe, analyzed it chemically, and found nothing at all unusual in it. One thing I can tell you: I've tried it and I think the taste is so bad that you would never eat it.

No, nobody has found that Yemenite spices of any kind have any influence on preventing disease. I truly believe that the most important point in favor of the Yemenites has been that they eat less. That small food intake is, with them, a custom. Or, at least, it was.

Q: What about the significance of triglycerides?

DR. BRUNNER: It seems to me that they are important—that elevated levels of them in the blood are indicators of trouble. American investigators have found them so; so have we in Israel.

Elevated triglyceride levels, as you know, can be brought

down. In some cases, the elevations are fat-dependent and the levels come down with reduction of fat intake. In some cases, they are carbohydrate-dependent and respond to reduced carbohydrate intake. Often, weight reduction brings them down.

Q: What of the role of sugar?

Dr. Brunner: I know there are good investigators, top-notch ones, who believe that the rise in coronary heart disease to epidemic proportions in recent years is traceable to a fabulous increase in sugar consumption. That could be. I wonder, though, if we can separate sugar out, without any doubt, as a prime malevolent influence. Who eats a lot of sugar? I think they could be the very same people who eat a lot of fats—the affluent people on rich diets. On a worldwide basis, I'd think of sugar as the food of the relatively rich man, with the poor man eating starch.

Smoking

Q: How do you regard smoking as a risk factor?

Dr. Brunner: Well, as you know, there have been many studies in the United States which indicate that it is a great risk factor. We have done some studies in the kibbutzim and propose to do more.

The kibbutzim provide an unusual opportunity for such investigations. In a kibbutz, any adult can draw weekly from supply as many cigarettes as he or she wants. If six packets are wanted, they're available; if fifty are wanted, they're available. And records are kept as a matter of routine. So if you're investigating smoking, you don't have to depend on what the smoker tells you he consumes. You have a written record going back years.

And so we investigated. It has been a relatively small study thus far and we need to expand it. But we have found evidence of a link between smoking and coronary heart disease.

In fact, we've produced what we call a "smoking index"—which represents the number of cigarettes smoked per day times the number of years of smoking. Thus, an index of two hundred could represent ten daily cigarettes over a twenty-year period or twenty daily cigarettes for ten years, for example. And we have found that the incidence of coronary heart disease goes up with increase in index.

EXERCISE

Q: Dan, I don't think there is any question but that you regard exercise—adequate physical activity—as a prime factor in combating coronary heart disease. If that's really so, why is it so?

DR. BRUNNER: Yes, there are many indications that the best way to reduce heart attack incidence or minimize the consequences if a heart attack does occur, is with physical activity. Time after time, study after study, in England, the United States and elsewhere—and certainly in Israel in the kibbutzim and other studies—activity, the nonsedentary life is what distinguishes the CHD-protected from the CHD-prone.

I think exercise is vital because it helps to control weight, control blood pressure, control blood fats and blood sugars. If it did no more, all this would be enough to make it a prime aid. But it does more.

Q: You mean the heart and circulatory system?

DR. BRUNNER: Those—and still more.

Look at the heart. It's a muscle. Any muscle degenerates when it isn't used. Now you might say that the heart is always being used—and that is so. But you can look at the heart as being in virtually an idle state when there is no physical activity going on. You exercise it when you exercise the body—when body demands put more demands on the heart. It's as if you're flexing the heart muscle when you exercise the body. And that, if done properly, is good for the heart. It tones that pumping muscle, gives it greater strength and endurance, encourages it to pump more blood with each beat, thus increasing its pumping efficiency. At the same time, exercise increases the heart's efficiency of use of oxygen. It becomes able to do more work with a given amount of oxygen or the same amount of work with less oxygen.

There's evidence, too, as you know, that exercise helps to open up collateral circulation, extra pathways for blood to reach and nourish the heart muscle. And if a coronary artery should be clogged, the collaterals may route blood around the clogged point, so it still gets to the heart, possibly avoiding an otherwise inevitable heart attack, or minimizing the effects of one if it does occur.

And then, on top of all this, there is the relaxation, the relief of stress and tension that exercise provides.

Q: You think that of major importance?

Dr. Brunner: I certainly do. I think physical effort is excellent relaxation. I wish I knew more of exactly how that works. I would like to investigate it. But I know that exercise does relax and soothe. And I know it not only from patients' experience but from my own.

I like to run rather long distances—six, eight, ten kilometers, which is up to about six miles. This is good physical effort. I would not recommend it to middle-aged people if they are not trained and prepared for such endurance activity. In Israel, there are good opportunities for such sport. You can run along the Mediterranean shore. If you are upset and go out for a good run, you will come home comfortably relaxed.

Q: That's a real run, Dan—not a jog?

Dr. Brunner: It's a real run. Ten kilometers—about an hour. You know, I think the difference between jogging and running is like the difference between artificial insemination and a love affair.

Q: You run regularly?

DR. BRUNNER: At least twice a week. You know, I'm an old Jew. Fifty-five. That's an old Jew. But I feel healthy.

Q: Does exercise, do you think, have any influence on aging?

DR. BRUNNER: When people ask me what I know about aging, I usually say I know only three things. First, that aging is a process you recognize much better in your neighbor than in yourself. Second, that there is an advantage in aging: our children grow more quickly when we grow old. And third, and most important, God has arranged the situation so that different organs grow old at different speeds. Seriously, I think exercise can have very beneficial effects on aging. Recently, with Dr. E. Jokl of the Exercise Research Laboratories of the University of Kentucky, I edited a medical book called *Physical Activity and Aging*. One of the most interesting contributions to that book, I think, was made by Dr. Hans Kreitler and his wife, Dr. Shulomic Kreitler of the Tel Aviv University Department of Psychology. I'd like to tell you a little about the Kreitlers' study.

Q: Please do. What was it called?

DR. BRUNNER: "Movement and Aging: A Psychological Approach." The Kreitlers' thesis is that while young people, especially children, enjoy movement for the sake of movement, in habitually sedentary older people this kind of pleasure is steadily reduced and they eventually may become reluctant to move at all. The inactivity not only leads to muscular degeneration but to distinct psychological changes, too. One of the changes is a distortion of the body image.

Physically inactive older people perceive their bodies as being broader and heavier than they actually are. They begin to experience bodily activities as more and more strenuous and that sets up a vicious circle in which progressive restriction of exercise leads to progressive alteration of body image which is followed by greater and greater clumsiness and fear of activity. I think you've seen this happen. It's characteristic of many aging people.

Q: Yes. And what then, Dan?

DR. BRUNNER: Well, as the Kreitlers put it, even though older people may be more interested in the emotional and intellectual spheres and find the conquest of them exciting, such interest and conquest do not involve the same discharge of energy as with bodily movement. And so there is an increase in internal tension. And it is this tension which creates geriatric symptoms such as insomnia of the old. The Kreitlers believe from their studies that fretfulness and restlessness, usually considered the cause of insomnia in the elderly, are in fact neurotic symptoms resulting from tensions due to physical inactivity. They find that such older people often turn their unreleased energies against themselves; that they experience a kind of internalized aggression which may lead to depression, which in turn may strengthen tendencies toward psychosomatic diseases or cause sudden outbursts of rage.

And the Kreitlers emphasize that regular bodily exercise can provide profound emotional satisfaction; it can break the vicious circle caused by distortions in body image due to prolonged inactivity, and it can reestablish a feeling of security.

I think their work is provocative, very much worth considering.

Q: You've done some studies on physical fitness in elderly people?

DR. BRUNNER: Yes. A colleague, Dr. N. Meshulam, and I did a study to check on a group of middle-aged and elderly men, all city dwellers, who participated regularly and over many years in an exercise program consisting of calisthenics and sports. You know, with advancing age, significant changes occur in the heart and blood vessel system but it is difficult to distinguish between the effects of aging and those of lack of exercise, for example, and we wanted to try to do this.

Q: And how did the study go?

DR. BRUNNER: Well, these were all middle-class men with a wide spectrum of occupations, ranging from very sedentary to moderate activity and manual labor. There were 45 men, fifty-five to seventy-one, and the only thing they had in common was that they were members of a health club and they exercised regularly for about half an hour a day or the equivalent per week.

We conducted fitness tests using a bicycle machine. Each test lasted six minutes and we started by braking the machine so the men had a workload that could be measured as 300 kilograms per minute and we gradually increased the braking until the workload was doubled to 600 kilograms.

We monitored the men carefully, taking electrocardiograms, blood pressure, pulse rate. If there were any abnormalities in these measurements, or if the men had any breathing difficulty, chest pain or felt exhausted, we stopped the test immediately.

And on the basis of the tests, we classified the men into three groups. Group A consisted of 21 who could complete a workload of 600 kilograms a minute for six minutes; B consisted of 17 who performed a workload of 600 for at least four minutes without having to stop or be stopped; C consisted of 7 who performed a workload of 450 kilograms per minute for six minutes.

When we took pulse rates at rest, those of the men in Groups A and B were significantly lower than for the men in C, indicating much greater heart efficiency. All in Groups A and B had normal blood pressure at rest; all in Group C had some elevation of pressure.

The men, we found, had lower cholesterol values than untrained men of comparable age. And while there was a decline of exercise tolerance with age, it was slight. Even in the age group sixty-five to seventy-one, 12 out of 17 men could perform at a load of 600 kilograms per minute for at least four minutes.

Q: What were your conclusions?

DR. BRUNNER: We came away from the study convinced that aging doesn't have to mean lack of fitness; that the elderly can be fit—and that regular training of just about 30 minutes a day seems to be sufficient to keep them in a state of high fitness and give them a feeling of well-being.

Q: You've also studied the influence of exercise on people with coronary disease—people who had had heart attacks. What happened?

DR. BRUNNER: Dr. Meshulam and I started with the idea that since the kibbutz studies had shown the incidence of coronary heart disease to be so much higher in sedentary than in nonsedentary people and also that there was a reduced death rate after a first heart attack in the nonsedentary, perhaps active reconditioning of coronary patients by physical exercises and sports might have a beneficial effect.

We began a project in 1966 and since then some 300 patients have participated in the twice-weekly exercise program. So far we have what we consider only preliminary results, but they are interesting.

When, for example, we compared the fitness of 42 patients who had participated in the program for at least one year with 42 others, matched by age, sex, and coronary history, who did not participate, we found the majority of the participants able to perform top workloads for six minutes in distinct contrast to the ability of the nonparticipants.

We did another comparison, too. In 64 patients who began to participate in the program three months after their first heart attack and continued for at least a year, there were two deaths and four second heart attacks during the year. None of the patients complained of severe angina during effort. On the other hand, among 65 comparable patients who did not participate, there were seven deaths and nine second heart attacks during the same period, and 30 patients complained of angina on effort.

Q: Any other aspects to the study?

Dr. Brunner: Yes. More recently, we tried a physical reconditioning approach in patients incapacitated by angina. They were getting severe chest pain after very short and mild effort. We treated them with daily exercises on a bicycle machine, beginning with a minimal workload and increasing the load step by step, always under close observation, including electrocardiographic studies. And we got remarkable improvement in the course of four to six weeks. In the beginning, the patients could perform the minimal workload task for less than four minutes. After six weeks, most were carrying four times that load for up to six minutes without pain.

Q: What do you think physical activity does in such cases?

Dr. Brunner: The mechanism isn't entirely clear. We have an idea. It could well be that while angina is caused by the heart muscle's lack of blood because of compromised coronary artery flow, the angina is actually compounded by anxiety. In other words, blood flow is compromised but it is adequate for a given amount of effort; beyond that amount angina develops. But with anxiety added, it takes far less effort to produce the angina. And we think that the psychological effect of the intensive reconditioning program alleviates conscious and unconscious anxiety and so angina appears only with far greater effort; it's no longer related to anxiety, only to effort and that real effort capacity, uncompromised by anxiety, is far greater than the patient ever thought.

Q: I take it that since you find exercise helpful even after a heart attack, you would not discourage sexual activity for patients who have had attacks?

Dr. Brunner: I certainly would not and do not discourage it. I think that one of the most important problems for the post-heart-attack patient is sex life—or rather, worry and inhibitions about it. It's a major problem—a stress factor for patient and spouse—and I've seen it often. I tell my patients emphatically: you may have to take it a little easier but you can have sexual intercourse. Don't abstain.

GUIDELINES ON EXERCISE AND FITNESS

Q: How do you think exercise is best approached by the average person? How can he go about getting maximum benefit from it?

DR. BRUNNER: He has to start, unquestionably, with a medical examination. It would be ridiculous to do otherwise, especially if he has been leading a sedentary life for a long time. In any case, it is wise to get a medical check, to make certain there are no immediate contraindications to starting a program of activity.

Q: Say the checkup is okay, what does he do?

DR. BRUNNER: I don't think it matters what activity he picks as long as it is an endurance activity—something continuous that works out not just a muscle or a small group of muscles but that provides a workout for the heart and the lungs. Walking, jogging, running, swimming—these are fine. So, after a bit of shape-up, can be tennis, volleyball, and other active sports. I would advise, except possibly for the very young, against contact sports. And, for older people, I hesitate even about tennis because it is competitive. A problem with sports like tennis is that the tempo is not solely dependent upon yourself but upon the opponent as well. Especially in coronary people, I do not like this. I prefer that they avoid competitive activities and set their own pace. I should add that I think bicycling is also an excellent activity—and I include use of a stationary bike at home. I think that a stationary bicycle can be particularly useful to people with limited time. Place the bicycle near a T.V. set and by the time you've watched the news, you have had a workout.

And running in place at home can be good exercise.

Q: Many people seem to feel that such activities are boring.

DR. BRUNNER: They can be, but they don't have to be. I have my best ideas when I'm running. I compose letters and speeches when I'm running. I couldn't stand running ten kilometers, an hour's worth of running, unless I could keep my mind running. Bicycling, running, jogging, walking, whatever —they don't have to be boring as long as your mind can be active.

Q: Could we put it another way, too, Dan? Some people are creative people; their business is to get ideas, create plans, etc. And they can be creative while exercising. Other people may not be creative or have any need for being. They might find that they can be creative, and enjoy being so, in the process of exercising. But if not, all of us love to fantasy—and so, many people could make the exercise time a fantasy time. Agree?

DR. BRUNNER: Indeed.

Q: More guidelines?

DR. BRUNNER: Whatever the activity, start slowly, work up gradually. Don't overdo the first day, the second week, or any time. If endurance exercising is to be of value for the heart and the lungs, it's necessary to work up to the point of feeling a little breathless. But it's not necessary to work up to the point of utter exhaustion. Exercise until you feel slightly out of breath. As the days go by, you can exercise longer or harder before the slightly out-of-breath feeling comes.

Q: Do you have any particular recommendation for a simple way to test for fitness?

DR. BRUNNER: Pulse rate return is good. It is not new but it is simple and, I think, dependable. It's just a matter of how long it takes the pulse to return to a rate of about 80. During activity, it may go up to 130 or 150. If it comes back to 80 or 90 in less than six minutes after activity is stopped, an individual is usually in good shape. And of course anyone can take his own pulse readily; no special equipment is needed.

Q: Dan, it would be nice, don't you think, if in this country, so urbanized and mechanized, we could have a kind of weekend kibbutz movement—places in the vicinity of cities where people could go on weekends, perhaps to rebuild farms or establish communities, to rough it, cut wood, do heavy physical work? And if such a scheme, which may sound implausible, could in fact succeed, would two days a week of heavy physical activity added to regular activity during the week be likely to make a real difference in the heart attack picture?

DR. BRUNNER: I think yes it would make a real difference. But I think there might be considerable difficulties in establishing such a movement to benefit sufficiently great numbers of people. Perhaps it would be more feasible to convince the great factories and offices to establish gyms and organize programs for workers before work or after work or during lunch hours. And perhaps communities or neighborhoods might be induced to establish such programs.

Q: You talked not so long ago about trying to get such community action in Israeli cities. Has anything happened?

DR. BRUNNER: We're working on that right now. We're making a start. We have convinced a few municipal administrations that there is merit in organizing mass sports for middle-aged people. We call the project the "forty-plus program."

We're going slow, experimenting many ways. We have the help of medical men and also of university sociologists and psychologists. We don't want to just start a program and hope it will work—start it on a big scale and if it doesn't work be set back for years. We are trying to determine the kind of program that would keep people interested and keep the drop-out rate low. Should the emphasis be on gymnastics or ball games? Indoor or outdoor activities? With men and women participating together or separately?

We have determined that people will have to pay fees. We think it's bad to give services without fees; it demeans the services. And there will be important services—provided by physical instructors from the universities and by doctors.

Our sociologists and psychologists are experimenting—to determine the best type of publicity or propaganda, how to approach people. Should they be approached on the basis of preventing heart disease or promoting health? To which appeal would they be more responsive?

We have chosen to begin, to do our first experimenting, in a small community near Tel Aviv. All school gyms have been put at our disposal. The community is sending literature to all citizens. Even before we've actually begun, we've had inquiries from other communities who have gotten wind of the project; they would like to start similar projects.

But we want to take it slowly and find out how best to do this. Maybe in a year or two we will have news for you. We think we're setting up a potentially important experiment in public health and we have high hopes of making it a pleasant experience for people which is the only way it could be successful.

13

Plan for Living: With a Guide Through the Maze of Gimmicks and Gadgets

---

What is the crux of our problem? How can we define it simply—with the kind of simplicity inherent in basic truths, and constantly astonishing to those who come upon them?

We have to recognize that in modern life we have been able to kill off many of the infectious plagues that once killed us early. But with our advances we have built up a degenerative plague that kills us a little later.

We have, at once, gone to two extremes because of our technological advances: we can and do eat luxuriously and we can and do live in a more and more akinetic, physically effortless state. And, in so doing, we have fostered a whole series of factors to destroy our hearts.

Analyze and what do you find?

Any propensity we may have for such disorders as hypertension and diabetes we encourage by eating too much and being physically active too little.

Atherosclerosis narrows our arteries, building up from fats— and the buildup is associated with excess of fats in the blood.

And we encourage this not only with diet but with lack of activity.

If stress is a factor, we often try—the phenomenon is common—to bury it with eating, but it is still there, under the surface. We have abandoned the activity that could help dissipate it, take the energy out of it.

We not only pollute the environment about us in many ways; we pollute our personal environment with smoking. Even as our hearts must work harder because of excess weight and blood pressure, we add to the demands through the heart-burdening influences of cigarette smoke while simultaneously, through the other influences of smoking, we reduce heart functioning capacity. There is much to be said for the likelihood that smoking, particularly in excess, is related to stress and to our failure to release stress through activity. And we keep busy with our hands, putting cigarettes to mouth, even as the evidence mounts that vigorous activity can reduce both the stress and the smoke craving.

What's open to us?

A basic change in way of life—and not too difficult, really, to make, because it involves moderation of excesses, not abandonment of pleasures.

We can eat—a bit less and a lot more wisely. And we can still enjoy eating.

We can find ways to be more active—and many of these can be little ways rather than formal sessions. Even the formal sessions can be more than rewarding physically; they can be mentally constructive and, for many of us, even creatively stimulating.

With these two alterations going for us, we can get rid of excess poundage; help bring down any elevations of pressure and keep them down; reduce elevated blood sugar levels, if present and prevent them if not yet present; and help release tension and stress.

Modern medicine has, indeed, much yet to learn. But it has something valuable to offer right now: increasingly sensitive and efficient tests to detect such heart-risk factors as elevated uric acid, blood sugar, and blood pressure—and when necessary, when they are beyond quick and adequate enough control by diet and exercise, medications to bring them under almost immediate control.

How Do We Start?

First, with a medical checkup—to accomplish many things.

Exactly where are we? How much atherosclerosis do we have? What are the levels of fats in our blood—and the levels of sugar and uric acid? And what is the blood pressure?

A checkup can uncover any immediate, hidden dangers. It can establish baseline values that can serve for future comparison, for measurements of progress.

It can determine if there is any need for specific, individual guidance for diet and activity. And if there is an emergency situation—say, a blood pressure level found to be so dangerously elevated that it must be brought down immediately to prevent serious damage—the emergency can be handled.

We can pass the burden of accurate measurements and comparisons and record-keeping to the doctor's office where they belong.

And we can then proceed to change, with good guidance, the record.

Sound Diet—And the Supermarket Minefield

The fundamental principles of good diet—the need for a proper balance between fats and proteins and carbohydrates; the need for variety; the need for moderation—have been detailed in earlier chapters.

We should note here some rather startling recent determinations that even in the broadest terms the diet of Americans has been deteriorating; that millions of even middle-class and upper-middle-class people are overfed but undernourished.

According to a recent government survey, "poor diets were found at higher income levels, even the highest." In a review of many studies made since 1950 of vitamin and mineral nutrition, physicians have found that "the nutrition of a significant proportion of the American public is inadequate and has become worse."

For the poor, nutritional deterioration is usually the result of lack of money to buy proper food. But for others, investigators report, the problem is that people are led or pushed into eating the wrong things through ignorance or confusion. They have only vague understanding of nutritional needs and the values provided by various foods—and the confusion has been increased by the flood of new foods and variations of old foods poured onto the market, usually with advertising campaigns that provide little nutritional information.

It is notable that a leading business newspaper was led to remark recently that "the flood of new food products has left even nutritionists bewildered. There are 'coffee creams' that contain no milk or cream, dried 'beef stroganoffs' that contain no meat, and a plethora of snack products whose nutritional values—if any—are uncertain. To find out just what they're eating themselves, many nutritionists report, they often have to write the manufacturer."

The newspaper also reported that according to one expert, "The American housewife entering a supermarket is, in a way, faced with a minefield for which she has no map."

Critics contend that snacks, soft drinks, and sweets are advertised more and more heavily. "In general, advertising promotes foods nobody needs and which are no good for you," declares Dr. Robert Mendelsohn of the University of Illinois College of Medicine.

One study indicates a 65 percent increase in the consumption of sweet foods over the period 1958 to 1968. Apart from what effect this may have on heart health, it is blamed in part for the dental decay epidemic among Americans, with one billion untreated cavities in 200 million mouths and with a need, for example, for army dentists to fill 600 cavities and pull 112 teeth for every 100 inductees.

As simple general advice, nutritionists are urging the public to eat a little bit of everything and not too much of any one thing. They are also urging that Americans cut down on the amount of sweet foods—candy, cake, pastry, and the like. They urge that housewives serve more green vegetables such as broccoli, spinach, and other leafy greens which are rich in the vitamins and iron many people chronically lack. They warn against overcooking vegetables which can destroy many of the natural vitamins.

That advice applies well to all of us determined to reduce heart attack risk.

At any weight, we need a sound, balanced, varied diet. If we're overweight, we need the same kind of diet but calculated to help produce weight loss in a reasonable period. As we've seen in earlier chapters, it should be calculated to make caloric input less than caloric output, and so the level of physical activity is very much a determinant of what the suitable level of caloric intake should be. Similarly, upon arrival at desirable weight, the weight can be maintained even as we eat more provided we maintain activity at a balancing level.

PHYSICAL ACTIVITY

Forget formal exercise for a moment.

For most of us, there are at least some opportunities every day, throughout the day, for little bits of action that add up in their good effects.

It's a matter of basic attitude, of recognition that it is all to the good to use the body as much as possible, and of seeking chances to do so.

Walk up and down a flight of stairs rather than take the elevator. If you have to go up or down six, eight, or a dozen or more flights, walk one or two or three of them and use the elevator the rest of the way. Walk part or much or sometimes all the way to the market, to the office. If transit dumps you at the office door, walk around the block before entering. If you have time for no more at lunch hour, take even just five minutes on a pleasant day for a walk.

Interrupt sedentary work with little bursts of activity, even if no more than getting up out of the chair and bending, stretching, moving about, flexing the arms, squatting, imitating a few golf swings. And if you don't have the privacy for that— though you may be surprised to find that you don't need it and that fellow workers will understand—take a trip to the lavatory.

As for formal activities, there are many possibilities. But let's understand the needs precisely.

DON'T RELY ON ISOMETRICS

If you want to be a "beach boy" with muscles bulging, you can choose such things as isometrics. These are the contraction exercises that work out a muscle by pushing or pulling against an immovable object such as a wall or by pitting it against the opposition of another muscle.

But they contribute nothing to solving the basic problem of building heart tone and endurance. Exercise any muscle and you strengthen that muscle. But isometric exercises, while strengthening biceps, triceps in the arms, and the like, don't help the heart or the lungs.

The heart and lungs are exercised by dynamic activities rather than static ones such as isometrics—by activities in which large groups of muscles participate and for longer periods. Among the many dynamic activities are walking, jogging, running, bicycling, swimming, tennis, volleyball.

Recently, many investigators—among them, Dr. Alexander R. Lind, chairman of the physiology department at St. Louis University's School of Medicine—have found that there is strikingly little increase in cardiovascular efficiency and little contribution to fitness for sustained dynamic exercise to be obtained from isometrics.

Moreover, while isometrics are safe for the physically fit, they may not be for others. Not long ago, Lord Moran, physician to Winston Churchill, told the story of Churchill's bringing on an episode of coronary insufficiency by straining to open a White House window during a 1941 visit. Such straining to budge an unmoving object is isometric activity, of course.

Isometrics also appear to be much more likely than dynamic exercise to produce rhythm disturbances in people who have coronary heart disease. Physicians at the University of Texas Southwestern Medical School, Dallas, have reported that almost one-half of a group of patients with coronary heart disease developed abnormal rhythms while undergoing a four-minute hand-grip isometric test whereas well under one-fourth of the same patients experienced any rhythm disturbances while performing dynamic exercise.

BEWARE GADGETS

Americans now spend more than $100 million yearly on exercise gadgets claimed to firm muscles and take off weight. They range in price from $1 to more than $1,000, and many require little or no effort on the user's part. Effortless exercises may be popular; their value, however, is another matter.

Physiologists and other authorities vehemently dispute the claims made for such devices. Not only do they provide no hidden benefits or values, as sometimes suggested; their most serious shortcoming is that most do little to improve the fitness of heart and lungs.

People use effortless exercising devices, thinking them an easy way of losing weight, for one thing, without realizing they have to use calories to burn fat. They don weighted belts and inflated belts even though, as authorities keep reminding them, spot reducing is merely pushing tissue fluid from one place to another and for any real reduction in total body weight there has to be a program of active exercise and diet.

Particularly in terms of preventing heart attacks, the need is not just to take off weight, even assuming this could be accomplished by some effortless means; the need is to take off any excess weight and simultaneously strengthen the heart, lungs, and circulatory system. By the very fact that an effortless exercise does not require active motion, it does not put healthful stress on heart, lungs, and other body organs.

But there is even more against exercise gimmicks that avoid exercise. They short-change the user of other values to be obtained from real exercise—the reductions in blood fat and blood sugar levels, the help in lowering elevated pressure, the aid to relaxation and anxiety-tempering.

ACTIVITIES TO CHOOSE FROM

Pick an activity—especially to begin with if you have been leading a sedentary life—that can gradually build up your endurance and stamina, that does not call for sudden tremendous effort but rather for a progressive increase in exertion. If many a flabby, unfit man has killed himself shoveling snow, for example, it was not because the shoveling intrinsically was dangerous, but because it involved sudden unprepared-for exertion. By starting slowly, easily, and progressing gradually to increased exertion, you can avoid pain and injury for muscles, joints, and your heart.

Later, if you like, you may be able to go on (once physically fit) to a sport you want to engage in that calls for playing with full speed and vigor—for example, soccer, basketball, handball, squash, tennis.

To build endurance and improve the condition of your heart and circulatory system gradually and safely, you need to choose an activity that provides repetitive movements. And it should be one you can engage in several times a week. So it helps to select an activity you can most readily fit into your schedule. It is all to the good if you can pick one you can use at any time of day or night—and one that, if necessary, you can engage in by yourself, without need for rounding up a partner or set of partners.

Among many activities that allow you to control the amount of exertion and to progress at your own rate are bicycling, hiking, skating, jogging, running, rowing, swimming.

Many people find that running in place has much to commend it. It can be done day in and day out, without regard to weather, at any convenient time, without special equipment. It can be done first thing in the morning before a shower, or at night before retirement, or at any other convenient time— in bedroom, bathroom, or anywhere.

One physician, Dr. Nathaniel Shafer of New York, favors indoor cycling for his heart patients. It could serve as well for those of us trying to avoid becoming heart patients.

As Dr. Shafer tells us: "When the patient with coronary disease is 'back on his feet' and regular daily exercise is considered essential to keeping him there, I prescribe indoor cycling, and the prescription is as specific as any written for his medication."

As Dr. Shafer notes, a patient housebound by wintry blasts or spring rains can exercise regularly on an indoor cycle. The exercise can be done at regular intervals throughout the day. If a patient is a busy executive, he can install a cycle in his office as well as at home and take his exercise on the job. While patients with back conditions may find some forms of exercise difficult, cycling seems to present no problem for them. And indoor cycling can be graded—so many minutes at so many miles an hour—gradually increasing with the individual's tolerance.

"Indoor cycles range in price from $40 to $300. My preference," Dr. Shafer says, "is for the inexpensive ones. A speedometer is the only extra equipment I favor. A friction device should be disengaged for the beginner. Later on it can be made operative if advisable. These cycles take up little room and can be set up in a living room, bedroom, or den, and can be easily hidden behind a screen or bookcase when not in use. A regular two-wheeler can be converted for indoor use by means of a special converter."

Dr. Shafer's procedure is to prescribe one-tenth of a mile at five miles per hour for one minute the first few days, then two-tenths of a mile, gradually increasing distance and time.

The same principle applies to other activities such as walking, jogging, running.

Don't Underestimate Walking

Walking is actually one of the best all-round physical activities. In their book, *The Magic of Walking* (Simon and Schuster, 1967), Aaron Sussman and Ruth Goode sing its praises this way: "Walking is the exercise that needs no gym. It is the prescription without medicine, the weight control without diet, the cosmetic that is sold in no drugstore. It is the tranquilizer without a pill, the therapy without a psychoanalyst, the fountain of youth that is no legend. A walk is the vacation that does not cost a cent."

They go on to add, "True walkers do not walk to make records or to win monuments. They walk for no reason but to enjoy the pleasure of walking. This may be the purely physical enjoyment of stretching muscles, expanding lungs, and the rhythmic relaxations from crown to toe in man's most natural exercise. Or it may be the psychological release of walking away from desk, telephone, automobile errands, shopping lists, the sheer dailiness of daily life, and enjoying the most available, least expensive of vacations, whether for an hour, an afternoon, or a weekend. It may be the esthetic and adventurous pleasure of seeing what one never can see except on foot, whether the course is along city streets, country roads, or wilderness trails. Any walk may be a blend of all these pleasures."

When you walk, the massaging action of leg muscles on the veins improves flow of blood back to the heart; when you walk, you improve not only your leg muscles but their pumping action. Develop a brisk step, swing the arms, breathe deeply—and, at once, you exercise many groups of muscles, the lungs, and the heart.

You can use a brisk walk, even a brief one, to discharge tensions, to get a change of pace, to set your thinking straight, and, before bed, as an aid to sleep.

On an occasional weekend, you can make walking a family enterprise, setting a goal—a walking tour to a park or other scenic area, or some place of historical interest.

Join—or Help Form—a Group

We can get the right kind of exercise on our own and, often, with other family members.

We can also participate in group activities.

The United States has lagged in any systematic, large-scale effort to reduce sedentary living. Ours differs from many other countries that maintain conditioning or recreation centers for their citizens and actively urge and encourage and make it more feasible for them to engage in physical activities habitually. The Soviet Union, for example, is a leader in this; it maintains 2,100 physical reconditioning centers and has 187,-

000 sports clubs with 33 million members. Czechoslovakia, East Germany, West Germany, Switzerland, Austria, and Israel also maintain physical conditioning centers.

Efforts in the United States have been less organized. The President's Council on Physical Fitness has actively worked to increase participation in physical activities for all ages. While participation by school children in school-supervised activities has gone up since 1961, participation by the adult population has been more difficult to assess. But groups are increasingly likely to be formed now; and we can help organize them and secure community cooperation for them.

Demonstrations of the values of group activities already are many. They've involved thousands of people willing to try to make what, in this country, has amounted to a pioneering effort, in addition to dedicated physicians and other health professionals willing to give their time and talents to showing what can be done.

For more than half a dozen years, for example, Dr. Herman K. Hellerstein and his associates of Case Western Reserve University, Cleveland, have made a fairly large-scale effort, as they put it, "to determine the feasibility and efficacy of activating *habitually sedentary, lazy, hypokinetic, hypercholesterolemic, cigarette-smoking, hypertensive, overweight males, with or without manifest coronary artery disease,* to participate in and adhere to a program of enhanced physical activity." (Italics are added.)

The subjects were 656 middle-aged, middle- and upper-class men. Thirty-two percent were physicians, dentists, engineers, lawyers, and other professionals; 22 percent were managers; 20 percent were businessmen and executives; 17 percent were salesmen; the remainder, semiskilled workers. Since the age of twenty-five, their body weight had increased an average of 19 pounds; 28 percent were at least 15 percent overweight. Seventy-two percent had behavioral characteristics of type-A personality. Four hundred and two were coronary-prone; 254 had coronary disease with either angina pectoris or a previous heart attack or both.

After each man was evaluated medically, a program was developed to enhance his fitness. The exercise prescription included walking, running, and calisthenics; and all men were advised to be physically active, to climb stairs, avoid use of elevators, walk whenever possible instead of ride.

Each subject was encouraged to attend exercise classes at the Jewish Community Center of Cleveland at least three times a week. Coronary-stricken subjects were carefully supervised during exercise by trained physical educators.

The men generally adhered well. Sixty-eight percent of them stuck with the training program, attending two or more hours a week, for an average follow-up period of 33 months. Others attended less often.

Improvement in fitness was determined by adherence. In the coronary-stricken, 86 percent of those adhering best showed marked improvement. Even among those with poorest adherence, 35 percent showed some improvement. The normal coronary-prone men showed a similar tendency for improvement to be related to adherence.

The results were analyzed in greater detail in 100 coronary-stricken and 58 coronary-prone men. The average loss of body weight was about five pounds in both groups. Cholesterol levels dropped an average of 21 points. Blood pressure reductions occurred. And in both coronary-prone and coronary-stricken, electrocardiograms showed distinct improvement.

Some of the individual men have demonstrated remarkable feats of performance. One forty-five-year-old executive, for example, with a previous heart attack, now runs five to ten miles several times a week and is in training for a well-known marathon race.

In another effort, Dr. George V. Mann and his associates of Vanderbilt University School of Medicine and the Department of Physical Education of George Peabody College for Teachers, Nashville, Tenn., recruited urban men, aged twenty-five to sixty, for a program of supervised activity.

The experimental program was publicized to men in six business, church, and social organizations. Those who responded were invited to a 6:00 A.M. clinic at which they were medically examined and tested for fitness on a treadmill. The 136 men were assigned randomly to five treatment groups of about 21 men each and the remainder were assigned to a control group and were asked to continue without a fitness program until summoned.

The subjects included professional men, white- and blue-collar workers, and a few laborers. The conditions of the program were expected to discourage the faint-hearted because they were asked to attend at least four of five training sessions each week. Four groups trained from 6:00 to 7:00 A.M. on Monday through Friday, and the other from 5:00 to 6:00 P.M. on those days.

The training, always led by an instructor, consisted of calisthenics and alternate periods of walking, jogging, and running. Each man was assigned to one of three intensity levels according to estimates of his competence based on physical examination and the initial treadmill test. These intensity levels were achieved by varying the cadence of activity. Thus, the men worked at different rates even though the activities were the same. Men were promoted to higher intensity levels as their proficiency increased. As fitness increased, the intensity of exercise for all the men was increased by diminishing the rest periods and making the exercise more strenuous. Each hour-long session was divided into a 15-minute warm-up period, 40-minute workout, and 5-minute recovery period.

Attendance and adherence varied among the groups. The men in group three, which was composed entirely of municipal firemen, were most enthusiastic at first but soon lost interest, and only 3 of the 24 completed the program. But in the other groups, 76 percent of the men stayed with the entire program, which lasted six months.

A questionnaire survey of men in the program at the end of the experiment showed that 96 percent would do it again. The improvement in fitness was marked and was associated not only with weight loss but also a reduction of cholesterol levels without dietary restrictions, and a significant fall in blood pressures. Older men, those in their fifties, showed changes just as favorable as those of younger men. One result of the program was the finding that only three training sessions a week are really necessary to produce measurable changes in fitness and in coronary heart disease risk factors. After such training, a lapse of two weeks or more will cause the benefits to disappear. But a trained person can maintain the improvements with as little as one intense training session per week requiring no more than 30 minutes.

The program demonstrated that both young and older men can be recruited and maintained in a fitness program. As Dr. Mann and his colleagues remark: "The enthusiasm encountered in recruitment and the adherence to a difficult regimen suggest that many men welcome an opportunity for systematic training. The reasons are numerous but the attractions of group training with leadership, in prearranged facilities, and with medical surveillance, seemed to be especially important inducements."

Here and there now, communities are beginning to aid in the setting up of programs that could become prototypes for use elsewhere.

In Glens Falls, N.Y., for example, a community-wide effort was inspired by Dr. Irving R. Juster, chief cardiologist of the Glens Falls Hospital, who enlisted the support of the hospital, board of education, Community Chest, local service clubs, and personnel directors of area industries. The aim was to develop an anticoronary program with physical reconditioning at a community level with a minimum of medical supervision and at low cost.

An initial group of participants consisted of 100 men, aged thirty to sixty, who joined with the approval of their personal physicians. Before being accepted, a man had to agree to attend the weekly two-hour supervised sessions of games, swimming, calisthenics, and other activities, perform daily physical activities at home, maintain his weight at a constant level, follow a low-saturated-fat diet, and stop smoking.

It was a seemingly tall order. But the board of education made available two gyms, a swimming pool, and funds to pay two physical education instructors for a year; the Community Chest supplied additional support. A physician was present during the first six sessions; after that close supervision was no longer necessary. And so successful was the project that within ten weeks another men's and women's group was started.

Because the public is beginning to be aware of how huge and serious the heart health problem is, it is no longer difficult to start a community anticoronary program. The need is to involve the whole community—medical profession, industry, education, clubs, etc. And the benefits even extend beyond those for the direct participants. For, as Dr. Juster points out, the publicity such a program generates causes many others to be more careful of their weight, diet, smoking, and exercise.

You may well find that, with the aid of a few interested friends or fellow-workers, you can get the ball rolling in your community.

Do It Before the Attack

If anyone of us were to get a heart attack today and survived it, we could count on a firm insistence by our physician that we embark on a program of caring for ourselves, that we make changes in our way of life in order to reduce our risk of having another attack.

And we would be frightened enough to try to do what we are told.

Why not now—in advance of an attack—to prevent the attack!

Not long ago, Dr. Thomas R. Dawber, who for many years directed the Framingham heart study and is now Associate Professor of Medicine and Program Planning Officer of the Boston University Medical Center, remarked that the treatment of many diseases that afflict us now—notably coronary heart disease but also many others including obesity, hypertension, diabetes, peptic ulcer, emphysema—is really as much up to the patient as the physician. Their prevention is even more so.

He noted that there are some wise people who, with due respect to *medical* care, are much more concerned with *health* care. To them, "the human body is a holy temple not to be defiled, a rule which if applied generally would have far more effect on the total health of our population than all the *medical* care we could possibly deliver."

That's what coronary heart disease is all about. It's not a transmissible disease, an infectious plague, or one to which we are doomed by heredity. It's the result of defilement. It's a disease we inflict upon ourselves—with the aid of our technology. But it's also one we can beat with our wits and our will.

The Whole Payoff

Beyond protection for your heart, the measures we've been discussing can help provide protection as well against strokes and kidney diseases stemming from atherosclerosis.

If they did no more, that would be plenty. But there are many dividends.

Many people discover that moderation in eating, replacing near-gluttonous shoveling in of food, actually adds to the enjoyment of eating.

Increased physical activity and the development of fitness bring diverse rewards: increased strength, endurance, and coordination; reduction of chronic fatigue; increased efficiency in performing both physical and mental daily tasks; reduction of minor aches, pains, stiffness, and soreness; correction of remediable postural defects; improvement in general appearance.

In addition to helping to prolong life, the fitness that comes from good diet, vigorous activity, and the other measures we have discussed prolongs the active years.

And when we set about achieving such fitness, we provide an endowment for our family. We become an example for health to our children and an example, too, of something else they can value—the ability of the individual to have some control over his destiny and not be a passive victim of circumstances.

14

What Hope for the Known Cardiac?

Even within the next hour, as things stand now, more than
125 men and women in the United States will experience heart
attacks; many others will go through the alarming experience
of a first attack of angina pectoris.

What do these people have to look forward to?

Until quite recently, the outlook for the known cardiac
patient was bleak. There was a pervading pessimism felt even
by many in the medical profession. It has been replaced by
optimism and activism.

The conviction now is that coronary heart disease, even
when manifested by severe angina and outright heart attack,
need not progress rapidly, inevitably to a fatal conclusion. Its
victims need not become invalids, withdrawn from life.

Not only are more and more heart attack patients being
saved from death that not many years ago almost certainly
would have followed their attacks, but they are being rescued
from death-in-living, and are being returned to work, to
sexual activity, to normal living. This is equally true for many
patients with even the most severe angina.

The very same measures worked out to help prevent the development of coronary heart disease and, when it is already under way, to help prevent its progress toward the angina and heart attack stage, are being applied with great promise even after the appearance of angina and heart attack.

In addition, for extreme cases, there are bold and promising new surgical techniques for revitalizing the heart. In the offing are heart transplantation techniques and artificial hearts, although there is increasing hope that with the use of immediately available measures there may be relatively little need for transplanted and artificial hearts.

Let's consider realistically the picture now for the known cardiac, beginning with the victim of angina and what can be done not merely to relieve the pain and frequency of attacks but also to help reduce very considerably the likelihood that a heart attack will occur.

Combating Angina Positively

At some point, coronary atherosclerosis, which has been a silent disease, may no longer remain so. The first terrifying attack of angina pectoris develops.

Almost 200 years ago, the English physician, William Heberden, described it succinctly: "They who are afflicted with it are seized while they are walking (more especially if it be uphill, and soon after eating) with a painful and most disagreeable sensation in the breast, which seems as if it would extinguish life, if it were to increase or continue; but the moment they stand still all this uneasiness vanishes."

Actually, angina pectoris—*angina* means suffocative pain, and *pectoris* refers to the breast—may make its first appearance and then repeated appearances not only as the result of exertion but of strong emotion. And the pain may not stay confined to the chest but may radiate to the fingertips, pit of the stomach, teeth, jaws.

What brings it on, as noted in Chapter 2, is clear enough. Atherosclerosis has been at work in the coronary system—in effect, rusting the heart-feeding arteries from within and diminishing the blood flow to the heart muscle. The process has been gradual but now has arrived at the point where, while blood flow is adequate for the heart to meet routine demands, any sudden extra demand may trigger angina.

It is not just a pain in the chest but the cry of the heart muscle. Not only is the heart not getting enough blood to supply its oxygen needs fully; the blood flow is not plentiful enough to carry away waste products. The waste product accumulation stimulates nerve endings; pain is felt.

An angina attack is brief. If chest pain continues for more than 15 to 20 minutes, it is not likely to be from angina. Usually, both the pain and the anxiety accompanying it are so intense the victim must stop activity immediately. The blood flow, inadequate for the activity, is now adequate when the victim is inactive, and the pain disappears.

Since 1879, nitroglycerin has been available to provide relief for angina. It appears to dilate the coronary arteries, increasing flow. It may also help by acting on other blood vessels in the body, reducing their resistance to blood flow and so easing the work of the heart.

Nitroglycerin is a remarkable drug—inexpensive and effective, and not likely to become less effective no matter how long used. Many physicians now advise patients to take a nitroglycerin tablet before doing anything they know is likely to trigger an angina attack. They may take it before going out into the cold, as a prelude to the sex act, as protection when they know they will be facing a trying business experience.

But there is much more that can be done for and by the person who has angina.

For one thing, every factor linked to the original development of atherosclerosis still operates in the person whose atherosclerosis has developed to the point of causing angina.

And there is still time to combat these factors—to prevent further inroads of the disease process.

For the angina victim who is overweight, appropriate calorie limitation to get rid of excess pounds can help. The heart does not have to work so hard if it need not pump a considerable amount of blood simply to feed excess fat. Moreover, the less weight the muscles and weight-bearing structures have to support, the less blood supply they need, further reducing the heart's burden.

Weight reduction also may help to reduce any blood pressure elevation and counter any diabetic tendency—and if reduction alone is inadequate for this, medication may be used. Change to a low-fat, low-cholesterol diet is indicated.

And now, too, there is increasing conviction among physicians that, however paradoxical it may seem at first blush to use exercise as treatment for a patient with angina, exercise may be of great help—especially when used with diet and other measures just mentioned.

This is why:

The coronary artery system, as noted in Chapter 2, has the capability of developing collateral circulation—new branch vessels and connections.

It is well-developed collateral circulation that seems to be the reason why some people, even though they have advanced atherosclerosis, live to seventy-five, eighty, and even longer without ever experiencing angina or a heart attack.

In their cases, fortunately, the formation of collateral circulation has kept pace with the atherosclerotic process. Even as blood flow through the major coronary vessels and branches is diminished, new collateral vessels form to bypass the narrowed areas and get blood through to the heart muscle.

Obviously, in the person who has angina, this has not happened. Atherosclerosis has advanced faster than collateral formation. But can the balance be redressed?

Suppose that with the help of weight reduction, low-fat

diet, and control of hypertension and high blood sugar if they exist, the atherosclerotic process is slowed. Suppose, too, that at the same time collateral formation can be speeded. The patient with angina could come out ahead. He might be freed of his angina. His risk of heart attack might be materially lessened.

How can collateral formation be speeded? There is evidence that exercise encourages the development of the new vessels.

But how can the person with angina produced by effort carry out any exercise?

In the past, under special circumstances, physicians have noted some seemingly remarkable cases. A man with great love for some activity—for example, golf—develops angina, refuses to give up the activity. Despite the angina, he tries to keep on playing. At first, he may play only one hole without triggering an anginal attack. But, persisting, he works up to the point of being able eventually to play 18 holes without an attack.

Is such activity dangerous? If carried to excess, it can be. Push hard despite the warning of angina and a heart attack may ensue. But go at the exercise gradually, starting very slowly, and there is a good chance that exercise tolerance will increase. Certainly, a patient who can become increasingly active will be happier than one who must remain an invalid or near-invalid. He may well be healthier, too.

And today many physicians are encouraging selected patients to become increasingly active.

Dr. Arthur M. Master of Mt. Sinai School of Medicine, New York, one of the nation's most distinguished cardiologists, has reported, after a special study, that patients with angina can learn to handle their angina constructively with a good chance of doing their hearts good.

Checking electrocardiographic records, Dr. Master has found that when a patient is put to exercising, feels an anginal attack is about to come on, and stops activity immediately, his electrocardiogram shows no abnormal changes. To that point, the heart has suffered no oxygen shortage. Let the exercise continue beyond that point, and abnormal changes do appear. Thus, impending angina is a warning that pain will follow if effort is continued.

Applying this to treatment, Dr. Master tells his angina patients to exert themselves but to stop the exertion the very moment they receive the slightest indication that chest pain is imminent. Patients become extremely discerning; they are able to sense that if they take even just another few steps chest pain will ensue.

And it is by being active, by refusing to become invalids, by exercising or engaging in other activities up to the point that angina is imminent, Dr. Master believes, that patients in time can improve their condition by stimulating the development of new collateral vessels.

While this, as Dr. Master notes, is still only a theory, he also notes that, "in a practical sense, the patient's condition frequently does improve, and he is gradually able to undertake more and more physical activity without having any symptoms. The success of this program is substantiated by the fact that we have never had to refer any of our patients to a cardiac surgeon for operation."

It must be emphasized that no patient with angina should undertake to start an exercise program on his own. It should be undertaken only with the approval and advice of a physician and with very careful attention to a very slow start and very gradual buildup. Perhaps the safest approach is to use walking, beginning at a slow pace and for limited distance, then gradually increasing the distance a little at a time, then gradually increasing (also very slowly) the pace of the walking.

RECOVERY FROM A HEART ATTACK

Heart attacks need not be fatal. Many are not. With prompt treatment, the vast majority of heart attack victims could be saved. Even after an attack, the heart may remain a strong organ—and may be made even stronger with measures now available.

Although a seemingly sudden event, a heart attack, as we know, is the result of a slowly developing disease process. And although it is a calamitous event, it often triggers successful body salvage maneuvers.

In an attack, as blood flow through a diseased and narrowed coronary artery or branch is shut off by a clot or debris, a part of the heart muscle supplied by that vessel suffers acute oxygen deprivation. It is the aching pain of this heart muscle area that is felt during an attack.

The pain continues while the damaged part of the muscle, not yet dead, tries to struggle along. Gradually, however, the muscle fibers in the damaged area stop contracting, swell, and die—and as this happens, the pain begins to disappear.

As this happens, too, healing starts. Whenever any part of the body is injured, leukocytes (white blood cells) are mustered. After a heart attack, they move in to engulf and remove dead muscle fibers. The clearing-away process, which is essential if remaining healthy heart muscle is to heal, may require a week or a little longer. During this time, there may be slight fever.

Other events are also taking place. The moment a coronary vessel actually becomes choked off, there is an intense stimulus for the development of new collateral vessels. Through them, blood is brought to the area around the site of damage in the heart muscle and the increased supply helps in healing. A dead area of heart muscle cannot be restored, but as healing takes place a scar forms, usually developing within the first two or three weeks after an attack. After another two to four weeks, the scar becomes firm and tough.

Many factors affect the outcome of a heart attack. One is the location of the artery blockage. Think of a river flowing hundreds of miles, providing water for scores of communities along the way. Suppose somebody thoughtlessly dams the river. Water for communities beyond the dam site would be cut off. If the dam is way upstream, many communities would be affected; if it is far downstream, few would be deprived.

The coronary arteries and their branches form an intricate network around and through the heart. A clot may lodge anywhere in the network and stop flow. If it blocks a main artery or a major branch, blood may be kept from flowing to the many smaller vessels that divide off—and a large portion of the heart muscle may be affected. If the clot blocks a small branch, only a small area of heart muscle may be affected.

Another factor is *when* the heart attack occurs. As atherosclerosis builds up over an extended period, collateral vessels begin to form. If the formation has had time to proceed to considerable degree before a blockage is produced by a clot, the collateral pathways may help to save much of the heart, making it a still viable organ.

Also, as the white blood cells are mustered, they may attack a clot, boring through and liquefying it. Sometimes, nearby vessels, growing to take on the blood circulation job, may even grow into a clot and help remove it. It is thus possible for a blocked artery sometimes to become unblocked.

Another mechanism may come into play. There are interconnections between coronary arteries through many branches and capillaries. Blood moves through arteries under pressure. Beyond a point of blockage in an artery, there is no longer any pressure. And, with normal pressure in unobstructed artery segments and no pressure beyond the site of blockage in the obstructed artery, there is a steep pressure gradient, tending to make blood rush over, crossing from good vessels, to enter the obstructed artery at a point beyond the obstruction. Thus, in effect, there is a built-in blood detour mechanism in the coronary system which may help save the day.

Indeed, it is sometimes possible, particularly when obstruction occurs in a minor coronary branch, for detoured blood to reach the small area of affected heart muscle quickly enough and in adequate quantities so that almost no lasting damage occurs. It may be this mechanism, in fact, that accounts for the many people who have silent heart attacks, so minor and producing so little discomfort that they remain unaware of them.

If there has been obstruction in a major artery, the detour mechanism may not provide enough blood in time to prevent serious oxygen deprivation for the heart muscle but it still may help to limit the damage and enable the heart to go on functioning.

The job of medical science today when a heart attack occurs is to give the coronary system a chance to adapt and the heart to heal, to tide the patient over while the adaptation and healing take place, and to prevent complications.

Pain relief, through a drug such as morphine, is important. Beyond its immediate discomfort for the patient, pain leads to spasm or contraction of the coronary arteries. It causes excess secretion of chemicals, called catecholamines, which increase heart rate and work; and it produces restlessness and excess activity. Relief of pain provides maximum heart rest.

Oxygen may be administered. It helps assure a richer supply for the heart muscle, diminishes pain, eases labored breathing, and makes the patient less restless. Bed rest in the early days after an attack also helps by reducing demands on the heart.

OVERCOMING COMPLICATIONS

For some patients, recovery after a heart attack goes smoothly. Others experience complications. There have been major strides recently in overcoming and even in preventing the more serious complications.

Sometimes, with injury to the heart muscle, there is a reflex nerve action which causes arteries distant in the body to open up wide. When this happens, blood pressure falls, the pulse rate shoots up, pallor develops. The patient is in what is called shock. Prompt treatment for shock with oxygen and other supportive measures, and with drugs to restore blood pressure, is often life-saving.

Another possible complication is pulmonary edema, or waterlogging of the lungs. This, too, can be treated effectively with medications, including morphine and digitalis. And a diuretic agent, which increases urinary excretion of fluids, may be used to prevent recurrences.

There is also the complication of irregularity of heart beat, or arrhythmia. There are many types of irregularity; some are of little consequence. They are fleeting, do no damage. But there are serious kinds which, in the past, have probably accounted for most deaths after heart attacks.

A major contribution of coronary care units, now to be found in thousands of hospitals, has been a great reduction in deaths from serious heartbeat irregularities. The irregularities may be set up by disturbances in the electrical pathways in the heart which may occur because of interference from a damaged section of heart muscle. If they are not checked, they can be fatal even though the heart is really still too good to die.

In coronary care units, patients are constantly monitored by means of electronic equipment so that there is immediate automatic warning when an irregularity develops. This permits prompt, effective treatment—sometimes with drugs, sometimes with electrical devices that instantly restore regular beat. Moreover, the monitoring picks up, in many cases, early, much less hazardous abnormal beats and allows them to be treated before there is any chance for the life-threatening irregularities to follow.

AVOIDING RECURRENCES AND INVALIDISM

Once a heart attack, inevitably another? Not inevitably at all. Nor is invalidism inevitable.

The heart has great reserve. Many heart attacks are relatively minor but even a massive attack may not so seriously impair heart function as to require invalidism.

One thing, however, is clear. With recovery from a heart attack, the underlying disease process—the atherosclerosis that led to the attack—is still a threat. And everything possible must be done to combat it.

For this, the same measures we have discussed earlier are very much in order. It is not too late to institute a change in diet, to abandon smoking, to treat any other problems such as hypertension or diabetes or gout that may be contributing to the atherosclerotic process. It is not too late to try to develop a more relaxed mental state and to get rid of excess weight.

And many physicians today encourage their heart patients to engage in physical activity once the damaged area of the heart has healed, and to work up gradually to quite vigorous activity, including sexual activity, and to return to work.

Many recent studies in this country have shown that after patients have recovered from heart attacks and have been carefully evaluated, medically prescribed programs of exercise are of great value. Dr. Herbert B. Rubin of the University of Southern California School of Medicine, for example, has reported that in the patient with healed myocardial infarct, exercise may increase work tolerance, decrease or relieve angina, and improve chances of surviving future attacks.

At a recent International Symposium on Coronary Disease, Dr. Henri Denolin of the Brussels Faculty of Medicine reported, "Early and continued physical retraining is extremely beneficial for coronary patients, and in particular for those recovering from a heart attack. Nearly 80 percent of patients without serious complications are capable of resuming their former or new activity after three months of rehabilitation."

Israel has produced evidence of the value of training for heart patients—for example, through an organization for rehabilitating them by carefully graded and ultimately strenuous sports activities. The organization, about which Dr. V. Gottheiner of Rhamat-Vhen recently reported, has been functioning since 1955. For several months, patients go through mild warm-up and strength-building exercises. Within about nine months, they qualify for systematic training in hiking, swimming, cycling, rowing, running, and volleyball. The program culminates in competitive team games. Of 1,103 trainees followed up for five years, only 49 died and in 9 death was due to a problem other than heart disease. That death rate of 3.6 percent compares with one of 12 percent for a comparable series of physically inactive heart patients in Israel.

RETURN TO WORK

Studies in Scandinavia, Britain, and Australia as well as the United States have shown that 72 to 88 percent of patients after heart attacks return to some form of employment, approximately 65 percent to their previous full-time occupation and 20 percent to either a part-time or a physically less demanding job.

Actually, recent studies indicate that many more could return to work. Not long ago, Canadian investigators checked on a series of patients recovered from heart attacks and found 81 percent back at work, happy to be, with obvious psychological as well as financial benefits for their families as well as themselves. When they also checked the unemployed, they found that over half need not have been out of work. They found that much of the disability of these men was functional, not organic—and due to inappropriate medical advice. "Misinterpretation of symptoms by the patient and his doctor," they reported, "is a frequent basis for unnecessary inactivity and subsequent failure to return to work." They urged physicians to discuss with patients the significance of heart attacks in relation to physical demands of work, to emphasize the therapeutic value of graduated activity, and to be aware of the need for continued patient counseling.

Except for the relatively uncommon instances of real and severe physical disability after a heart attack, patients can be happier—and may well be healthier—by returning to work.

SEXUAL ACTIVITY

The importance of the sexual act goes far beyond mere physical expression. It has great and profound symbolic significance and, for this reason, as two distinguished American heart researchers, Drs. Herman K. Hellerstein and Ernest H. Friedman note, "Deprivation or loss of this function due to heart disease may be catastrophic."

Recently, they have reported one of the most thorough studies ever made of the conjugal sexual activities of men who had suffered heart attacks. They used electrocardiograms to monitor the men, both during work and sexual activities.

They found that the cardiovascular cost of sexual activity— in terms of heart rate, oxygen use, and electrocardiographic changes—was relatively low. In fact, it was comparable to that of many other longer lasting daily living and ordinary work activities well tolerated by most postcoronary patients.

They found that over 80 percent of postcoronary patients can fulfill the demands of sexual activity, as well as a majority of jobs, without symptoms or evidence of significant strain.

They also found that sexual activity could be influenced favorably by increasing fitness through systematic physical training. Among men who developed angina during sexual activity, two-thirds showed a marked decrease in the frequency and severity of anginal symptoms after participating in a physical conditioning program.

REVITALIZING SURGERY

There are some patients with such far-advanced coronary heart disease that they suffer from unyielding angina which makes invalids of them or they experience repeated heart attacks.

For many of them, there may be new hope now in the major advances recently made in heart-revitalizing surgery.

Not long ago, for example, a fifty-year-old man was wheeled into an operating room after having suffered six heart attacks. For nine hours, surgeons worked to rehabilitate his seemingly doomed heart. As the result of his attacks, part of his weakened heart had ballooned out. The ballooned-out section was the size of an orange. The surgeons cut it away and stitched together the remaining relatively healthy heart muscle. They removed a vein from one of his legs, cut it in two, and grafted the two sections so they bypassed severely obstructed areas in two coronary arteries. They went on to implant an artery moved over from the chest wall (where it wasn't urgently needed) into a tunnel made in the heart muscle—as another means of getting more circulation to his starved heart.

Today, he is back at work full time. Unable before to take even a few steps without angina, he now keeps himself in trim with a daily exercise routine in which he jogs, does pushups, situps, and toe touches.

He is one of the beneficiaries of a bold new approach to helping patients, many of whom not long ago would have been considered beyond hope unless heart transplantation could be made successful or an artificial heart became a practical reality.

Modern surgical efforts to combat advanced coronary heart disease go back as far as 1929 when Dr. Claude Beck tried irritating the heart with talc and scraping procedures, hoping to stimulate new blood channel formation. The amount of increased blood flow, if any, could not be determined.

In 1946, Dr. Arthur Vineberg of the Royal Victoria Hospital, Montreal, thought of using the internal mammary artery as a new source of blood for the heart. The artery runs down in back of the chest wall. It supplies certain chest areas with blood. Because other arteries also supply the areas, the internal mammary could be spared. Dr. Vineberg freed it from its attachments and placed it in a tunnel made in the wall of the left ventricle, the hardest-working part of the heart which pumps blood out into the main trunk, the aorta, and then to the whole arterial system of the body. The hope was that when so implanted the internal mammary might become hooked up with unblocked branch coronary arteries and thus provide blood through a new network. Over the years Dr. Vineberg has been able to show that this often does happen. It may take as long as six months, however, before the hookup is established and the patient benefits.

Other surgeons sought ways to provide more immediate help for patients who might not survive that long. They opened a blocked segment of coronary artery and reamed out clogging material. In another technique, they slit an artery, left the clogging material in place, and grafted a patch of vein on to enlarge the vessel, on the gusset principle well known to seamstresses. But both procedures had limited use—in the relatively few cases in which obstruction was confined to only a short length of artery.

In May, 1967, Dr. Rene G. Favaloro of the Cleveland Clinic developed a saphenous vein graft technique. The saphenous vein is a large vein running the length of each leg. It returns only about 10 percent of the blood in the leg to the heart. It can be spared and other veins can take over its work. In fact, this is the vein often removed in varicose vein surgery. Dr. Favaloro removed a segment of diseased coronary artery and interposed a section of vein to restore continuity. This technique was soon followed by another in which one end of a saphenous vein was inserted into the aorta and the other beyond a point of obstruction in a coronary artery.

But still only a limited number of patients could be helped. Two main coronary arteries, a right and a left, come off the aorta. The right runs a moderately long course down the front of the heart before dividing into two main branches, one of which continues down while the other goes around to the back. The left coronary runs a short course and divides into an anterior descending branch which supplies the front part of the heart, and another branch, the circumflex, which goes around to the back.

In vein grafting, surgeons had been able to bypass blocks high up in the right coronary artery, a relatively easy area to reach. Also, the artery diameter is larger here and stitching a vein to it is a less formidable task. But while such bypasses help 5 to 10 percent of patients, others have obstructions lower down and often in both left and right coronary arteries.

Then, one day in July, 1968, Dr. W. Dudley Johnson of Marquette University faced a grave emergency during a heart operation. His patient had an aneurysm, a ballooned-out portion of the front of the left ventricle. Undernourished muscle had softened and bulged and was impairing the ventricle's pumping action. Johnson had removed the aneurysm when suddenly the diseased right coronary artery closed off at a point around in back of the heart. With its back wall no longer receiving blood, the ventricle could not contract. The patient was still on the heart-lung machine, which temporarily takes over the work of heart and lungs, but could not come off the machine. There was only one hope: a long vein graft from the aorta to a clear, unblocked portion of the small right coronary artery branch in back of the heart. It worked.

Johnson had attached the vein to a tiny coronary branch— a vessel only 1½ millimeters in diameter ($\frac{6}{100}$ inch). If that could be done in back of the heart, it should be possible elsewhere, in front of the heart. If an artery had a major obstruction high up but also had smaller blocks lower down, it should be possible to go beyond the last diseased segment and graft to healthy vessel where the diameter might be as small as 1½ millimeters.

Johnson tried, was successful in patients with right coronary artery disease and then in those with left coronary artery disease. In November, 1968, another forward step was the first double bypass. Within 11 months after that, 90 patients had been given double and triple vein bypasses. In many cases, too, aneurysms had been removed. The mortality, 22 percent, was high but acceptable since almost half the patients would have been considered candidates for transplantation and at that time only 23 of 153 heart transplant recipients throughout the world survived. More recently, mortality has been reduced to 7 percent.

Before being considered for operation, a patient is studied with x-ray movies. Under local anesthesia, a catheter—a slender, flexible tube—is inserted into a vessel at the crease of the elbow and carefully maneuvered up to a coronary artery. A dye is then injected through the catheter. Quickly, the dye reaches the coronary artery and quickly is washed away. But x-rays are taken and a movie camera records the fleeting events appearing on an x-ray image amplifier. When the movies are studied later, they reveal any areas where there is any interference to the flow of the dye, a sign of artery narrowing.

It will require years before there can be a definitive evaluation of the results of such operations. The immediate results are clearly promising. The operations are now being performed by surgeons in many major medical centers. Most patients show marked, often dramatic improvement. The questions yet to be answered are, how much long-term benefits do patients derive, and how long-term are they?

Even at best, surgery can only be palliative. The scalpel may help to overcome consequences of atherosclerotic disease but it does not end the disease process. The real solution to coronary heart disease must lie in preventing it to begin with or preventing its progression when it already exists.

HEART TRANSPLANTATION

Man has long dreamed of a time when diseased or damaged body organs could be replaced with healthy ones. Recently, at least part of the dream has become reality. Kidney transplants now are used for patients otherwise doomed to die of irreversible kidney damage. Corneas of the eye have been transplanted successfully.

The first heart transplantation, which took place in Cape Town, South Africa, in December, 1967, using the heart of a girl automobile accident victim, added 18 days to the life of a man dying of an irreversible heart condition.

Since then there have been more than 100 heart transplantations—always in desperate cases, usually with brief benefits, occasionally with extension of life for a year or longer.

The problem is not with surgical technique but with rejection, the body's blind fight to slough off anything foreign to it.

Many years of laboratory research preceded the first human heart transplant. Repeatedly, animal hearts had been transplanted with successful immediate results. A dog with a damaged heart, for example, could be placed on a heart-lung machine, the bad heart removed, a healthy heart from a donor dog could be stitched in place. With one quick electric shock, the donor heart could be made to start beating effectively.

As a technical procedure, human heart transplantation was expected to be even simpler than dog heart transplantation since the human aorta is sturdier than the dog aorta. If a dog aorta could be connected up to a transplanted heart, it seemed likely that the human aorta could be.

Moreover, hearts had been removed from people dying of massive brain injuries, perfused with blood, stored for an hour, then made to beat again.

As expected, when the Cape Town operation was performed, there was less trouble than with dogs. But as expected the big problem was rejection.

Rejection is part and parcel of a body protective mechanism. When infectious organisms gain entry into the body, the defense system is alerted by antigens, chemicals produced by the organisms. White blood cells, or lymphocytes, are rushed to the site. The lymphocytes produce antibodies, chemicals able to lock onto and destroy the invading organisms.

But the same system goes into action when a heart, kidney, or other organ is transplanted. Organ cells, like bacterial or viral cells, produce antigens, inviting destruction by antibody-producing lymphocytes.

At first, briefly, an implanted organ may function well. It has a healthy pink look. But then, as lymphocytes attack, the organ begins to swell. Eventually as an army of lymphocytes infiltrate and overwhelm the transplanted tissue, the graft stops functioning, shrivels, and dies. The organ has been rejected.

Transplantation efforts had long foundered because of rejection. It was not until December, 1954, that Dr. Joseph E. Murray in Boston achieved a successful internal organ transplant—a kidney donated by one identical twin and implanted in the other. Being identical twins, the brothers were identical in genetic makeup, and an organ from one was not regarded by the body of the other as foreign. The first successful transplant of a kidney between nonidentical twins came in 1958—and two more years went by before there was a successful transplant between less closely related donor and recipient.

Hoping to prevent rejection, surgeons used massive doses of radiation. But as the radiation destroyed the tissues that produce lymphocytes, the patient was left without defense against disease germs, prone to death from pneumonia or other infection.

Then, cortisone-like agents such as prednisone and some anticancer chemicals such as Imuran were found to help suppress rejection. Combining such agents with low-dosage radiation, surgeons tried to find a happy medium, some combination that could keep a kidney or other organ from being rejected without so impairing body defenses that the patient died of infection. It was an elusive goal.

Matching—for better compatibility between donors and recipients—could help. Blood typing is a familiar form of matching. Before a blood transfusion, red cells of the recipient are classified so donor blood with the same type of cells can be used to avoid transfusion reaction, a kind of rejection process. For transplantation, blood typing was of limited value but a step in the right direction.

White cells are more helpful for transplantation matching. The idea behind matching is that the closer the compatibility between organ donor and recipient, the less rejection-suppressing treatment will be needed and so the less likelihood of death from infection.

As matching techniques have improved, there have been heart transplant patients who have survived for a year or more. Currently, there is intensive research to improve matching techniques further, and to find other useful methods of combating rejection. Among many possibilities being explored is the development of special serums that introduce antibodies directed against the lymphocytes that turn out the antibodies directed against transplanted organs.

Human heart transplantation remains an investigative procedure. Undoubtedly, there will be advances in overcoming the rejection problem. The day may come when heart transplantation can be counted upon as a practical procedure. But there is increasing optimism among many surgeons that the need for transplants may be greatly limited by current vein-bypassing techniques and refinements of these techniques yet to come. The need may be further limited if a successful artificial heart can be developed.

THE ARTIFICIAL HEART

More than two dozen types of artificial hearts developed at various centers have had preliminary trials in animals. In each, the operating principle is the same as that of the natural organ: alternate compression and relaxation of blood-filled chambers. The devices are essentially mechanical pumps that try to duplicate the actions of the right and left sides of the natural heart.

The feasibility of substituting a mechanical pump for the human heart was demonstrated with the advent of the heart-lung machine, now in daily use in operating rooms around the world. The machine has shown that a mechanical substitute can provide adequate circulation for at least a few hours. But the development of a mechanical substitute capable of maintaining circulation for years is yet to be achieved.

Actually, three difficult problems must be solved. When blood comes in contact with any surface other than the lining of the heart or blood vessels, its vital elements are gradually destroyed. Many efforts have been made to prevent these destructive changes by using different types of lining for the artificial heart but no lining yet tried has prevented them satisfactorily. A flocked Dacron surface, for example, very nicely lends itself to infiltration by blood material so that it soon presents a more-nearly natural surface that greatly reduces destruction. Unhappily, such a surface keeps on building, thickening until it ultimately blocks the pump.

A second problem has to do with the proper control of the output of the right and left ventricles of the mechanical heart —with the stroke volume and balancing of the two sides of the heart. An automatic control is needed and much work will have to be done before such a control can be developed.

The third major problem is the power source. Several possibilities are being pursued experimentally. They include high-capacity, long-lived batteries to be implanted in the body; thermoelectric devices that would convert body heat to electricity; other devices that would convert motion, such as the movement of the rib cage during breathing, into electricity. A nuclear-powered battery eventually may be the answer. The possibility of transmitting energy across the skin from an outside source also is under study.

BOOSTER HEARTS

Closer to practical reality are booster hearts designed not as replacements for, but as aids to, sick hearts.

There are several such devices which promise to save many lives by taking over part of the job of an ailing heart for hours, days, or weeks.

The left ventricle, which is the heart's main pumping chamber, moves oxygen-bearing blood out to the body. Any heart disease that undermines the efficiency of the left ventricle can be critical. Most heart attacks inflict some damage on the left ventricle.

One booster heart, called a left ventricle pump, is a chamber about the size of an apple, with a flexible membrane. During open-heart surgery, it can be connected up so blood flows into it, bypassing the ailing left ventricle. Gas is pumped in to move the membrane and the device does the work of the left ventricle and gives it a chance to recover.

Another booster heart works with, instead of in place of, the left ventricle. It's a rigid case containing a flexible inner lining which can be made to collapse and expand by means of gas flow. The device is connected across the arch of the aorta so that blood flows through it after leaving the ventricle. As the left ventricle pumps out the blood, the booster heart expands to receive the blood—and since the ventricle now is pumping blood into an agreeably expanding chamber, it can pump much more easily. The booster, activated by a pulse of gas, then pumps the blood onward.

Still another device, the balloon pump, consists of a balloon on the end of a long tube which is attached to a pump. Balloon and tube are inserted into a leg artery and pushed upward into the aorta. The system is timed to allow the balloon to collapse as the ventricle pumps blood and, as with the rigid case device mentioned above, the collapsing makes room so that the ventricle can pump blood more easily. Then, in the next phase of the cycle, the balloon is inflated to pump the blood onward.

Before the era of coronary care units, heart rhythm abnormalities were the chief cause of death in hospitalized heart attack victims. Now that dubious honor has fallen to cardiogenic shock, or pumping failure. If, during the critical period when the heart is in shock, it could be assisted in its work, its load lightened, there might be a better chance for the patient to survive and for the heart to recover its efficiency.

In one of its first human trials, the balloon assist device was used for a forty-five-year-old housewife who, after being hospitalized for a heart attack, went into cardiogenic shock. She lost consciousness; her blood pressure slipped almost to the vanishing point. She was expected to die within less than 30 minutes when the balloon system was inserted through a leg artery. As it began to function, she came out of shock and regained consciousness. Five hours later, the device could be removed. The woman left the hospital alive and well.

Not all patients can be expected to respond as well. When damage to the heart has been very extensive, it may not be able to recover its pumping efficiency. In early trials with more than 20 other patients, the balloon assist did bring all out of shock. About half recovered; the others eventually died because their hearts had been too severely damaged. But a 50 percent recovery rate is a notable achievement.

So booster hearts, especially as they are further refined, promise to be life-savers in themselves for many patients. And, as heart transplants become more practical or when a complete artificial heart is developed, the boosters may save many more patients by supporting them until a transplant can be achieved or an artificial heart inserted.

APPENDIX I

Table of Spending Calories

Activity	Calories per hour
REST AND LIGHT ACTIVITY	
lying down or sleeping	80
sitting	100
driving a car	120
standing	140
domestic work	180

Activity	Calories per hour
walking (3¾ mph)	300
badminton	350
horseback riding (trotting)	350
square dancing	350
volleyball	350
roller skating	350

MODERATE ACTIVITY	
bicycling (5½ mph)	210
walking (2½ mph)	210
gardening	220
canoeing (2½ mph)	230
golf	250
lawn mowing (power mower)	250
bowling	270
lawn mowing (hand mower)	270
fencing	300
rowboating (2½ mph)	300
swimming (¼ mph)	300

VIGOROUS ACTIVITY	
table tennis	360
ditch digging	400
ice skating (10 mph)	400
wood chopping or sawing	400
tennis	420
water skiing	480
hill climbing (100 ft. per hour)	490
skiing (10 mph)	600
squash and handball	600
bicycling (13 mph)	660
scull rowing (race)	840
running (10 mph)	900

NOTE: The caloric expenditures shown in the above table are for an individual weighing 150 pounds. The heavier the person, the more calories expended in each activity.

APPENDIX II

Common Foods and Their Cholesterol Content

The tabulation below shows the cholesterol content in milligrams of 100-gram (3½-ounce) portions of common foods:

Beef, raw	70	Ice cream	45
Brains, raw	2,000-plus	Kidney, raw	375
Butter	250	Lamb, raw	70
Caviar or fish roe	300-plus	Lard and animal fat	95
Cheddar cheese	100	Liver, raw	300
Creamed cottage cheese	15	Lobster meat	200
Cream cheese	120	Margarine, vegetable fat	0
Cheese spread	65	Margarine, ⅔ animal fat	65
Chicken, raw	60	Milk, whole	11
Crab	125	Milk, skim	3
Egg whole	550	Mutton	65
Egg white	0	Oysters	200-plus
Egg yolk, fresh	1,500	Pork	70
Egg yolk, frozen	1,280	Shrimp	125
Egg yolk, dried	2,950	Sweetbreads	250
Fish fillet	70	Veal	90
Heart, raw	150		

Caloric Content of Foods and Beverages

Foods	Amount	Calories
SOUP		
Bouillon or consommé	1 cup	30
Cream soups	1 cup	150
Split-pea	1 cup	200
Vegetable-beef or chicken	1 cup	70
Tomato	1 cup	90
Chicken noodle	1 cup	65
Clam chowder	1 cup	85
MEAT AND FISH		
Beef steak	3 oz.	300
Roast beef	3 oz.	300
Ground beef	3 oz.	245
Roast leg of lamb	3 oz.	250
Rib lamb chop	1 medium	130
Loin pork chop	1 medium	235
Ham, smoked or boiled	2 slices	240
Bacon	2 strips	100
Frankfurter	5½″ x ¾″	125
Tongue, kidney	average portion	150

Foods	Amount	Calories
Chicken	6 oz.	190
Turkey	3½ oz.	200
Salami	2 oz.	260
Bologna	4 oz.	260
Veal cutlet (unbreaded)	3 oz.	185
Hamburger patty	3 oz.	245
Beef liver, fried	2 oz.	130
Bluefish, baked	3 oz.	135
Fish sticks, breaded (with fat for frying)	4 oz.	200
Tuna fish, canned, drained	⅖ cup	170
Salmon, drained	⅔ cup	140
Sardines, drained	4 oz.	260
Shrimp, canned	4 to 6	65
Trout	average portion	250
Fish (cod, haddock, mackerel, halibut, white, broiled or baked)	average portion	190
Whole lobster	1 lb.	145
VEGETABLES		
Asparagus	6–7 stalks	20
Beans, green	½ cup	15
kidney	½ cup	335
lima	½ cup	80
Beets	½ cup	30
Broccoli	1 large stalk	30
Cabbage, raw	½ cup	12
cooked	½ cup	20
Carrots	1 medium or ½ cup	25
Cauliflower	½ cup	15
Celery	1 large stalk	5
Corn	5″ ear or ½ cup	70
Cucumber	½ medium	5
Eggplant	2 slices or ½ cup	25
Green pepper	1	20

Foods	Amount	Calories
Lettuce	3 small leaves	3
Peas	½ cup	55
Potato, sweet	1 medium	200
white	1 medium	100
Potato chips	10	100
Radishes	2 small	4
Spinach	½ cup	25
Squash, summer	½ cup	15
winter	¼ cup	45
Tomato, raw	1 medium	30
canned or cooked	½ cup	25
FRUITS		
Apple	medium	75
Applesauce, unsweetened	½ cup	50
sweetened	½ cup	95
Apricots, raw	2 to 3	50
canned or dried	halves, 4 to 6	85
Avocado	½ small	250
Banana	medium	85
Cantaloupe	⅓ medium	35
Cherries, fresh	15 large	60
canned, syrup	½ cup	100
Cranberry sauce	½ cup	250
Fruit cocktail, canned	½ cup	90
Grapefruit	½ medium	55
Olive	1 large	8
Orange	1 medium	70
Peach, fresh	1 medium	45
canned, syrup	2 halves, 1 tbsp. juice	70
Pear, fresh	1 medium	45
canned, syrup	2 halves, 1 tbsp. juice	70
Pineapple, canned, with syrup	1 slice	90
Plums, fresh	2 medium	50
canned, syrup	2 medium	75
Prunes, cooked with sugar	5 large	135

Foods	Amount	Calories
Raisins, dried	½ cup	200
Tangerine	1 large	45
CEREAL, BREAD, CRACKERS		
Puffed wheat	1 cup	45
Other dry cereal	average portion	100
Farina, cooked	¾ cup	100
Oatmeal, cooked	1 cup	135
Rice, cooked	1 cup	200
Macaroni or spaghetti, cooked	1 cup	200
Egg noodles, cooked	1 cup	100
Flour	1 cup	400
Bread, white, rye or		
whole wheat	1 slice	70
Ry-Krisp	1 double square	20
Saltine	1, 2″ square	15
Ritz cracker	1	15
Biscuit	1, 2″ diameter	110
Hard roll	1 average	95
Pancakes	2 medium	130
Waffles	1 medium	230
Bun, cinnamon with raisins	1 average	185
Danish pastry	1 small	140
Muffin	1 medium	130
DAIRY PRODUCTS		
Whole milk	1 cup	160
Evaporated milk	½ cup	170
Skim milk	1 cup	90
Buttermilk (from skim milk)	1 cup	90
Light cream, sweet or sour	1 tbsp.	30
Heavy cream	1 tbsp.	50
Yoghurt	1 cup	120
Whipped cream	1 tbsp.	50
Ice cream	⅛ quart	200
Cottage cheese	½ cup	100
Cheese	1 oz. or 1 slice	100
Butter	1 tbsp.	100
	1 pat	60

Foods	Amount	Calories
Egg, plain		80
fried or scrambled		110

CAKE AND OTHER DESSERTS

Chocolate layer	½₂ cake	350
Angel	½₂ cake	115
Sponge	2" x 2¾" x ½"	100
Fruit pie	⅛ pie	375
Cream pie	⅛ pie	200
Lemon meringue	⅛ pie	280
Chocolate pudding	½ cup	220
Jell-O	1 serving (⅙ pkg.)	65
Fruit ice	½ cup	145
Doughnut, plain	1	130
Brownie	2" square	140
Cookie, plain	3" diameter	75

MISCELLANEOUS

Sugar	1 level tbsp. or 3 level tsp.	50
Jam or jelly	1 level tbsp.	60
Peanut butter	1 tbsp.	100
Catsup or chili sauce	2 tbsp.	35
White sauce, medium	¼ cup	100
Brown gravy	½ cup	80
Boiled dressing (cooked)	1 tbsp.	30
Mayonnaise	1 tbsp.	100
French dressing	1 tbsp.	60
Salad oil, olive oil, etc.	1 tbsp.	125
Margarine	1 tbsp.	100
Herbs and spices		0
Chocolate sauce	2 tbsp.	90
Cheese sauce	2 tbsp.	65
Butterscotch sauce	2 tbsp.	200

SNACKS

Chocolate bar	1 small	155
Chocolate creams	1 average size	50
Popcorn	1 cup popped	55

Foods	Amount	Calories
Potato chips	10 or ½ cup	100
Peanut or pistachio nut	1	5
Walnuts, pecans, filberts, or cashews	4 whole	40
Brazil nut	1	50
Butternut	1	25
Pickles	1 large sour	10
	1 average sweet	15
Chocolate nut sundae		270
BEVERAGES		
Chocolate milk	8 oz. glass	185
Cocoa made with milk	1 cup	175
Ice cream soda		255
Chocolate malted milk	1 glass	450
Eggnog (without liquor)	1 glass	235
Tea or coffee, plain		0
Apple juice or cider	½ cup	65
Grape juice	½ cup	90
Cola drink	8 oz.	95
Ginger ale	8 oz.	70
Grapefruit juice, unsweetened	½ cup	40
Pineapple juice	½ cup	55
Prune juice	½ cup	85
Tomato juice	½ cup	25
ALCOHOLIC BEVERAGES		
Beer	8 oz.	120
Wine	1 wine glass	75
Gin	1 jigger	115
Rum	1 jigger	125
Whiskey	1 jigger	120
Brandy	1 brandy glass	80
Cocktail	1 cocktail glass	150

The American Heart Association's Fat-Controlled, Low-Cholesterol Meal Plan

This plan is mainly for adults from their twenties on who have a family history of heart disease, or who may have increased their risks through a regular diet high in saturated fat and cholesterol. Children and adolescents, especially from susceptible families, can also benefit from this meal plan by forming tastes for food early in life that may protect them from heart disease when they reach adulthood.

The types of food recommended here are suitable for most people from childhood through maturity. The *amounts* of food specified in the food list, however, are recommended mainly for the average adult. Nutritional needs differ during growth periods of infants, children, and adolescents, and during pregnancy and breast feeding; at these times, the amounts of food to be eaten should be regulated by a physician.

To use this plan, simply select, every day, foods from each of the basic food groups in lists 1–5, and follow the recommendations for number and size of servings.

MEAT, POULTRY, FISH, DRIED BEANS AND PEAS, NUTS, EGGS

One serving: 3–4 ounces of cooked meat or fish (not including bone or fat) or 3–4 ounces of a vegetable listed here. Use two or more servings (a total of 6–8 ounces) daily.

RECOMMENDED

Chicken — turkey — veal — fish — in most of your meat meals for the week.

Shellfish: clams, crab, lobster, oysters, scallops, shrimp, are low in fat but high in cholesterol. Use a 4-ounce serving as a substitute for meat no more than twice a week.

Beef — lamb — pork — ham — in no more than 5 meals per week. Choose lean ground meat and lean cuts of meat; trim all visible fat before cooking; bake, broil, roast or stew so that you can discard the fat that cooks out of the meat.

Nuts and dried beans and peas. Kidney beans, lima beans, baked beans, lentils, chick peas (garbanzos), split peas, are high in vegetable protein and may be used in place of meat occasionally.

Egg whites as desired.

AVOID OR USE SPARINGLY

Duck–goose.

Heavily marbled and fatty meats, spare ribs, mutton, frankfurters, sausages, fatty hamburgers, bacon, luncheon meats.

Organ meats: liver, kidney, heart, sweetbreads, are very high in cholesterol. Since liver is very rich in vitamins and iron, it should not be eliminated from the diet completely. Use a 4-ounce serving in a meat meal no more than once a week.

Egg yolks: limit to 3 per week including eggs used in cooking.

Cakes, batters, sauces, and other foods containing egg yolks.

VEGETABLES AND FRUIT (Fresh, frozen, or canned)

One serving: ½ cup. Use at least 4 servings daily.

RECOMMENDED

One serving should be a source of Vitamin C.
Broccoli, cabbage (raw), tomatoes. Berries, cantaloupe, grapefruit (or juice), mango, melon, orange (or juice), papaya, strawberries, tangerines.

One serving should be a source of Vitamin A—dark green leafy or yellow vegetables, or yellow fruits.
Broccoli, carrots, chard, chicory, escarole, greens (beet, collard, dandelion, mustard, turnip), kale, peas, rutabagas, spinach, string beans, sweet potatoes and yams, watercress, winter squash, yellow corn.
Apricots, cantaloupe, mango, papaya.

Other vegetables and fruits are also very nutritious; they should be eaten in salads, main dishes, snacks, and desserts, *in addition* to the recommended daily allowances of high vitamin A and C vegetables and fruits.

AVOID OR USE SPARINGLY

Olives and avocados are very high in fat calories and should be used in moderation.

If you must limit your calories, use vegetables such as potatoes, corn or lima beans sparingly. To add variety to your diet, one serving (½ cup) of any one of these may be substituted for one serving of bread or cereals.

BREADS AND CEREALS (Whole grain, enriched, or restored)

One serving of bread: 1 slice. One serving of cereal: ½ cup, cooked; 1 cup, cold, with skimmed milk. Use at least 4 servings daily.

RECOMMENDED

Breads made with a minimum of saturated fat.

AVOID OR USE SPARINGLY

Butter rolls; commercial biscuits, muffins, doughnuts, sweet rolls,

White enriched (including raisin bread), whole wheat, English muffins, French bread, Italian bread, oatmeal bread, pumpernickel, rye bread.

cakes, crackers; egg bread, cheese bread; commercial mixes containing dried eggs and whole milk.

Biscuits, muffins, and griddle cakes made at home, using an allowed liquid oil as shortening.

Cereal (hot and cold), rice, melba toast, matzo, pretzels.

Pasta: macaroni, noodles (except egg noodles), spaghetti.

Milk Products

One serving: 8 ounces (1 cup). Buy only skimmed milk that has been fortified with Vitamins A and D. Daily servings: Children up to 12, 3 or more cups; Adults, 2 or more cups.

RECOMMENDED
Milk products that are low in dairy fats.
Fortified skimmed (nonfat) milk and fortified skimmed milk powder, low-fat milk. The label on the container should show that the milk is fortified with Vitamins A and D. The word "fortified" alone is not enough.

Buttermilk made from skimmed milk, yoghurt made from skimmed milk, canned evaporated skimmed milk, cocoa made with low-fat milk.

AVOID OR USE SPARINGLY
Whole milk and whole milk products.
Chocolate milk; canned whole milk; ice cream; all creams including sour, half and half, whipped; whole milk yoghurt.

Nondairy cream substitutes (usually coconut oil which is very high in saturated fat).

Cheeses made from cream or whole milk.

Butter.

Cheeses made from skimmed or partially skimmed milk, such as cottage cheese, creamed or uncreamed (uncreamed, preferably); farmer's, baker's or hoop cheese; mozzarella and sapsago cheeses made with partially skimmed milk.

FATS AND OILS (Polyunsaturated)

An individual allowance should include about 2–4 tablespoons daily (depending on how many calories you can afford) in the form of margarine, salad dressing, and shortening.

RECOMMENDED

Margarines, liquid oil shortenings, salad dressings, and mayonnaise containing any of these polyunsaturated vegetable oils.
Corn oil, cottonseed oil, safflower oil, sesame seed oil, soybean oil, sunflower seed oil.
Margarines and other products highly polyunsaturated usually can be identified by their label which lists a recommended *liquid* vegetable oil as the *first* ingredient, and one or more partially hydrogenated vegetable oils as additional ingredients.

Diet margarines are low in calories because they are low in fat. Therefore it takes twice as much diet margarine to supply the polyunsaturates contained in a recommended margarine.

AVOID OR USE SPARINGLY

Solid fats and shortenings.
Butter, lard, salt pork fat, meat fat, completely hydrogenated margarines and vegetable shortenings, products containing coconut oil.

Peanut oil and olive oil may be used occasionally for flavor, but they are low in polyunsaturates and do not take the place of the recommended oils.

DESSERTS, BEVERAGES, SNACKS, CONDIMENTS

The foods on this list are acceptable because they are low in saturated fat and cholesterol. If you have eaten your daily allowance from the first five lists, however, these foods will be in excess of your nutritional needs, and many of them may also exceed your calorie limits for maintaining a desirable weight. If you must limit your calories, limit your portions of the foods on this list as well.

Moderation should be observed especially in the use of alcoholic drinks, ice milk, sherbet, sweets, and bottled drinks.

ACCEPTABLE
Low in calories or no calories.
Fresh fruit and fruit canned without sugar; teá, coffee (no cream), cocoa powder; water ices; gelatin; fruit whip; puddings made with nonfat milk; sweets and bottled drinks made with artificial sweeteners; vinegar, mustard, ketchup, herbs, spices.

High in calories.
Frozen or canned fruit with sugar added; jelly, jam, marmalade, honey; pure sugar candy such as gum drops, hard candy, mint patties (not chocolate); imitation ice cream made with safflower oil; cakes, pies, cookies, and puddings made with polyunsaturated fat in place of solid shortening; angel food cake; nuts, especially walnuts; nonhydrogenated peanut butter; bottled drinks, fruit drinks; ice milk; sherbet; wine, beer, whiskey.

AVOID OR USE SPARINGLY
Coconut and coconut oil; commercial cakes, pies, cookies, and mixes; frozen cream pies; commercially fried foods such as potato chips and other deep fried snacks; whole milk puddings; chocolate pudding (high in cocoa butter and therefore high in saturated fat); ice cream.

If You Want To Give Up Cigarettes

(*From the American Cancer Society booklet, reproduced here with the Society's permission*)

If you want to give up cigarettes: Congratulations! This pamphlet seeks to round up helpful suggestions from experimental projects that have been carefully evaluated. No sure techniques are offered, no absolute laws of human behavior provided. There are different kinds of smokers and what helps one may not work with another. Individuals must choose for themselves from what is presented here.

Each man (and woman) makes a personal decision on the important matter of smoking cigarettes. The fact that you are reading this pamphlet indicates that you are properly concerned.

Many millions have given up cigarette smoking. Although for some people it is surprisingly easy to quit, most find it rather difficult. Psychologists estimate that half of all cigarette smokers can stop without too much difficulty once they make up their minds to try. They feel only minor or temporary discomfort. Others suffer intensely, almost unbearably for days and weeks. Remember that those who have tried to stop a number of times may succeed this time.

Will you really make the effort? We hope so.

The American Cancer Society

This pamphlet developed out of discussions at a two-day conference called by the American Cancer Society on withdrawal programs and cigarette smoking. Participating, and contributing ideas and materials, but not responsible for the content selected here, were Borje E. V. Ejrup, M.D., Clinical Associate Professor of Medicine, Director, Anti-Smoking Clinic, The New York Hospital Cornell Medical Center, New York, N.Y.; Donald T. Frederickson, M.D., Director, Smoking Control Program, New York City Department of Health; Judith S. Mausner, M.D., Assistant Professor of Epidemiology, Department of Preventive Medicine, Woman's Medical College, Philadelphia; Bernard Mausner, Ph.D., Professor of Psychology, Chairman, Department of Psychology, Beaver College, Glenside, Pa.; Charles A. Ross, M.D., Chief, Department of Thoracic Surgery, Roswell Park Memorial Institute, Buffalo, N.Y.; David Sharp, M.D., Medical Consultant, National Clearinghouse for Smoking and Health, United States Public Health Service, Arlington, Va.; and Jerome L. Schwartz, Dr. P.H., Project Director, Smoking Control Research Project, Berkeley, California. We have also drawn on ideas from others including Donald Pumroy, Ph.D., Counselling Center, University of Maryland, and Silvan Tomkins, Ph.D., Center for Research in Cognition and Affect, City University of New York, and a member of the American Cancer Society's Committee on Tobacco and Cancer. Representing the American Cancer Society were Harold S. Diehl, M.D., at that time Deputy Executive Vice President for Research and Medical Affairs; Walter James, Vice President for Public Education, and Clifton R. Read, Senior Editor-Consultant.

Once You Have Stopped

If you are like most cigarette smokers, you will in two weeks or less say farewell to that hacking, shattering morning cough, good-by to ugly thick phlegm, adios to smoker's headaches and unpleasant cigarette-induced mouth and stomach complaints.

You will be saving—how much? Well, how much do you smoke up in dollars every week? Could be considerable.

You will no longer burn cigarette holes in clothing, furniture, rugs, or tablecloths. (The National Fire Protection Association says that "smoking and matches" caused a property loss of $80,400,000 in 1965.)

Food will tend to taste better and your sense of smell will return to normal.

Cigarette breath (it can be very offensive) will disappear.

Q Day, cigarette quitting day, might well be renamed K Day—kindness day for both you and your friends.

By quitting cigarettes you are instituting an immediate program of kindness to your lungs, your heart, your stomach, your nose, your throat.

A GARLAND OF FACTS

Since you have decided to give up cigarette smoking, you probably know the risks of the habit. However, a brief selection from the mountains of facts that have developed through research, published since 1954, may be useful.

NOT A GAMBLE

Cigarette smoking used to be compared to Russian roulette. Now we know better. Every regular cigarette smoker is injured, though not in the same degree. Cigarette smoking kills some, makes others lung cripples, gives still others far more than their share of illness and loss of work days. Cigarette smoking is not a gamble; regular cigarette smokers studied at autopsy all show the effects.

THE MORE CIGARETTES, THE MORE CANCER OF THE LUNG

The regular cigarette smoker runs a risk of death from lung cancer ten times greater than the nonsmoker, men who smoke more than a pack a day have about 20 times as much lung cancer as nonsmokers have. Unfortunately, early diagnosis of lung cancer is very difficult; only about one in 20 cases is cured.

SIX AND ONE-HALF YEARS, 78 MONTHS, 23,725 DAYS

Men aged twenty-five who have never smoked regularly can expect six-and-a-half years more of life than men who smoke one pack or more a day. Twice as many heavy smokers (two packs a day) will die between twenty-five and sixty-five years of age, as nonsmokers.

THOSE MINUTES OF LIFE

The average heavy smoker (two or more packs a day) smokes about three-quarters of a million cigarettes during his lifetime. As a result, he loses about 4.4 million minutes—8.3 years—of life compared with nonsmokers. This amounts to a loss of almost six minutes per cigarette smoked; a minute of life for a minute of smoking.

Give Your Heart a Break

Male smokers (ten or more cigarettes a day) between forty-five and fifty-four have more than three times the death rate from heart attacks than nonsmokers do. In the ages between forty and sixty-four, heart attacks prematurely kill some 45,000 cigarette-smoking men.

How to Escape Work

Cigarette smokers between forty-five and sixty-four miss 50 percent more days at work than do nonsmokers. Or, to say it another way: According to the Public Health Service, if cigarette smokers had the same rate of illness as nonsmokers, some 77 million working days would not be lost annually.

A Deep Breath

Emphysema, a relatively rare disease a few years ago, is now a major cause of medical disability in this country. Most emphysema is caused by cigarette smoking. The disease is both a crippler and a killer causing the lungs to lose their elasticity. Eventually the effort to breathe becomes a constant, agonizing struggle.

Live a Little More

A longer and healthier life is high on our priorities: giving up cigarette smoking is the most important action that the average individual can take that will improve the physical quality of his daily life, extend his life expectancy, and increase his chances of avoiding lung cancer, heart disease, emphysema, and a number of other nasty complaints.

Some of the Millions Who Make It

(The following brief sketches are based on fact from letters, conversations, reports, but with names and details altered. They have been selected with the intention of helping others to go and do likewise.)

William is a psychiatrist who decided soon after the Report of the Advisory Committee to the Surgeon General that he ought to stop cigarettes. What triggered his actual decision? He suspects it was a morning cough, but he is not sure! In any case, he stopped and reports that he watched television for several evenings (which he rarely did), ate rather more often than was his custom, did some strenuous skiing, and was happy that his wife cleared the house at once of all cigarettes and ashtrays. He was uncomfortable for a few days but not climbing any walls. He hasn't smoked for three years.

Joan is a writer who reads seriously. After the Surgeon General's report she stopped smoking cigarettes. Cold turkey. No gum, no candy, no gaining of weight. Some bad temper for a few days but it was not a big or difficult deal.

Pete is a carpenter who smoked two packs a day for 25 years. He was proud, however, that his three sons did not smoke. He wanted to quit but was hooked, he knew it, and he told his boys never to take up the habit. When they believed and obeyed him, he was delighted. He stopped only after an operation in which two-thirds of his stomach was taken out because of an ulcer. He still doesn't discuss the fact that he has given up smoking but he hasn't smoked for a year and he was in the hospital long enough so that when he went back on the job and people began offering him a smoke, he was able to say "no" calmly.

John was a brilliantly successful advertising man who smoked two packs of cigarettes a day; when he began to cough, and this happened half a dozen times in a work day, it took him embarrassed moments to get over it. He had thought of stopping cigarettes, even made half-hearted trials—but at last he decided to go for broke. His first step was to keep a careful record of when he smoked each cigarette, and how much he wanted it. Then he selected a future Q Day and told his family and friends what he was doing. He began to cut down, 50 percent each week for four weeks, and he laid in mints and gum.

When Q Day arrived he stopped. It was a rough experience and at one time he was in such a serious depression that he frightened his wife. After a visit to his physician, however, he stood by his decision. During the first three months he gained 15 pounds, but he lost all of this later, his cough is gone, and he feels a hundred percent better. He hasn't smoked a cigarette for two years.

George is a television announcer who never smoked on camera. But, during his tense, challenging work, he consumed more than two packs of cigarettes a day. Finally, he and a lawyer friend bet each other $1,000 that each could stay off cigarettes longer than the other. They deposited the money in a special bank account and agreed that after 18 months they would take the money and go to Europe. Neither has smoked for six months. George found that he couldn't sleep, that his food didn't taste any better and that he passionately hated all cigarette advertising. But George was Scotch and he wasn't out to lose one thousand dollars. His bad time lasted for almost four weeks—now he is convinced that he will never smoke again.

Linda reports she really puffed away at cigarettes when she was worried or tense. She was disturbed by stories of the risks of smoking and wished she could stop but continued until (she says) one of the American Cancer Society's announcements gave her just the push she needed. That was three months ago, about the same time her husband lost his job, her four-year-old child broke her arm, her baby had his first nasty cold. Linda wrote the Society that despite all the tensions she "came through with a smile and a prayer, but no cigarette."

Harold—a reporter of considerable distinction—smoked three packs a day: at the typewriter, before and after breakfast, during lunch, in the afternoon and evening. Any tests would have shown him as a habituated smoker, a bad risk for a withdrawal program. However, he stopped, cold turkey, and has not smoked for 10 years. Why? His specialty was science writing and he decided that if the scientists he trusted were right he was a fool to go on smoking. For two weeks he was in considerable discomfort, but with gum and candy he kept going. He says he feels great since he stopped smoking.

There are twenty-one million ex-cigarette smokers in the United States; about one in five adult men in this country has dropped the habit. Those who give up cigarettes report a great sense of satisfaction, of tremendous pride in being able to do it. To learn a new way of living, a way without cigarette smoking, is very rewarding to the ego—and to the ego's mate. *You can kick the habit!*

As You Approach Q Day

Many stress willpower as the decisive factor in giving up cigarettes. For them the sense that they can manage their own lives is of great importance. They enjoy challenging themselves and, with an effort of will, they break the cigarette habit.

Thus, some psychologists describe stopping cigarettes as an exercise in self-mastery, one that introduces a new dimension of self-control.

Others, often successful in many aspects of living, find that will-power does not help them in giving up cigarettes. They try to stop, they do not, and they feel guilty over their weakness. This is a mistake, since many smokers fail in their first and second, even their fifth attempts, and then finally succeed. Those whose "will" fails in breaking the habit are not weak but different. Their approach must be less through determination and more through relearning new behavior with patience and perseverance.

Self-suggestion, when one is relaxed, aimed at changing one's feelings and thoughts about cigarettes can be useful.

One health educator remarked recently, "nothing succeeds like will-power and a little blood in the sputum."

To think of stopping smoking as self-denial is an error: the ex-smoker should not believe that he is giving up an object of value, however dependent he may be on it. If he begins to feel sorry for himself and broods on his sufferings, they may well become more severe and indeed unendurable. He must recognize that he is teaching himself a more positive, more constructive, more rewarding behavior.

TRY CUTTING DOWN

An important first step in the process of giving up cigarettes for many smokers is to set the date for Q Day, when you are going to stop completely and, as it approaches, to gradually reduce the number of cigarettes you smoke, day by day, or week by week.

A good system is to decide only to smoke once an hour—or to stop smoking between the hours of 9 and 10 o'clock, 11 and 12, 1 and 2, 3 and 4, etc. And then to extend the nonsmoking time by half an hour, an hour, two hours.

You may decide to halve the cigarettes you smoke week by week, giving yourself four weeks to Q Day.

How about smoking only half of each cigarette?

In the process of reducing the number of daily cigarettes, try various possibilities: if you have one pocket in which you always carry your pack, put it in another so that you will have to fumble for it. If you always use your right hand to bring your cigarette to your mouth, use the left hand. Is it your custom to rest the cigarette in the right corner of the mouth? Try the left side.

Make it a real effort to get a cigarette:

Wrap your package in several sheets of paper or place it in a tightly covered box. If you leave your change at home you won't be able to use a cigarette machine.

Shift from cigarettes you like to an unpalatable brand.

Before you light up, ask yourself "Do I really want this cigarette or am I just acting out of empty habit?"

A smoker may find an unlighted cigarette in the mouth is helpful. Others enjoy handling and playing with a cigarette.

Cigarette smoking is a habit that is usually very well learned—learning the habit of not smoking can be difficult. It can help in breaking into your habit chain to make yourself aware of the nature and frequency of your smoking behavior.

KEEP A TRACK RECORD

Many smokers have found that a useful step in understanding their smoking is the keeping of a daily record on a scale like this:

Score Card

Copy this record sheet seven times for seven days. Make a check for each cigarette you smoke, hour by hour, and indicate how much you need it: a mark in the box opposite 1 shows low need, a mark opposite 6 high need; opposite 4, moderate need, etc. Then decide which cigarette you wish to eliminate.

NEED	MORNING HOURS (A.M.)							AFTERNOON					EVENING HOURS (P.M.)							
	6	7	8	9	10	11	12	1	2	3	4	5	6	7	8	9	10	11	12	1
1																				
2																				
3																				
4																				
5																				
6																				

In your gradual withdrawal you may decide to eliminate those daily cigarettes that you find are rated 1, 2, or 3, i.e., ones you want least.

Or you may wish to give up first the cigarettes you like most. In any case keeping a smoking log will give you information about yourself, make you more aware of what your smoking habits are.

You may find that you are largely a social smoker, that smoking makes you feel closer to others, more welcome at a party, that you seem to have more friends. A cigarette may play a surprisingly large part in your picture of yourself as a mature and successful person.

How do you convince yourself that people like and respect you for more important reasons than for your cigarette? Try not smoking and see.

PLUS AND MINUS

Write down carefully, after some thought, in one column the reasons why you smoke and in another all the reasons why you should give up cigarettes.

As you turn this exercise over in your mind, new material will occur to you for one or the other columns. Thoughtful concentration on your reasons for giving up cigarettes is important in changing your behavior.

FOUR SMOKING STYLES

Dr. Silvan Tomkins distinguishes four general types of smoking behavior. An abbreviated summary of the types follows:

Habitual smoking. Here the smoker may hardly be aware that he has a cigarette in his mouth. He smokes as if it made him feel good, or feel better, but in fact it does neither. He may once have regarded smoking as an important sign of status. But now smoking is automatic. The habitual smoker who wants to give up must first become aware of when he is smoking. Knowledge of the pattern of his smoking is a first step toward change.

Positive-affect smoking. Here smoking seems to serve as a stimulant that produces exciting pleasure, or is used as a relaxant, to heighten enjoyment, as at the end of a meal. Here a youngster demonstrates his manhood or his defiance of his parents. This smoker may enjoy most the handling of a cigarette or the sense and sight of smoke curling out of his mouth. If these smokers can be persuaded to make an effort, they may find giving up cigarettes relatively painless.

Negative-affect smoking. This is sedative smoking, using the habit to reduce feelings of distress, fear, shame, or disgust or any combination of them. This person may not smoke at all when things go well, on vacation, or at a party, but under tension, when things go badly, at the office or at home, he reaches for a cigarette. These smokers give up often, but when the heat and pressure of the day hit them, when there's a challenge, they find it very hard to resist a cigarette. A strong substitute, like nibbling ginger root, may be useful.

Addictive smoking. The smoker is always aware when he is not smoking. The absence of a cigarette is uncomfortably obvious. The lack of a cigarette builds need, desire, and discomfort at not smoking. With this increasing need is the expectation that a cigarette will reduce discomfort—and the cigarette does give relief—for a moment. Pleasure at smoking is real, just as the buildup of discomfort at not smoking is real, sometimes rapid and intolerable. The enjoyment of the cigarette, however, is very brief, and may be disappointing—but the suffering for lack of slight relief is considerable. For this smoker, tapering off doesn't seem to work: the only solution is to quit cold. Once you have been through the intense pain of breaking your psychological addiction, you are unlikely to start smoking again. The experience of giving up has been too uncomfortable—and too memorable for you to risk having to go through it again.

Some such smokers have found it useful to increase during the week before Q Day the number of cigarettes smoked, to go from two packs to four packs, to force themselves to smoke so that their bodies will be in actual revolt against the double dose of tar and nicotine.

For information on a Smoker's Self-Testing Kit (four questionnaires, etc., to help one to understand personal reasons for, and style of, smoking) write to the National Clearinghouse for Smoking and Health, United States Public Health Service, 40404 North Fairfax Drive, Arlington, Va. 22203.

THE WEEK BEFORE Q DAY

Think over your list of reasons why you should not smoke: the risk of disease, the blurring of the taste of food, the cost, the cough, the bad breath, the mess and smell of morning-after ashtrays.

Concentrate each evening when you are relaxed, just before you fall asleep, on one result of cigarette smoking. Repeat and repeat and repeat that single fact. Drive home another fact the next night and another the next.

Review the facts that you know about the risks of cigarette smoking. Remind yourself that there, but for the grace of God, go you;

that you may indeed, if you continue smoking, lose six and a half years of life; that—if you are a heavy smoker—your chances of dying between twenty-five and sixty-five years of age are twice as great as those of the nonsmoker. Are the six minutes of pleasure in a cigarette worth six minutes fewer of life to a heavy smoker? Would you fly in an airplane if the chances of crash and death were even close to the risks of cigarette smoking? Think over why it is that 100,000 physicians have quit cigarette smoking.

ACTION: Q DAY

Let us suppose that you know, now, when and where and how you smoke. You have suggested again and again to your tired mind that smoking is a dangerous business.

"But what will I do the morning of Q Day when, mind or no mind, I desperately want a cigarette?"

We hope you will prove that you are stronger than your dependence. Here are some tips that may prove useful when you have an impulse to smoke. They are not scientifically proven, but many smokers have found one or another of them helpful.

For the mouth. Drink frequent glasses of water.

Nibble fruit, cookies, eat somewhat self-pleasing food.

Suck candy mints and/or chew gum (sugarless gum will be easier on your teeth).

Chew bits of fresh ginger when you start to reach for a cigarette. (Take this gently, ginger root is aromatic and pervasive—some experience it as burning, others as clean and satisfying.)

Bite a clove.

Nicotine replacement. Lobeline sulphate tablets, available without prescription, are reported to make it easier for some people to stop cigarettes. Authorities disagree as to whether they provide a substitute that will help satisfy your body's craving for nicotine!

(Since some individuals—those with stomach ulcers for instance—should not use these tablets, check with your physician before trying them.)

Be vigorous: exercise. Strenuous physical activity that demands effort and keeps you busy can be very helpful.

Vacation is a good time for some people to stop: camping, mountain climbing, tennis.

Stretching exercises or long walks can be relaxing.

Go *"no smoking."* For a few days, spend as much time as possible in libraries or other places where smoking is forbidden. Ride in "No Smoking" cars.

A spurt of motion picture or theater-going will pass many hours.

Keep away for two weeks from friends who are heavy smokers.

Use your lungs. Deep breaths of air can be wonderfully calming.

Inhalers—that reduce nasal stuffiness—may help tide you over the first few days.

After meals. For some the cigarette after breakfast coffee, at the end of lunch or dinner, is most important. Instead of a cigarette try a mouth wash after each meal.

If you have had a specific pattern that you have followed after dinner you may want to change it: read a book instead of a newspaper, skip familiar television programs, sit in another comfortable chair, try crossword puzzles or take care of some household task you have been putting off, take your dog out for a walk.

On the other hand, you may prefer to do all the things that are familiar and comfortable for you and to which you are used—except to smoke cigarettes. Take your choice.

Reward yourself. Be sure you have your favorite food on Q Day.

Give yourself all the things that you like best—except cigarettes.

When you have saved a bit of money by not smoking, buy yourself a present: perhaps a new record, or a blouse, or necktie, or book, or a trinket.

So—Now You Are on Your Own

When the impulse to smoke is strong, try a substitute: a drink of water, a piece of gum, a walk around the block, stretching, and deep breathing.

These substitutes may only satisfy you temporarily—but they will keep you alert and aware and will soften the strength of your desire to smoke. Equally important are constant reminders to yourself of why you are stopping cigarettes. Remember the reasons that you put down for not smoking? Recall the basic data about disease, disability, and death that are caused by cigarettes.

You may be very uncomfortable but "this too shall pass" relates to cigarette-less shakes, irritation and temper, the urge to climb walls, depression, anxiety. Time is a great healer.

A minority of cigarette smokers go through the terrors of the damned after they quit. Even these—when they come on the fresh air side—report great pride at having been able to give up.

Unfortunately, fear of failure to make it seems to deter very many men and women from even trying—but for many, giving up cigarettes, while uncomfortable and a strain, is by no means agony. After all their terrible expectations, stopping can seem relatively easy.

QUESTIONS AND ANSWERS

Do you believe in cold turkey quitting? Yes, for some, no, for others. If you are a really "addicted" smoker, psychologists favor the sudden, decisive break.

For some, gradual withdrawal is less painful and entirely satisfactory.

Some cigarette smokers shift to pipes and cigars—there is of course some risk of mouth cancer from these but over-all mortality of cigar and pipe smokers is only a little higher than among nonsmokers, provided the smoke is not inhaled.

What about going to a cigarette withdrawal clinic for help? If there is a clinic or program in your community, you may find it useful. The American Cancer Society favors such efforts.

Sharing your withdrawal experiences with others and working with them on a common problem can be very helpful. The clinic may make it considerably easier in various ways to stop cigarette smoking.

However, remember, no clinic can provide a sure result. In this matter you must be both patient and physician.

Shall I make a big thing of Q Day? Some find it most satisfactory to work on a schedule in which Q Day, quitting day, is singled out as the important, decisive day in their personal lives—that indeed it is.

Others who have known for a long time that cigarettes are bad for them and that sooner or later they will stop, wake up one morning and say to themselves "This is it. No more cigarettes."

What motivates them? An obituary, an antismoking commercial on television, a magazine article, a leaflet brought home from school by a child, a worried look from their son, being fed up with a repeated cough. There are many possible stimuli to stop, but almost always beneath the casual-seeming but bold decision are months, often years, of thought and worry.

What if I fail to make it? Don't be discouraged; many thousands who stopped did so only after several attempts.

Some people prefer to stop for just one day at a time. They promise themselves 24 hours of freedom from cigarettes and when the day is over they make a commitment to themselves for one more day. And another. And another. At the end of any 24-hour period they can go back to cigarettes without betraying themselves—but they usually do not.

Is smoking a real addiction? This depends on your definition of words. In any case, smokers obviously can become very strongly, very tragically dependent on cigarettes.

However, the discomfort that most feel at giving up cigarettes is not like the painful withdrawal symptoms that drug addicts report.

Giving up cigarettes is much closer to the discomfort and the irritation produced by dieting than to the agony of stopping drugs. As so many know, dieting in an effort to lose fifteen or twenty pounds can be a most uncomfortable experience—but when you have done it, you have a fine feeling.

Shall I throw out our ashtrays? One school of thought asks, do you leave a bottle of whiskey near an alcoholic? Their recommendation is to get rid of cigarettes, ashtrays, anything that might remind a smoker of his former habit.

Others take a different view and even suggest carrying cigarettes to demonstrate to yourself that you can resist temptation. Choose for yourself.

Shall I tell others of my decision? Some do, some don't. Some find that the wider they spread the news of their decision the easier it is for them to make it stick. Others regard not smoking as their own personal business and keep it almost entirely to themselves. Will you strengthen your decision if your wife and friends know that you have committed yourself?

Will I gain weight? Many do. Food is a substitute for cigarettes for many people. And your appetite may be fresher and stronger.

During the first few weeks of giving up cigarettes some psychologists recommend pampering yourself: eating well, drinking well, enjoying those things that are pleasant and fulfilling.

Some people, those to whom self-mastery is vital, get rewards out of controlling their wish for fattening food at the same time they are licking the urge for cigarettes.

Again, it depends upon the person and his approach.

How about hypnosis? There is much interest in this technique by some physicians who report success, particularly with hard-core smokers. Why not discuss the matter with a physician, if you are interested.

Shall I see my physician? Yes. However, the problem is yours, not his, and he may not feel that he can be helpful. On the other hand he may be able to give you sympathetic support and may prescribe medication. He can be helpful, also, in suggesting a diet which will prevent you from gaining too much weight.

Physicians as a profession have been leaders in acting on the risks of cigarette smoking: the Public Health Service estimates that 100,000 physicians (half the physicians who once were cigarette smokers) have kicked the habit. A California study shows that only 21.3 percent of all physicians in the state are cigarette smokers now.

Why do so many people smoke cigarettes? Surely one reason is that the cigarette industry spends about $300,000,000 a year in promoting the habit and in challenging the facts that scientists have produced that point to the dangers of the habit.

Another reason is that something in cigarettes, probably nicotine, is habit-forming: smokers become dependent rather rapidly on cigarettes.

Cigarette smoking is essentially a twentieth-century habit, encouraged by wars, by brilliant advertising, and by the development of remarkably efficient automatic machinery that produces those millions of round firmly packed cigarettes.

It is only within the last 15 years that we have learned, through research pioneered by the American Cancer Society, that this personal and socially accepted habit is extremely dangerous. Cigarette smoking is deeply embedded in our life: agriculture, industry, government, the communications media, all have a stake in it. It is still widely accepted, even though proven to be a most certain hazard to health.

Because promotion is important in maintaining the habit's popularity, the Society believes all cigarette advertising in all media should be terminated. We hope that this goal will be achieved voluntarily and that governmental action won't be necessary.

APPROACHES TO GIVING UP CIGARETTE SMOKING

If you don't stop immediately and permanently:
1. List the reasons for and against smoking.
2. Select Q Day—change to a low tar and nicotine cigarette.
3. Chart your smoking habits for at least two weeks: how many cigarettes, when, the most and least important.
4. Repeat each night, at least ten times, one of your reasons for not smoking cigarettes.
5. Eliminate one category of cigarettes: the most or the least desired.
6. Secure a supply of substitutes: mints, gum, an inhaler, ginger root, etc.
7. Quit on Q Day—try the different substitutes as the wish to smoke

recurs—enlist your wife or a friend in a busy series of events: eating well, going to the movies or theater, exercise and many long walks, moderate drinking.

8. If you are depressed, see your physician and discuss your symptoms.
9. Keep reminding yourself, again and again, of all the shocking risks in cigarette smoking.

To Smoke or Not to Smoke?

A story is told of two boys who knew a man who was supposed to be wise and were determined to challenge him. They caught a small bird and decided on a formula that they felt could not fail. They would go to the wise man with their hands cupped and say: "Tell us, wise man, is the bird that one of us holds in his hands alive or dead?" If he said "dead" they would release the bird. If he said "alive" a squeeze of the hands would prove him wrong. When they confronted him and asked the question, the wise man smiled, and considered, and finally said, "The answer is in your hands."

Index